Communication
& Organizational Culture

Communication
& Organizational Culture

A KEY TO UNDERSTANDING WORK EXPERIENCES

JOANN KEYTON
The University of Kansas

SAGE Publications
Thousand Oaks ▪ London ▪ New Delhi

For information:

Sage Publications, Inc.
2455 Teller Road
Thousand Oaks, California 91320
E-mail: order@sagepub.com

Sage Publications Ltd.
1 Oliver's Yard
55 City Road
London EC1Y 1SP
United Kingdom

Sage Publications India Pvt. Ltd.
B-42, Panchsheel Enclave
Post Box 4109
New Delhi 110 017 India

Printed in the United States of America

Library of Congress Cataloging-in-Publication Data

Keyton, Joann.
Communication and organizational culture : a key to understanding work experiences / Joann Keyton.
      p. cm.
Includes bibliographical references and index.
ISBN 0–7619–3017–5 (cloth)—ISBN 0–7619–3016–7 (pbk.)
      1. Organizational behavior. 2. Corporate culture.
3. Communication in organizations. 4. Communication
in management. 5. Organizational change. I. Title.
  HD58.7.K49 2005
302.3'5—dc22

                                                    2004015961

04   05   06   07   08   10   9   8   7   6   5   4   3   2   1

Acquiring Editor:	Todd Armstrong
Editorial Assistant:	Deya Saoud
Production Editor:	Sanford Robinson
Typesetter:	C&M Digitals (P) Ltd.
Copy Editor:	David Yurkovich
Cover Designer:	Michelle Kenny

Contents

Acknowledgments

This book would not have been completed without the support of Jeff, Bill, faye, Tracy . . . and of course, Maggie and Sally.

This book would not have been completed had I not stumbled into a job at the Federal Reserve Bank of Kansas City many years ago.

This book would not have been completed had people not been willing to tell me their organizational stories. I appreciate each and every person who jumps in when I say, "I study organizational communication." My network of friends across the country also contributed examples used in this book. Thank you for taking the time to share your work experiences.

This book would not have been completed without the many students who take my seminar in organizational culture and ask questions to get me to explain concepts repeatedly. Those classroom conversations helped shape my views about organizational culture and led me to pedagogy for teaching it. I am especially grateful to Jennie Bledsoe who allowed me to use the cultural pyramid concept she developed as a class assignment. The pyramid has become a splendid tool for introducing organizational members to their organizational culture and for guiding students with limited research exposure into cultural analysis.

This book would not have been completed without gaining access to organizations. For each of those organizational gatekeepers, I appreciate the risk you took in allowing me in.

This book would not have been completed . . . well, it isn't complete. Organizations and their cultures will continue to evolve; and our understanding of organizations and their cultures will continue to be challenged.

Sage Publications gratefully acknowledges the contributions of the following reviewers:

Sue Easton
Rollins College

Angela Trethewey
Arizona State University

Karen Lee Ashcraft
University of Utah

Erika L. Kirby
Creighton University

Linda Putnam
Texas A&M University

Steve May
University of North Carolina at Chapel Hill

Jennifer Thackaberry
Purdue University

Alexandra Murphy
DePaul University

Heather Walter
University of Akron

Robert Brower
Florida State University

Mark Peterson
Florida Atlantic University

1

Positioning
Organizational Culture

INTRODUCTION

If asked to do so, you could name many organizations. It is likely that you would first name the school you attend, where you work, and companies that manufacture products or provide services that you purchase and use. You might also name government institutions at local, state, and federal levels, nonprofits like the American Cancer Society, and civic and religious institutions, such as neighborhood associations and churches. Each type of organization contributes to our collective economic, civic, community, and social lives in some fundamental way. Organizations are the building blocks of our society.

   Each organization has a culture, and that is the focus of this book. *Organizational culture* is the set of artifacts, values, and assumptions that emerge from the interactions of organizational members. Although often difficult to describe, as an employee we *know* what it's like in our organization. Whether we buy into them entirely or not, we are intuitively aware of values and beliefs that our coworkers, subordinates, and superiors hold about the work they perform in our particular organization. You may have even decided to join a company because it *felt* like an environment in which you could be successful. As a customer or client, we encounter an organization's culture through

1

our interactions with organizational members. Perhaps you return to a specific store—even though you have many other choices—because the service is good and the employees are friendly and personable. Or, perhaps you vow "to never return" because the store's return policy distinctively advantages their rights over yours. As an employee or in the role of customer or client, you are exposed to the culture of every organization you encounter.

Managers and executives are particularly interested in organizational culture, often as a means for improving productivity, effectiveness, or efficiency. Other managers pay attention because they believe their organization's culture is unique and can be an effective tool in attracting quality employees or distinguishing the organization from competitors.

Employees can be interested in organizational culture, particularly when they make employment choices. Most of us need to work, and want to work in environments that resonate with our values and ideas.

Trainers and consultants are interested in organizational culture. A Web search for *organizational culture* using the search engine Google (www.google.com) resulted in over 1.5 million hits. Clearly, organizational culture has become part of the business lexicon and stories about organizational culture are regularly reported in the business press. Many commercial websites promote trainers and consultants' strategies for implementing, changing, or improving organizational culture. For example, these websites promote their advice for shaping a positive and productive culture, identifying the dimensions of an organization's culture, or turning an organization's culture into a competitive advantage. Scholars from a number of disciplines are also interested in organizational culture. Obviously, scholars who study management and organizational communication view organizational culture as central to their interest in organizations. In addition, psychologists, sociologists, and anthropologists also study and explore organizational culture.

With this level and type of attention from practitioners, trainers, consultants, and scholars, one would think that we know all that we need to know about organizational culture. To the contrary, interest in organizational culture exists and continues to be stimulated because organizational culture is both changeable and complex, as it emerges from the interactions of organizational members. Moreover, as new organizational structures appear (for example, a workforce of virtually connected employees), they continue to challenge our understanding of organizational culture.

Based on the research literature, this book treats organizational culture as a complex, communicative, and multidimensional process, and introduces differing research and practical perspectives. The text reveals conclusions that scholars have drawn from different research approaches. The text also has a practical side drawing realistic applications from research findings. The focus of this book is limited to U.S. organizations. However, material in Section 3 does address the influence of globalization on U.S. organizations. The primary objective of this book is to help you make sense of organizational culture, and thereby help you to make informed work and employment decisions. Thus, this text encourages you to develop answers for four questions:

1. What is organizational culture?

2. How is organizational culture created?

3. Why does organizational culture matter?

4. What is my role in creating organizational culture?

Material in the text is presented in five sections. This first section—Positioning Organizational Culture—answers four questions: (a) What is an organization?, (b) What is organizational communication?, (c) What is culture?, and (d) What is organizational culture? This section concludes with the argument that understanding organizational culture is a primary means for understanding organizations and their communication practices.

The second section—Unpacking Organizational Culture—explores five core characteristics of organizational culture: that is, that organizational culture is inextricably linked to its employees; that it is dynamic; that it can hold competing values and assumptions; that it is emotionally charged; and that it is both the foreground and the background of the organization's communication system. This section also explores how organizational members communicate (and create) culture, and how communication among organizational members reveals cultural elements. Central to the exploration of organizational culture is subcultures. Thus, this section also addresses subcultures: how subcultures are both a part of the culture yet also distinct, and how subcultures are identified and structured relative to one another. This section closes by addressing what organizational culture is *not* and some common myths about organizational culture.

The third section—Lenses for Understanding Organizational Culture—starts with a description of the development of the organizational culture construct to show us how to position our different lenses, or perspectives, for investigating and understanding organizational culture. Subsequent parts of this section explore the reflexive relationship of communication and organizational culture from the lenses of symbolic performance, narrative and textual reproduction, management, power and politics, technology, and globalization.

The fourth section—Developing, Managing, and Changing Organizational Culture—addresses the pragmatic issues of communication's constitutive role in developing and managing organizational culture. A significant part of this section explores the ways in which organizational culture can change, intentionally or not. The role of formal and informal leaders and the role of ethics are explored for their influence on organizational culture.

The Culture Toolkit concludes the book by providing descriptive and analytical tools to use in the exploration of organizational culture. The Toolkit provides methodologies for conducting basic research studies of organizational culture or for use in applied studies with pragmatic consequences.

WHAT IS AN ORGANIZATION?

Ordered and Purposeful Interaction Among People

One way to define *organization* is to identify its common elements. First, an organization is comprised of people. Without people, an organization could not exist. Moreover, people, whether as salaried or hourly employees or volunteers, or the organization's clients, engage one another in purposeful and ordered activity (Shockley-Zalabak, 2002). Interaction in organizations is purposeful because people interact with organizations with a goal in mind. For example, cashiers at the grocery store have the expectation that they will scan the products that customers bring to their checkout lanes. Customers visit the grocery store to buy items and expect products to be on the shelves in a reasonable order. Whether you are the cashier or the customer, you have an expectation about the communication that will occur as you engage in these organizational roles of store clerk and customer. The point here is that people in organizations do not act randomly. Rather, organizations are sites of controlled and coordinated activity.

Our organizational role provides us with expectations and structures for our behaviors while we are engaged in that role. Admittedly, there may be occasional variations in expectations, but when I take on the role of professor at my university I expect to teach students in a prescribed set of classes for a specified period. Communicating with others at the university (i.e., administrators, faculty colleagues, staff members, and students) helps me to both understand and enact my role. My set of interactions combined with the sets of interactions of other organizational role-players (e.g., the department chair, the dean, other faculty, the computer technician, the librarian, and students) become the purposeful and ordered interactions that facilitate the university's achievement of its organizational goals.

Despite the organization's overall goals and ordered patterns of interaction, it is very likely that not all organizational members are directly connected to one another. It is possible even in small organizations that some employees will never communicate with each other. However the patterns of ordered activity and the communication channels that support that activity in and of themselves create links among organizational members, so that despite the lack of direct connection, employees are indirectly linked through some type of network structure (Stohl, 1995).

Communicating Within and Across Structures

In most organizations, what we label as organizational structure is the way in which organizational activities are organized into functional or operational units. For example, employees who provide services to other employees are often part of a human resources or personnel department while employees who create the goods an organization sells are part of the production or manufacturing unit. This type of deliberate structure is based on functional expertise. It is common for organizational structures to be delineated in this way. Common structural labels include manufacturing, research and development, client services, accounting, human resources, and so on. However, an organization's structure could also be delineated by timeframe or geographical region. Manufacturing plants that operate 24 hours a day, 7 days a week are structured by shifts (e.g., the first shift starts work at 7:00 a.m. and is relieved by the second shift at 3:00 p.m., which is relieved by the third shift at 11:00 p.m.) Conversely, an organization's structure could be geographically determined. For example, a company that refines and sells commercial grade solvents is organized by employees who work in the home office in Detroit, and those who work as sales representatives in Northern, Eastern, Southern, and Western regional offices. Of course, some organizations are so large that their structures are organized and identified by function, timeframe, and geography (e.g., reservation clerks who work the overnight shift at the Phoenix call center). In all organizations some type of hierarchy is created, and the power associated with hierarchical levels is distributed through the organizational structure with some members having more rights, responsibilities, and power than others. Traditionally, there is a distinction between the organization's executive, supervisory, and employee levels. We can identify the power and responsibility associated with each by examining the messages communicated between levels as well as looking at how those messages are communicated. Executives administer the organization and are responsible for its overall direction and strategy. Supervisors facilitate groups of employees in the day-to-day work that supports this direction and strategy, and employees engage in the work to create the organization's product or service. Even alternative organizational forms that include greater employee participation or are team-based have some type of organizational structure that creates and maintains power (Harter, 2004). Thus, organizational "structure is the architect of organized participation" (Stohl & Cheney, 2001, p. 359).

Regardless of how an organization is structured, organizational members are distributed across space and time in different units, shifts, or locations by division of labor, and by position or hierarchical level. While most organizational members regularly communicate to others within their unit, organizations cannot survive without their employees communicating across units as well. For example, the interdependence required to achieve continuous plant production demands a shift change meeting so that the operators on the first shift can describe how the equipment is working to those on the second shift. The organization's vice presidents, each responsible for a specific organizational function, will need to meet periodically as an executive team to discuss how functional goals in each area interact as they will influence the success of an organization's long-term strategic goals. And, even though sales reps are responsible for different geographical territories, periodic sales meetings will be scheduled at the home office so that home office and field employees can address procedural issues to create better working relationships and serve customers more effectively. Thus, communication interdependencies within and across organizational structures create and maintain organizations.

A Superordinate Goal

Interdependent interaction is required because organizations are created to achieve superordinate goals. A superordinate goal is one that is so difficult, time-consuming, and complex that it is beyond the capacity of one person. By bringing together people with different strengths and skills, an organization is able to achieve its goal. Few organizations can operate effectively using the resources of only one person. Even small or family businesses are dependent on the skills and talents of several organizational members, or contract employees, to achieve their goals.

Whether profit or nonprofit, an organization must have its economic viability as part of its goal. For-profit organizations, like The Gap, McDonald's, and VISA, have superordinate goals of selling clothes, fast food, and financial services, respectively. However, these goals are intended to accomplish another superordinate goal, that is, to make money to pay operating expenses and deliver profits, which are then distributed to the organization's owners, and perhaps the stockholders or employees. In a capitalistic society, making money is always an underlying organizational goal regardless of what type of product or service the organization manufactures or provides.

Even nonprofit organizations, whose purposes might be to provide services to children who have been abused or to protect the oceans and forests, must be concerned about their economic viability. While nonprofits typically do not make money by selling products or services, they cannot operate without capital. In the case of nonprofits, capital and operating expenses are raised through donations, earned from invested monies, or provided by institutional grantors or individuals who want the nonprofit to continue to provide services. The United Way and your local humane shelter are examples of nonprofits. Other nonprofits are more dependent upon cash received for services. Hospitals are a good example, as they bill patients and insurance companies for services provided. However, regardless of the income source, and regardless of the nature of their mission, whether it is charitable, religious, scientific, or educational, a nonprofit organization cannot legally make distributions to organizational members, officers, or directors. Rather, any surplus monies must be spent on providing the services for which the nonprofit organization was initially formed.

Government institutions and agencies at all levels must also raise monies to pay employees to provide us with our public services, such as trash collection, fire and police protection, emergency services, public school education, and highway maintenance. These institutions and agencies levy taxes on the people who use or benefit from their services, or raise money through fees, such as the fee you pay to obtain your driver's license, register your car, or use a campsite.

Accordingly, economic viability is a part of any organization's superordinate goal. While it may appear that an organization's goal is to manufacture and sell computers at retail outlets, the unstated part of this goal is to make a profit. If a municipality's goal is to provide quality K-12 education, the unstated part of this goal is to provide the best quality of education that the municipality's educational budget will allow. Even if we were to remove the monetary aspect, the superordinate goals implicit in running a computer manufacturing and retail operation or in providing public education are so complex that no one person could efficiently and effectively achieve them. Regardless of the size of the organization, a superordinate goal implies that two or more individuals will work interdependently and cooperatively to facilitate the achievement of the organizational goals, which, in turn, serve as a vehicle or purpose for obtaining monies or the other resources required to sustain goal-directed activities.

A Dynamic System

Considering these first three characteristics of organizations—organized and purposeful interaction, communication within and across structural units, and a superordinate goal—it is easy to see that organizations are dynamic systems. Despite the ordered and purposeful interaction employees pursue in achieving a superordinate goal, communication within and across structural units is not predictable. An organizational system is dynamic because an organization must be responsive to and interact with its customers and clients, suppliers, and regulatory and economic environments. Although an organization has a target audience, or public, for its products and services, other stakeholders interact with and influence the organization. For example, General Motors expects suppliers to deliver components as they are needed in the car manufacturing process rather than stockpiling parts ahead of time and warehousing them until needed. This type of just-in-time manufacturing creates interdependencies between a GM auto assembly plant and the supplying organizations. Likewise, GM, whose employees are members of the UAW (The International Union, United Automobile, Aerospace and Agricultural Implement Workers of America), must manufacture cars that meet emissions control standards set by the federal government. Working with these organizations, the suppliers, the union, and the government agency, GM is part of a dynamic system through which it influences other organizations, and at the same time is influenced by them.

The dynamics of these interdependent systems are further enhanced when GM considers its customers, the auto buying public. Simply because GM manufactures certain models does not ensure that these are the cars people want to purchase. Customers have preferences that may or may not be satisfied by GM's current car designs. Moreover, the economic environment (e.g., the cost of living, the unemployment rate) can make it more or less likely that people will have money to spend on a major purchase such as a car.

Just as the needs of its external public contribute to the interdependencies and dynamics of the GM organization, the internal public (GM's employees), contributes to its dynamic nature. Organizations lose and gain employees on a regular basis (through firing, layoffs, and retirements). Although job functions and the number of employees may remain fairly stable across a period of time, the people who hold jobs in the organization can have different levels of skill and motivation. A successful employee can be promoted or transferred, temporarily or permanently, to another position. Employees take vacations and other types of leaves of absence. New employees take on the responsibilities of those who quit or are terminated. While the job functions are arguably the same, the people performing them are not.

Think of a retail store you visit on a regular basis. There is probably one employee whom you prefer to have serve you. Perhaps this employee is friendly and remembers your name, or knows your product preferences and helps you find just the right thing. Now think of your shopping experience in this same store when your favorite employee is not working. Although ostensibly your interaction is with the same organization, your subjective experience may be considerably different. Because organizations are dynamic, different people can perform the same functions, but the communication experience will not be the same.

Thus, an organization is an open social system (Weick, 2001), which creates a dynamic as it develops and maintains interdependencies with both internal and external stakeholders. Internally, an organization is dynamic because employees move in and out of the organizational structure as they are promoted, hired, or fired. The relationships among employees can also differ based on which employees are promoted and which are scheduled for a particular shift or task. Because the contingent of employees is not stable, an organization's relationships among its external stakeholders are also dynamic.

Organization Defined

Thus, an *organization* is a dynamic system of organizational members, influenced by external stakeholders, who communicate within and across organizational structures in a purposeful and ordered way to achieve a superordinate goal. With this definition, an organization is not defined by its size, purpose, or structure. Rather, an organization is defined by the linguistic properties that reside in its internal and external communication interdependencies (Deetz, 1992; Weick, 1979). An organization can change its physical location and replace its members without breaking down because it is essentially a patterned set of discourses that at some point in time were created by the members and codified into norms and practices that are later inherited, accepted, and adapted to by newcomers. Because an organization emerges through communication, it is always being constituted; it is "a property of communication" (Taylor & Van Every, 2000, p. 37).

An organization is also a real and practical place (Boden, 1994; Kuhn & Ashcraft, 2003). Several streams of communication through multiple channels in multiple contexts continually constitute the organization. Face-to-face informal conversations among a group of coworkers, a written performance evaluation of a subordinate by a superior, telephone conversations between customer service agents and clients, a formal meeting among executives with others sitting in via electronic conferencing, and a persuasive plea by an employee to a boss for an extra day of vacation prior to a holiday—all constitute ongoing moments of the organization. It is a flexible, interactional system comprised of layers of ongoing conversations. Although it is common to reference *the* organization, it is not necessarily a monolithic or unified actor (Martin, 2002; Trice & Beyer, 1993; Weick, 1985). It is a symbolic and social construction of the ongoing and overlapping conversations of its members (Taylor & Van Every, 2000).

Assumptions About Organizations

In any study or discussion of organizations, two assumptions about them must be addressed (Weick, 2001). First, organizations are open social systems. Everything an organization does is done through its members who process and communicate information from both internal and external sources. Yet an organization does have a memory of sorts. "Individuals come and go, but organizations preserve knowledge, behaviors mental maps, norms, and values over time" (Weick, 2001, p. 243). When information is shared among organizational members and codified or captured in some way, an organizational interpretation exists beyond that of its individual members. These interpretations get passed from employee to employee creating a "thread of coherence" (Weick, 2001, p. 243) even though there may not be full convergence. The interactions of individuals create an organizational-level interpretation that can be passed on to others and acted on by others.

Second, organizational-level interpretations more commonly reflect the views of upper-level managers. Charged with the strategic operation of the organization, executives (e.g., vice president level and higher) have multiple opportunities to purposely direct or unintentionally influence what the organizational-level interpretation will become. In most organizations, top-level executives are a relatively small proportion of employees, yet their influence is disproportionately large. Because their job responsibilities include analyzing information drawn from a variety of sources, departments, or functions, top-level executives create interpretations that speak for the organization as a whole.

Defining an organization as a dynamic system of organizational members, influenced by external stakeholders, who communicate within and across organizational structures in a purposeful and ordered way to achieve a superordinate goal, forces us to take a closer look at what constitutes organizational communication. Although communication is required for an organization to exist, it is common for us to refer to *the organization* separately from the communication processes that sustain it.

WHAT IS ORGANIZATIONAL COMMUNICATION?

Without communication, could an organization . . .

- Create products or provide services?
- Market or sell its products and services?
- Respond to the concerns of its customers or clients?
- Respond to the demands and influences of external stakeholders?
- Coordinate employees?
- Plan and manage its internal affairs?

It should be obvious that organizations cannot exist without communication. Even before the members are communicating with potential customers and clients, they must communicate with one another to create and develop the organization's products and services. Thus, an organization emerges from communication and continues to emerge from the communication of its members (Taylor & Van Every, 2000).

Organization communication is not confined to messages within or to any particular stakeholder group. For an organization to exist, communication must occur with all stakeholder groups—current and potential employees, current and potential clients and customers, current and potential suppliers, and regulators or those who may have a regulatory role in the future. Some organizational communication is devoted solely to socializing new members or negotiating one's position in the organization. Some organizational communication, particularly that of management, is devoted to structuring or controlling the organization. Some organizational communication is devoted to negotiating and coordinating work activities—in other words, the communication that produces the work. Finally, some organizational communication is devoted to positioning the organization within the marketplace and society. Although initially directed to different stakeholders, these four types of role-related or work-related communication are likely to be interrelated or to overlap (McPhee & Zaug, 2001).

Frequently, business communication is confused with organizational communication. Organizational communication includes business communication, which includes formalized and planned messages codified in letters, memos, reports, websites, and advertising campaigns. Thus, business communication is what we refer to as the activities of leadership, supervision, decision making, managing conflict, hiring, firing, and so on.

However, organizational communication also includes informal and day-to-day interactions among organizational members. Informal conversations include personal stories, gossip, rumors, and socializing that also reveal important cultural information (Ibarra & Andrews, 1993), especially when informal or casual talk is intertwined with task talk, such as when casual conversation begins or ends professional meetings (Boden, 1994).

Together the formal and informal message systems across many channels create a context in which any one message is interpreted and understood relative to the others. A message cannot be isolated or dis-associated from an organization's context. Rather, any message sent or received by an organizational member is interpreted for meaning against the background of all other messages sent and received. A more complete picture of organizational communication is created when we think of messages in a pattern of coordinated moves among organiza-tional members. Interaction requires two or more people, and, from a transactional view of communication, one person cannot dictate how others will respond to or initiate conversations. Viewing organizational communication in this way reminds us that new possibilities are con-tinually being realized because the conversation can never be controlled (Barge & Little, 2002).

Organizational Communication Defined

Thus, *organizational communication* is a complex and continuous process through which organizational members create, maintain, and change the organization. Two important issues need to be addressed with this definition. First, it is important to note that all organizational members participate in this process. Communication is not the sole responsibility or privilege of managers. Even if managers create and send most of the messages, their subordinates and peers create mean-ing from those messages. Second, while the process is said to be trans-actional in which all parties enact both sender and receiver roles to create mutual and shared meanings of messages, shared meaning is not always achieved in organizational settings. Certainly, the process is mutual, and understandings are created. However, the interpreta-tions created or derived from these interactions may not be mutual (Stohl, 1995).

Because organizations must address and meet their monetary needs, organizations are also sites of hierarchy, dominance, and power, with organizational members having varying degrees of power and status and varying degrees of control over message creation and message meaning. For example, Cedric, the family member who manages his family's specialty retail store has more power and status than non-family members employed there. In this role, Cedric will create more of the organizational messages intended to prescribe organizational policies and practices. However, of the non-family employees, Sarah, who has worked there the longest, is likely to be perceived as having more power and status than the others have. Indeed, other employees look to Sarah for her advice about interacting with customers, and as a result of her mentoring, increase their commissions. However, what if a new employee who is also a family member has just been hired? Would this new employee have more power and status due to his familial connections? Or would non-family employees have more power and status due to their experience at the store? This example identifies two realities of organizational life. First, that power and status vary among organizational members. Second, that power and status vary along a number of dimensions. Thus, it is likely that on some level you will have more power and status than other employees.

Certainly, the varying degrees of organizational power and status will influence how you create meaning for and from organizational messages. Other factors will also influence what you communicate about, how you communicate, and how you create meaning in an organization. These include your interest in the job you perform or the profession with which you identify, your interest in the organization you work for, the people you work with, and the rewards work provides to you.

Finally, the number and nature of competing roles you are enacting will also influence what you communicate about, how you communicate, and how you create meaning in an organization. Many students who work part time consider their work roles secondary to their roles as students. Employees with families or employees who are heavily vested in a hobby or volunteering may also view their work roles as secondary to their other commitments. However, there are individuals in every organization who view their organizational role as primary over all others. Although we are voluntary members of organizations, our membership in organizations differs along a number of characteristics, each of which influences our level of participation in the communication process.

As a result of these characteristics, organizational messages vary across several dimensions. Some organizational messages are intended to be strategic and task oriented. For example, imagine that you are the afternoon supervisor at a restaurant. It is your responsibility to oversee three simultaneous goals. First, you must ensure that the customers are served. Second, you must check that your employees prepare the ingredients needed for dinner meals. Third, you must be certain the restaurant is kept clean because it is subject to random inspection by your manager or the health inspector. As you have gained experience as a supervisor, you have learned which employees can be relied upon to effectively perform specific tasks, how the tasks are interrelated, and how to estimate the flow of dining traffic during the afternoon hours. Therefore, as you start your shift, you are able to give specific instructions to your employees. These are strategic messages because you are instructing employees on *what* to focus on and how to carry out these tasks. Your communication with the employees is strategic in nature because as their supervisor you want to control their behavior and work performance. Other instances of communication that you have with them are informal and more personally oriented. Examples of this type of communication include talking with your employees during breaks about their personal lives, or chatting with your manager about your weekend plans while waiting for a conference call to begin.

Some information in organizations is communicated verbally or nonverbally, while other messages are communicated in writing or electronically. Certain messages are communicated solely to an individual; others are communicated to groups. Some messages are internal, as they are communicated to other employees; some are external, as they are communicated to people external to the organization, such as customers or suppliers.

To illustrate these varied message types, return to the previous restaurant scenario. As the afternoon supervisor, you start the shift with a brief shift meeting explaining the prep work that needs to be done for the evening shift and the cleaning tasks that need to be accomplished. Once given their instructions, the employees conduct their duties and you return to the office to finish your month-end reports and to put the candles on a cake to celebrate one server's upcoming college graduation. Before you can surprise your employee with the graduation celebration, you notice that the buzz in the restaurant is louder than what is customary for this time of day. You walk toward the serving area to find that a bus of tourists is visiting your restaurant. These patrons are waiting to have their orders taken. By observing the wait staff's hurried movements, you can tell that they are overwhelmed, so you pitch in by taking orders from the large tables the tourists have pushed together for themselves. After writing down the orders, you deliver them to the cooks and begin assisting in preparing the food. As one server prepares a salad, you look at the monitor for other salad orders and see that a second customer has ordered the same item. To save time, you ask this employee to prepare the salad needed by the other server. As the cook finishes the meals and places them under the serving lights, you let another server know that you will help her to deliver her customers' meals. As you empty your tray, you notice a raised hand from a customer whose order you took. You walk over to answer her question. Finally, all the orders have been delivered and the unexpected afternoon rush is over. The restaurant traffic returns to normal and you determine that the afternoon crew can handle the remaining customers and prep tasks. You return to your office and write out a procedure for handling a large volume of customers. However, before you print it out, you email the procedure to your manager to obtain her feedback and approval. Once approved, you intend to use the new procedure as a training tool. After all this is done, you look around to see what should be done next and notice that you have forgotten the graduation cake. Meekly you take the cake out to the serving area, hoping to gather enough employees to celebrate the server's graduation from college even though the afternoon and evening shifts are changing places.

Within these few minutes, you have sent and received strategic and spontaneous, formal and informal, verbal, nonverbal, written, and electronic messages. You have communicated internally with other employees and your manager, and externally with customers, and you have communicated with individuals and groups of people. Moreover, like most employees, you moved flexibly among these types and methods of communicating without even thinking of them in this discrete way. Although you sent specific and distinct messages, the messages were not independent. Rather, the messages were part of a communication system in which meaning was derived from the communication context that included the roles (e.g., manager, wait staff, cook, customer) in which individuals were engaged. Some of your messages were strategic. For example, you instructed one server to prepare a salad for an order taken by another to save time. Some of your messages were spontaneous. You noticed a customer's raised hand and responded immediately to his request.

Thus, *organizational communication* is a complex and continuous process through which organizational members create, maintain, and change the organization by communicating verbally, nonverbally, electronically, and in writing with individuals and groups of people engaged in roles as internal and external stakeholders. It is important to note here that this definition views communication as consequential. Real consequences, intended or not, arise from our communication in organizations.

Do you notice the similarity in the definitions of *organization* and *organizational communication?* These two concepts are inextricably linked. Communication is not superimposed on an organization. Rather organizations emerge from communication, making all communication organizational (Taylor & Van Every, 2000).

WHAT IS CULTURE?

Culture was initially a concept applied to social groupings that were geographically distinguished from one another, and became the focus of anthropological studies. One early definition provides that culture:

> consists in patterned ways of thinking, feeling and reacting, acquired and transmitted mainly by symbols, constitute the distinctive achievements of human groups, including their embodiments in artifacts; the essential core of culture consists of traditional (i.e., historically derived and selected) ideas and especially their attached values. (Kroeber & Kluckhohn, 1952, p. 181)

From early anthropological studies, the focus was on the complex whole, not any one element and culture, and culture was synonymous with societal boundaries. Over time as the discipline of anthropology evolved, so did the concept of culture.

More recently, Hofstede (2001) offered that culture was "the collective programming of the mind that distinguishes the members of one group or category of people from another" (p. 11). With this definition, we can view culture as a system of values for any group of people, not just societies or nations. Regardless of perspective, anthropologists search for the "meaning underlying human creations, behaviors, and thoughts . . . by observing cultural aspects" (Sackmann, 1991, p. 14). The primary contribution of anthropologists to the study of culture has been their integrated and detailed accounts of cultural phenomena, which have been adopted by communication scholars.

Sociologists also study culture, but they do so in a different way. The sociological tradition is to focus on subgroups of society (e.g., first year college students, blue-collar workers). From this perspective, culture is conceptualized as a collection of the ideas, themes, and values expressed by a particular social group (Sackmann, 1991). Thus, a sociological view of culture examines culture across a type of person (many of whom do not interact with each other, not even indirectly), while an anthropological view of culture examines the integrated patterns within an interacting community.

In today's society, references to culture are many. We commonly speak about national culture (e.g., American culture), ethnic or racial cultures (e.g., African American culture, Jewish culture), regional culture (e.g., southern culture), and more localized cultures (e.g., Memphis, Tennessee, your university, or even your neighborhood). In each of these instances, people interacting in these social structures create their culture. Culture is not produced for them; it is produced by them as they interact with one another. Moreover, a culture is continually reproduced by its members. Thus, the patterns, expectations, and norms emerge as meanings, and are negotiated and re-negotiated as members enter and exit the social structure.

Like any social group, the complex web of messages sent and received by members in an organization is interpreted by these members, and the interpretation results in patterns and expectations. The interplay of messages and meanings creates a culture, or a set of artifacts, values, and assumptions, by which people choose their subsequent behaviors and messages, and against which the behaviors and messages are interpreted. Hence, culture is both a process and a product (Bantz, 1993).

Furthermore, just as culture is both a process and a product, culture is also confining and facilitating. Culture is confining because it acts as a perspective or framework, limiting what we see and how we interpret what we see. On the other hand, culture is also facilitating, as it allows us to make sense of what is happening so that we can function in that setting. The social reality of any group is simultaneously tied to its traditions anchored in the past, and open to revised or new interpretations based on the interactions of its members. Indeed, culture is learned and passed on from one generation to another, and defines groups and distinguishes them from other social groups (Stohl, 2001).

How do we know when something becomes a part of culture? Three criteria guide our acceptance of something as culture. These are when meanings are: (a) deeply felt or held, (b) commonly intelligible, and (c) widely accessible to the cultural group (Carbaugh, 1988a). At the same time, any specific aspect of culture is intertwined with other cultural aspects. No one symbol or value exists in isolation; rather, a combination of symbols and values create culture.

Cultural symbols—physical indicators of organizational life (Rafaeli & Worline, 2000)—are deeply felt or held when they tap into emotions or identity. For example, students at the University of Kansas identify strongly with the Jayhawk, the university's mascot. Students, staff, and faculty proudly display Jayhawks on their hats, sweatshirts, and jackets. The Jayhawk appears on university posters, business cards, and websites. Jayhawk statues are on display on campus and in the community. The Jayhawk is a cultural symbol at the university. Students, staff, faculty, alumni, and local businesspeople identify with the Jayhawk symbol. It identifies them as belonging to a specific university, and as a result, ties them to others who are part of the Jayhawk community.

Classifying or referring to someone as a Jayhawk separates people into two cultural groups: those who are Jayhawks and those who are not. Not only do those in the University of Kansas community identify themselves as Jayhawks, others outside this group are able to label them as Jayhawks as well. Within the University of Kansas community, the Jayhawk is more than just a convenient way to identify team and school loyalty. The legend of the Jayhawk and how it became the university's mascot is retold every fall during student and faculty orientations. The meaning of the Jayhawk is commonly understood. No one would point at another mascot and say, "That's a Jayhawk."

However, while there is a common identification of what a Jayhawk is, and acknowledgment that this symbol stands for the University of Kansas, there is some variety about what beliefs and values are represented by the Jayhawk. For some, the Jayhawk denotes excellence in college basketball. For others, the Jayhawk represents democratic values championed by the Civil War era individuals who made Kansas a free state. For still others, the Jayhawk is simply a way to label oneself as being part of the University of Kansas community. Each of these interpretations is generated from the same Jayhawk symbol. Some individuals may carry multiple interpretations of the symbol; others may carry only one. Often the interpretation is context dependent.

The Jayhawk itself is not the culture; it is a physical identifier of the University of Kansas community and a symbolic representation of the artifacts, values, and assumptions created by the individuals who comprise the University of Kansas social structure. A symbol always represents something different or more than itself because it combines the concrete or direct experience with an abstract feeling or attitude (Alvesson & Berg, 1991). In summary, a symbol is a collective representation of a culture when the symbol or meaning is deeply felt or held, is interpretable within a community, and is widely accessible to members of the community.

Thus, it would be impossible for any culture to be stagnant. Although some cultures change more dramatically or frequently than others, there is always opportunity for new cultural interpretations to be generated as individuals enter and exit a community and as members interact to make sense of their environment. The culture creation process is not simple. Members of the community influence it as they interact with one another and as they respond to threats and opportunities in both their internal and external environments.

WHAT IS ORGANIZATIONAL CULTURE?

Given the definitions of organization, organizational communication, and culture introduced in this section, it should be clear that some type of culture would emerge from any collection of individuals who comprise themselves as an organization. Individuals in an organization are held together—positively or negatively, loosely or tightly—by their communication within and across the organizational structure as they work to satisfy the organization's superordinate goal, as well as their personal or professional goals. Just as an organization is enacted through the interactions of its members, an organizational culture emerges from the complex and continuous web of communication among members of the organization.

There are many definitions of *organizational culture*. Schein (1992) defines it as:

A pattern of shared basic assumptions that the group [social units of all sizes] learned as it solved its problems of external adaptation and internal integration, that has worked well enough to be considered valid and, therefore, to be taught to new members as the correct way to perceive, think, and feel in relation to those problems. (p. 12)

His definition focuses on three elements: (a) socialization, or the way in which new organizational members learn the culture; (b) deeply held assumptions; and (c) recognition that any organization may have more than one culture. Schein further argues that culture can be analyzed at three different levels: artifacts, espoused values, and basic underlying assumptions.

Martin (2002) defines organizational culture as "patterns of interpretation composed of the meanings associated with various cultural manifestations, such as stories, rituals, formal and informal practices, jargon, and physical arrangements" (p. 330). Further characterizing the boundaries of organizational culture as fluctuating, permeable, and blurred, Martin argues that organizational culture is a subjective phenomenon viewed differently by different people. Her perspective cautions us in making quick decisions about who is in or out of an organizational culture simply by identifying employees as organizational members. She argues that we should not assume that organizational culture is tied to a physical location or to a collection of bodies.

For example, a sales representative for a footwear manufacturer travels throughout his territory west of the Mississippi River; the other sales rep covers the territory east of the Mississippi. The manufacturer's headquarters, or home office, is in South Carolina, which the two sales reps visit only three times per year. If we were to view organizational culture as residing in a location, then the two sales reps would not be part of it. To the contrary, their frequent phone and email contact with one another and home office employees contributes to the creation of the organization's culture just as much as the more frequent and face-to-face interactions among home office employees contribute to the organization's culture. Are the sales reps influenced by the organization's culture? Yes, but the intensity of that cultural connection is likely to be different from the cultural influences felt by employees in the home office. The intensity of the employee-cultural connection can also vary among home office employees, some employees are more connected to and more influenced by the organization's culture than others. There must be some degree of collective interaction to create and share patterns of interpretation, yet what is shared is not complete or total.

Parker (2000) argues for a perspective in which *culture* and *organization* fold into one another with the culture making process occurring in organizations and the organizing process occurring in culture. His view also stresses that culture is not a mechanism internal to an organization. Rather, "culture making processes take place 'inside,' 'outside' and 'between' formal organizations" resulting in many different senses of culture (p. 82). He points out that neither organization nor culture are cohesive or definitive wholes with stable references because history and everyday practice are being drawn together. This results, he argues, in a continual process of creating shifting and temporary meanings that are often contested or competing. Thus, Parker's definition of organizational culture is "a continually contested process of making claims of difference within and between groups of people who are formally constituted as members of a defined group" (p. 233).

Common to these definitions are several features. First, organizational culture must be shared by a collective. That collective, or group, can vary in size from a small work unit to a division, or from a handful of employees to all employees. Those who share cultural elements may not be confined to any one department or unit. Organizational members who share cultural elements are drawn together by their meaningful and shared interpretation, not necessarily by their job function or location. Those organizational members who share these interpretations are likely to say, "It's how *we* do things around here."

Second, organizational culture is a multilevel construct comprising many elements—primarily artifacts, values, and assumptions. As a set, these elements guide our organizational behavior, help us make sense of the organizational world in which we operate, and create a mechanism for identifying with others at work. Although the artifact, value, and assumption categorization scheme is commonly referenced, organizational culture phenomena are not so neatly identified.

These categories are hardly ever seen as exclusive. Instead, they may be associated with different layers of social practice and consciousness, some visible and accessible, while others are hidden and, for that reason, thought to be much harder to change. (Schoenberger, 1997, p. 117)

Any cultural phenomenon may exist at one, two, or all three levels. An organizational culture is a system of artifacts, values, and assumptions—not any one artifact, value, or assumption. For example, an artifact (e.g., Monday morning sales meetings with a buffet breakfast) may reflect values (e.g., a strong emphasis on employee participation, leadership visibility) that, in turn, reflect underlying ideological assumptions (e.g., get employees together on Monday morning while they are fresh; motivate them with this week's goals so that the organization can meet its annual sales forecast). In this case, the artifacts, values, and assumptions create a congruent pattern of understanding.

It is also possible that an artifactual representation of organizational values is not meaningfully or similarly held by all employees. For example, at a global transportation company, all employees are given a card to carry in their wallet and a plaque for their desks. On one side is the organization's vision statement. On the other side are the company's guiding principles about leadership. Despite the presence of the artifact, and some would say despite the top management's obvious preoccupation with having the organization's vision and leadership principles in front of the organization's managers—not all managers adhere to the leadership principles. Some even scoff at them or interpret them in humorous ways among trusted colleagues. Top management expects all managers to have the vision and principles memorized. However, doing so does not move the vision and leadership principles from roles as artifacts to enacted values. The following sections provide a more detailed explanation of artifacts, values, and assumptions, and their roles in the process of creating organizational culture.

Artifacts

Artifacts are visible or tangible—anything that one can see, hear, or feel in the organizational experience, and often the first things we notice about an organization when we enter it. Norms, standards, and customs are artifacts just like the more physical attributes of organizational life. Social conventions (e.g., celebrations, forms of address) of the organization are easy to observe, but can be difficult to decipher because the path back to the value that prompted the artifact is not always direct or clear. Interpretation of artifacts is further complicated because organizational life produces a great number of artifacts and observers cannot focus on all of them. Thus, most analyses of an organization's artifacts are partial. Thus, a valid interpretation of an organization's culture cannot be constructed from its artifacts alone (Schein, 1992).

One artifact that becomes especially important in studying organizational culture is norms. A norm is a way in which a collective, or group of people, engage in routine behavior. More specifically, a norm is a (a) pattern of behavior or communication (b) that indicates what people should do in a specific setting. It is also a (c) collective expectation of what behavior should be or what reaction should be given to a particular behavior. Thus, norms are informal or unconsciously held rules for how people should behave and communicate (Bantz, 1983; Feldman, 1984; Gibbs, 1965), and powerful forms of social control (Bettenhausen & Murnigham, 1985).

Despite this power, norms are rarely explicitly or directly addressed or acknowledged. Rather, norms become routine and unstated expectations about behavior. Organizational members do not regularly discuss what the norms are, but they are likely to admit that a particular communication practice is a norm if it is pointed out to them. In many organizations, the normative practice is to use first names when speaking with other members of your work group. However, the norm shifts to using a person's last name when that individual is not present. For example, in a meeting, my colleagues will use "Joann" to get my attention or ask me a question, but when referring to me in my absence, the norm is to say, "I'll talk to Keyton about that." As with assumptions and values, artifacts are derived from symbols, and as such, are the basis of organizational culture.

Values

Individual organizational members can hold values, but it is the values shared by organizational members that are of importance to organizational culture. A value is "a broad tendency to prefer certain states of affairs over others" (Hofstede, 2001, p. 5) and determines our view of reality. *Values* are strategies, goals, principles, or qualities that are considered ideal, worthwhile, or desirable, and, as a result, create guidelines for organizational behavior. Values have both intensity and direction. Thus, values can be seen as being dimensional with each having a plus and minus pole, for example, rational vs. irrational and dangerous vs. safe. Frequently, we talk about organizations having values. More accurately, individuals within organization share values. Values are human properties, thus when we talk about organizations having values, we mean so only metaphorically (Stackman, Pinder, & Connor, 2000).

Values that are often associated with work and organizations include prestige, wealth, control, authority, ambition, pleasure, independence, creativity, equality, tolerance, respect, commitment, politeness, and harmony. Organizational cultures comprise many values that are interdependent in some way. While one set of values may support one another (e.g., independence and personal achievement); other values may conflict (e.g., autonomy and team work).

Despite their importance to understanding an organization's culture, values are invisible and difficult to discern until they are manifested in behavior (Hofstede, 2001) and shared by organizational members (Schein, 1992). Some values are subconsciously held and become assumptions that we use in choosing our behavior and communication without consciously considering the choices we are making. Thus, the values of an organization are often visible in the actions of its employees and the values influence how organizational members facilitate and practice communication.

For example, Josh, a new marketing employee would probably have difficulty discovering why accounting processes are discussed at every meeting, especially those meetings that ostensibly have little to do with accounting. The discussions of accounting are so frequent and central to the flow of the meetings that Josh believes he is missing a critical piece of information. His observations of the work environment do not provide any clues, and he is hesitant to ask because, to him, it looks like he is asking about the obvious. In a lunch conversation, a colleague says to him casually while talking about his potential promotion:

> You do know that our CEO was an accountant, so, he likes all of the vice presidents to be accountants, or at least have considerable accounting knowledge? Even Lurinda, our VP, has an accounting background. So, I took some accounting courses so I could feel more confident making contributions in the meeting. What kind of accounting background do you have?

In this organization, accounting skills are obviously highly valued and this value creates assumptions about what people should know, what is important to discuss, and who should be promoted. This example illustrates another characteristic about values. Values that are shared inevitably become transformed into assumptions that seldom are overtly discussed in conversation.

Assumptions

Assumptions are beliefs that are taken for granted, so deeply entrenched that organizational members no longer discuss them.

Although deeply held, these tacit assumptions are subtle, abstract, and implicit. Organizational members can hold assumptions about themselves (e.g., as professionals, employees); about their relationships to other organizational members, clients, customers, vendors, and other external stakeholders; about the organization itself; or about the work that they perform. For example, one assumption held by printing press operators of a plant that produces and prints magazines is that any errors that make it into print are the responsibility of the editorial side of the operation located in another city. Even if a press operator notices an error as she checks the initial copies for the quality of printing, she dismisses it without notifying anyone. The "we just print what they give us" attitude allows the press operators to produce the magazine "on schedule 'cause that's our job." The assumption about the division of work is so deeply held that press operators, and even their supervisors, do not recognize printing thousands of copies of magazines with errors in them as a problem.

As this example demonstrates, basic assumptions are acted on with such little variation that any other action is inconceivable. In this way, assumptions guide behavior by directing how organizational members should perceive, think, feel, and act. Because assumptions do not rise to the level of conversation, they are extremely difficult to change. In fact, assumptions are so ingrained that the organizational members who hold the assumptions are often unable to articulate them until they are confronted with a different set of assumptions such as they might encounter when changing jobs, or when an organization undergoes radical change (Schein, 1996).

As an integrated set, basic assumptions provide a map by which we engage our organizational lives. Assumptions are so powerful that we run the risk of not understanding or misinterpreting the actions of others who behave according to a different set of assumptions (Schein, 1992). Interviews with employees who work for a company that designs and produces packaged holiday-themed gifts revealed that they are so accustomed to doing whatever it takes to get the product out that they are stumped when someone asks, "Who do you report to?" Stephanie, a gift designer, explained:

> Sometimes I report to my boss. But other times I don't report to anyone. Our business demands that we work quickly to take advantage of purchasing deals and to accommodate our retail customers' objectives, and to create gifts within specific price points.

So, my reporting structure isn't necessarily hierarchical . . . I get an okay if there's someone who can approve what I'm doing. But really, the reporting structure is really based on what aspect of gift design is a problem at the moment. You know . . . sometimes, my VP doesn't even know what I'm doing.

Thus, for this organization, the assumption of "do whatever is necessary to make the customer happy" is the foundation of the approval process, quite different from an organization in which employees work within a strict hierarchical structure with different levels of approval. Stephanie explained further,

Vendors and customers sometimes ask me, "Who needs to approve this concept?" Frankly, that's me . . . I'm the one who designs it and has to bring it to market within a certain margin of the retail price. That's just how we operate. I'm not sure I could even draw an organization chart out. When we hire someone new, this is really hard to explain. They [the newcomer] expect that we have some type of chart that tells them who does what. The bottom line: If you have to have approval to feel confident about your work, this probably isn't the place for you.

The profit-centered assumption, or focus on the bottom line, is so embedded in this organization and accepted by Stephanie and other employees that making decisions in any other manner would not make sense to them. Watching Stephanie create a gift product reinforces her deep acceptance of the profit-centered assumption. Rather than starting with a design concept or stylized drawing, Stephanie starts the design process for each gift product with a price point—that is, how much a retail customer will pay measured against how much the retailer will pay the gift design company relative to the profit the design company will make selling 10,000 copies of the gift. With these numbers, or margins, in mind, Stephanie phones her suppliers to ask, for example, "What ceramic mug or bowl do you have that I can buy for 16 cents? I need 10,000." If her price is accepted, she gives the supplier a purchase order number without consulting the vice president she reports to, and starts to identify and negotiate for the elements of the gift that can fit into the purchased mug or bowl. In this company, a gift is *designed* based primarily on profit-centered assumptions and purchasing opportunities rather than on creative or artistic features.

INTEGRATION OF ARTIFACTS, VALUES, AND ASSUMPTIONS

Although an organization's culture comprises of artifacts, values, and assumptions, organizational members seldom talk directly about any of these. More typically, organizational members *reveal* their assumptions and values through their communication—communicating about the organization and what happened in the organization. Thus, organizational culture is revealed through day-to-day conversations organizational members have with other insiders and outsiders. Moreover, much of that communication revolves around the artifact manifestations of culture. By creating and enacting rites, rituals, and ceremonies; practicing norms or procedures; using specialized language; and telling stories or using metaphors, organizational culture is revealed.

It is important to recognize that no single artifact, value, or assumption is, or can create, an organization's culture. Rather, culture emerges from the complex interplay of these elements in the organizational communication of all the organization's members, at all levels, in all job functions. As a result, culture is an extremely subtle phenomenon (Isaac & Pitt, 2001) that is not entirely obvious to those in or outside of the organization. Because all organizational members help to create and sustain it, culture permeates all levels and functions of an organization making it nearly impossible to see its totality in one set of interactions.

Organizational Culture Defined

From these commonalities, this book uses the following definition of organizational culture: *Organizational culture is the set(s) of artifacts, values, and assumptions that emerge from the interactions of organizational members.* An organization's culture becomes the framework against which organizational communication is evaluated and is the avenue for creating ongoing collective and individual action. This definition embraces the notion that organizations are "evolving, dynamic, complex cultural systems with inconsistencies and paradoxes, and several cultural groupings or meaning systems" (Sackmann, 1990, p. 138). An organization does not have a culture; it *is* culture (Smircich, 1983).

ORGANIZATIONAL CULTURE AND YOU

Why should you be interested in the study of organizational culture? Inevitably you will be a member of many organizational cultures: the culture of the profit, nonprofit, or government organization for which you work, the civic and social organizations in which you volunteer your time, and the community and religious organizations in which you celebrate and create social ties. You will contribute to the creation, maintenance, and development of these organizational cultures. As a member of these organizations, your communication with other organizational members will influence the cultures that are created. Studying the intersection of organizational communication and organizational culture is central to your role as an organizational member. In organizations, communication functions both as the instrument that operationalizes and as a means of interpreting it (Mills, Boylstein, & Lorean, 2001). Thus, your communicative role as an organizational member is central to both the emergent nature of the organization and its culture. Understanding organizational culture and your role in its creation and maintenance could help you cope with issues at work, and, potentially, help you succeed in or manage that environment.

The link between organizational culture and communication becomes salient when employees or managers want to change something about the organization. Indeed, employees across many levels frequently report that communication *is* an issue in their organization (e.g., Sobo & Sadler, 2002). Despite this awareness, communication is often taken for granted and simultaneously lauded as being responsible for achieving organizational goals or blamed as the root of organizational problems. Given the role of organizational communication in developing and sustaining organizational culture, developing an understanding of organizational culture will help you achieve your personal and professional goals, and influence organizational goals.

Additionally, even if you did not care about your work environment, it is shaping your interactions within it. Anything with that much influence on your communication is worthy of your attention. And finally, organizational members frequently point to an organization's culture as what distinguishes their organization from others. For example, Rich Panico, president of Integrated Project Management Company, points to the way in which the culture of his organization helps him recruit new employees.

When we hire people we will ask them why they joined us. I will tell you that 98 or 99 times out of 100 they will tell us it's because of our culture. Talk to our people, you'll learn that this company lives up to Our Mission and Beliefs. To me this is the strongest endorsement. (Mathys, 2002, pp. 96–97)

An organization's culture is what sets one organization apart from similar others. Churches of the same denomination, fast food restaurants of the same chain, home improvement retailers with similar product lines, manufacturers of desktop and laptop computers, universities of similar sizes and student populations, county governments in the same state—all distinguish themselves from one another by the organizational culture that emerges from the interactions of its organizational members. You are a part of that process.

Most of us have to work. Feeling comfortable in that environment can be important. Indeed, the level of congruence between an organization's culture and employees' value preferences can predict employee job satisfaction and turnover (O'Reilly, Chatman, & Caldwell, 1991; Vandenberghe, 1999).

Does Organizational Culture Really Matter?

This is a difficult question to answer because qualitative scholarly studies of organizational culture tend to examine the way in which organizational members create and enact their organizational culture with particular emphasis on (a) members' influence on the culture, and (b) the culture's influences on them. Despite the richness and detail of the data and the contextualization of the findings, these types of studies generally do not assess organizational cultural relative to organizational outcomes. This is primarily because the link between culture and performance is believed to be indirect or too multiply linked to be coherent. There are some quantitative studies that attempt to compare types of organizational cultures and examine the influences of cultural types on outcomes, but often the type of data collected only allows for a surface or partial view of culture, as it is quite difficult to get to the deep meanings of cultural assumptions and values in questionnaire items. Thus, answering *if* organizational culture matters and *how* it differs based upon these methodological and ideological choices is a difficult endeavor.

If you look at the organizational cultural studies as a whole across disciplines, however, it is easier to conclude that organizational culture really does matter. Of course, individuals who have work experience in several organizations can confirm this. Despite similarities in occupations and professions, different organizations *are* different—sometimes subtly; other times to a great degree. However, because our focus as an organizational member is on our personal view of the culture, it can be difficult to see the full extent to which these differences matter. Sometimes we will not see the influence on ourselves until we leave that environment, until another person brings it to our attention, or until a situation occurs in which there is a prominent clash of personal and organizational values.

Which brings us back to the question: Does organizational culture really matter?

Yes, it does.

A study using ethnographic and survey data of social control mechanisms on workplace drinking norms demonstrated the way in which organizational culture can matter on both organizational (e.g., absenteeism, safety, quality) and individual (e.g., aggression, health) outcomes (Ames, Grube, & Moore, 2000). The study was conducted in two large U.S. manufacturing plants—both manufactured the same product in the same industry; workers were represented by the same union. One plant in the Western U.S. employed approximately 4,000 employees; the plant in the Midwest employed approximately 6,000 employees. In both settings, 90% of the workers were employed in hourly positions; most worked on assembly lines, as skilled tradespeople, or in support services.

Despite these similarities, there were significant structural differences between the two plants. The Western plant was jointly owned by Japanese and U.S. corporations and, as a result, used some aspects of Japanese management principles. Employees, including management, were organized into teams and had greater responsibility for delivering quality products, finding solutions to problems, and improving production. Consensual decision making was encouraged, and union-management relationships were cooperative. The Midwest plant was owned by a U.S. corporation and reflected a more traditional bureaucratic structure and principles. This plant had a hierarchical organizational structure and a rigid division of job tasks. Managers, not employees, were responsible for decision making and performance issues, and there was an adversarial relationship between union and management.

The objective of this study was to examine how workplace drinking norms compared in the two cultures. In the survey portion of the study, the research team found that 72% and 81% of male and female employees at the Midwestern plant drank, whereas 80% and 77% of male and female employees at the Western plant drank. Thus, overall, employees did not differ in their alcohol consumption. However, employees did differ considerably in *where* they drank. At the Midwestern plant, men (23%) and women (26%) were far more likely to report drinking while on the job than employees at the Western plant (3% for both men and women).

What could account for this difference?

Organizational culture.

Norms about workplace drinking differed dramatically between the sets of employees. Overwhelmingly, employees at the Midwestern plant were more likely than employees at the Western plant to get alcohol from others at work, bring alcohol into the plant, drink while at their work stations, or drink at breaks. At the same time, employees at the Western plant reported with greater frequency than employees at the Midwestern plant that their coworkers, team members, and supervisors disapproved of drinking at work. Employees at the Western plant also differed dramatically in their reporting that it was very likely that they would get caught if they drank at work or in the parking lot at work, and would be disciplined for doing so.

Because individuals' drinking patterns outside of work did not transfer uniformly to drinking at work, the research team investigated cultural elements that could encourage or inhibit work-related drinking. Both plants had a formal alcohol policy in place (including statements about bringing alcohol into the workplace, drinking during work hours, and being at work in an impaired condition, and both policies contained procedures for disciplinary action), but the policies were differently revered and enforced. At the Midwestern plant, supervisors did not enforce the policy because it was incompatible with other organizational policies, and this incompatibility was a low priority for union officials and management. Other work environment problems were more pressing. At the Western plant, the alcohol policy complemented other policies (e.g., drug use policy, attendance policy), and, despite the team environment, other aspects of the Western plant appeared rigid and controlling; yet, employees seemed comfortable with these structures. For example, employees could take their lunch break on the premises to earn an additional hour's pay. This, of course, kept employees from leaving the premises to buy or drink alcohol.

Informal social controls were more prominent at the Western plant due to the team structure because team concepts were evident at all levels of the organization. Employees in this plant experienced greater cohesion and solidarity with their team and other organizational members, as teams, not individuals, were responsible for productivity and quality. Thus, peer accountability for worker performance and safety was significantly more pronounced at the Western plant. Conversely, at the Midwestern plant, peer accountability was weakened due to the autonomous work structure, which did not encourage cohesiveness to develop among organizational members.

Does organizational culture matter? In this study, the formal and informal social control mechanisms about drinking differed considerably. Moreover, the social control mechanisms acted as norms in either facilitating or inhibiting workplace drinking.

Does organizational culture matter?

Yes.

SUMMARY

This section introduces the concepts of *organization, organizational communication, culture,* and *organizational culture.* An organization is a dynamic system of organizational members, influenced by external stakeholders, who communicate within and across organizational structures in a purposeful and ordered way to achieve a superordinate goal. Without communication, an organization could not exist. Thus, organizational communication is the complex and continuous process through which organizational members create, maintain, and change the organization. This definition presumes that all organizational members participate in this process, and organizational members can create shared meanings of messages, but not all meanings will be shared.

Culture is defined as both a process and product—the complex set of messages and meanings by which people choose their subsequent behaviors and messages, and against which behaviors and messages are interpreted. Culture distinguishes people in one group or collective from people in another group or collective. Artifacts, values, and assumptions are the three broad categories of cultural elements that comprise the pattern of symbols interpreted as organizational culture.

Artifacts are visible—anything that one can see, hear, or feel in the organizational experience—and often the first things we notice about an organization when we enter it. Norms, standards, and customs are artifacts just like the more physical attributes of organizational life. Values are broad tendencies to prefer certain states of affairs over others, and have both intensity and direction. Despite their importance to understanding an organization's culture, values are invisible and difficult to discern until they are manifested in behavior and shared by organizational members. Assumptions guide behavior by directing how organizational members should perceive, think, feel, and act. Because they do not rise to the level of conversation, they are extremely difficult to change. Artifacts, values, and assumptions are symbolic representations of an organization's culture. Together, they reflect organizational culture, influence behavior by triggering internalized values and norms, facilitate organizational members' communication about their organizational experiences, and integrate organizational systems of meaning.

Inevitably, you will be a member of many organizational cultures. You will contribute to the creation, maintenance, and development of these organizational cultures through your communication with other organizational members. Your communicative role as an organizational member is central to both the emergent nature of the organization and its culture.

Because organizations are central to our society and organizational cultures are complex, scholars use multiple theoretical and methodological lenses to illuminate the complexity of organizational culture—revealing it for what it is rather than for what managers want or expect it to be. Scholars focus on the way in which culture is developed, maintained, or changed in order to identify frames or scripts that managers can credibly use to bridge the different assumptions held by organizational members. Scholars from a variety of fields—anthropology, communication, education, management, psychology, sociology—have contributed to the conversation. Common to all contemporary views on organizational culture is acknowledgement of the role of communication in its creation. Thus, this book focuses on the communicative and performative aspects of organizational culture.

2

Unpacking
Organizational Culture

CORE CHARACTERISTICS OF ORGANIZATIONAL CULTURE

If an organization's culture emerges from the complex and continuous web of communication among members of the organization, then what exactly is a culture? Rather than being something tangible or something that someone can easily point to, *organizational culture* is the set of artifacts, values, and assumptions that emerge from the interactions of organizational members. In other words, an organization's culture is its belief system—created and managed by the organization's members. Using a communicative perspective, organizational culture has five important characteristics: inextricably linked to organizational members; dynamic, not static; competing assumptions and values; emotionally charged; and foreground and background. Each of these is explained below.

Inextricably Linked to Organizational Members

First, organizational culture cannot exist independently of the organizational members who create it. Nor is organizational culture a result of the actions of one organizational member (Trice & Beyer, 1993). Everyone who participates in the organization symbolically and socially constructs the culture. While it may seem that organizational members react to an existing culture, all organizational members, by virtue of their interactions, help develop or sustain it. Think of an organization as having a language system with its own specialized symbols and vernacular. People who comprise this language system produce a set of typical actions or normative procedures, and a set of explanations for those actions and procedures. Often, these take on the form of stories or myths about *how work is done* or *what it means to work here*. When new members join the organization, current members use these stories and myths to explain the job and the organization. In one sense, culture is inherited from the community—in this case, previous and current organizational members—who comprise the language system (Taylor & Van Every, 2000). However, as new members learn the language system, and adopt the stories and myths, they have the potential to alter them or create new ones. Thus, an organization's culture is a mix of accepted practices by a collective and dependent on organizational members, past and present (Trice & Beyer, 1993).

Dynamic, Not Static

Second, an organization's culture is dynamic, not static (Trice & Beyer, 1993). This happens largely because there is an infinite number of combinations of verbal and nonverbal messages that can be sent and received (Bantz, 1993). Even when managers try to direct an organization's culture, employees can accept, reject, or in some way modify these cultural directives. Moreover, organizational culture is not developed from the isolated interactions of any two organizational members, regardless of their level. Multiple dyads, triads, and small groups interact in a variety of ways creating a synergy that is impossible to fully predict (Bantz, 1993). Of course, organizational membership is also not static. Organizational cultures change as people come into and out of organizations. Essentially, an organization's culture can change as organizational members change their belief systems or modify norms.

An organization's culture can also change as executives address internal problems and opportunities, or as organizations respond to or create their external environments. For example, Larson and Pepper (2003) describe value change at JAR Technologies, an aerospace company. Over time JAR had grown into a medium-sized company that designed and produced one-of-a-kind instruments for government and commercial customers. As the government space market shrunk, the global commercial space market expanded causing JAR to reprioritize its values to meet the demands of its commercial customers. While some employees embraced the new vision, others with longer tenure fought to retain the values and practices that helped make the company successful with government contracts. Using three communication strategies—comparison, logic, and support—many employees were able to manage the internal pressures related to the market shift experienced by the organization. Still, some long-term employees did leave the company because they could not identify with the new values.

Alvesson (2002) uses the term *cultural traffic* to describe the variety of influences on organizational culture. Not only is culture influenced by people entering and leaving the organization, organizational culture is also influenced by societal values. "Changes regarding environmental protection, gender and ethnic relations, age, attitudes toward work, new ideas on business and management, and so on, affect people not only outside but also inside their workplaces" (p. 160).

Because change can occur in so many venues—the manner in which messages intersect and are interpreted, fluctuations in membership, or revisions of organizational goals—the type and level of change is variable. Changes to an ongoing culture may be significant departures from existing practices, or subtle variations that build over time into a new way of doing things. Regardless of their source, quality, intensity, or direction, changes in organizational culture are inherent to the process of organizing.

Competing Values and Assumptions

Third, there may be multiple and potentially competing patterns of values and assumptions. From any one position in the organization, it may look like the culture is consistently singular. However, it is more typical for organizations to structure themselves into networks based on tasks, relationships, information, and functions with organizational members identifying with, and belonging to, more than one network (Kuhn & Nelson, 2002). As a result, organizational members have the opportunity to create many belief systems, or subcultures, with both overlapping and distinguishing elements. At the center of the organization's culture, clarity may reign, but at the periphery, competing assumptions and values create a fuzziness where assumptions and values are contradictory (Trice & Beyer, 1993).

Two reasons account for this potential. First, recall that organizations emerge from the interactions of their members. And, second, while organizational members commonly take on the vernacular and linguistic forms of the organization, individuals can also modify the vernacular and linguistic forms, as well as create new vernacular and linguistic forms as new situations arise.

For example, as Amazon.com, Inc. moves from being an online retailer to being an online retailer *and* a technology company, it is likely that different sets of employees will view this move in different ways. Technology employees whose day-to-day work creates the e-commerce software that Amazon sells online to independent programmers will likely view this organizational change differently than employees whose work is more directly tied to the book operation central to Amazon's initial operation and public image. Some employees will view this move to add an e-commerce side of the business as progressive, innovative, and necessary for maintaining its industry leadership position. Others are likely to view this move as risky as Amazon sells its underlying technology. These two sets of employees will create their own interpretations and explanations of the e-commerce addition, and these explanations will find their way into the conversations of employees.

From one event, two explanations emerge, each seen as valid by the organizational community that contributes to and maintains a particular view. Continuing this hypothetical situation further, the two views of Amazon's culture have the potential to become further entrenched and more distinguished as interdependencies between the two groups encourage employee debate about the e-commerce addition. Worse, if information about the technology move is not shared with employees on the retail side of the operation, there is the potential for these employees to create a cultural view consistent with their organizational position and not one grounded in the realities of the e-commerce activities.

Also recall that organizational members can identify with and belong to more than one network or group. You may identify with your work group that values doing just enough work to get by. At the same time you could identify with a social group at work that is based on common values—and one of those values is to be productive at all tasks. As an employee, you structure your work activities and your communication about those activities to address and manage this competing set of beliefs. Of course, your strength of identification with these two groups is changeable based on situational elements and communication within the groups (Kuhn & Nelson, 2002). For example, if your work group adopts a value that you believe is unethical, you are likely to weaken your identification with that group and those beliefs, while you strengthen your identification with the other group.

Emotionally Charged

Fourth, the meanings that create organizational culture are by definition not neutral. Artifacts, values, and assumptions that carry cultural meaning also carry the emotions organizational members experience in their work and express about their work environments. Indeed, artifacts, values, and assumptions are only meaningful if we have some feeling or emotion about the artifact and what it means, positively or negatively. Clearly, emotion influences how we make sense of our work environments (Weick, 1995). For example, an assumption about how one works, if questioned, will likely draw emotion from the organizational member defending the practice. Such emotions can be heightened when employees report that they are more identified with their work role than with family roles (Hochschild, 1997).

Emotions—positive and negative—are prevalent in all work contexts (Miller, 2002). Indeed, Ashforth and Humphrey (1995) claim that emotion saturates our work experiences. One need not work as a 911 emergency responder, a first grade teacher, or a flight attendant to experience emotion at work. In performing emotional labor jobs like the three just described emotions are likely to be more heightened, and more controlled, by the organization as they demand the performance or management of certain emotions or feelings to meet organizational and role expectations (Sutton, 1991). However, employees express genuine and spontaneous emotion in their relationships with other organizational members (Waldron, 2000), or about their work, in all types of work environments. The emotions organizational members express—or control—influence the cultural meanings or cultural norms derived from those interactions (Ashforth & Humphrey, 1995; Callahan, 2002). Thus, organizational culture is emotionally charged (Trice & Beyer, 1993).

Foreground and Background

Fifth, organizational culture is simultaneously the foreground and the background of organization life. Organizational members make sense of their current interactions—the foreground—based on their understanding of the existing culture—the background. At the same time, current communication creates, enhances, sustains, or contradicts the existing culture, which in turn creates a new background against which future interactions are interpreted. This cycle is continuous and never complete. As a result, organizational culture is a representation of the social order of an organization.

Organizational culture emerges from the interactions of organizational members as they use messages and symbols to pursue their personal and professional goals and objectives relative to the organization's goals and objectives. The interaction that is required to make an organization function creates the organizational reality in which people work. That is, organizational culture is communicatively constructed (Pacanowsky & O'Donnell-Trujillo 1982; Smircich, 1983). So while we may commonly talk about an organization as a thing, from this perspective its members communicatively construct it and the interactions of its members create its social and symbolic reality (Bantz, 1993). Simply stated, language use and other communicative performances drive organizational culture. What is said and done, and how it is said and done in the present is interpreted by organizational members against what was said and done, and how it was said and done in the past to create the culture. The process is a continuous communicative performance. As Alvesson argues, "culture is not primarily 'inside' people's heads, but somewhere 'between' the heads of a group of people where symbols and meanings are publicly expressed, e.g., in work group interactions, in board meetings but also in material objects" (2002, p. 4).

Symbols, messages, and meaning are inherent parts of the communicative processes that create an organization. Individuals use symbols—words, behaviors, objects—to create messages. Meanings are created as messages—sent and received—and are interpreted by organizational members. Through this process, organizational culture is symbolically performed (Trice & Beyer, 1993).

COMMUNICATING CULTURE

Two examples explain how organizational members use symbols, messages, and meanings to communicate (and create) their organizational cultures. In the first example, imagine that you have just been hired as a manager of a credit card product with a large financial services organization. To socialize you to your new position and the organization, you are required to attend a weeklong orientation program at the corporate office. The day before you go, the assistant vice president who hired you presents you with a notebook that includes the company's mission statement and its history, a glossary of industry relevant terms, a description of the protocols you are to follow in developing and marketing products, and a complete set of the company's policies. As he hands you the notebook, he gives you his "going to orientation" speech, meant to encourage you and demonstrate that you are already a valued member of the organization.

In this case, the symbols—the notebook with the organization's logo, the words and drawings on the pages of the notebooks, and the words your manager uses in giving you the notebook—create messages. Some of the messages are intentional. For example, the messages that describe the policies and protocols are clear and direct. Without question, you are to follow these. Some of the policies even include messages about the consequences if you do not. Other symbols create unintentional messages. The weight and professional presentation of the notebook sends a message that working for this financial services company is serious business. Moreover, the symbols associated with the costs of you attending a weeklong orientation rather than developing new customer groups for the company create a message that there is a great deal to learn about being a manager in this company.

Meanings are created as you interpret these messages singly and collectively. It is important here to recognize that multiple meanings can exist from the same set of messages. While it is likely that you and others going through the orientation will create similar meanings from the experience, it is unlikely that everyone will create the same meanings. Your previous experiences, motivation for and interest in doing this job for this organization, and your relationship with your superior are just some of the elements that are unique to you and can result in creating meanings that differ from others at the same orientation.

How did the symbols, messages, and meanings contribute to the creation of culture? The interaction between you and the assistant vice president was a dialogue. Although you might not have said much, just by nodding your head and mumbling "okay" and "yes sir," you were an integral part of the interaction. In this interaction, your boss raised your awareness about certain organizational norms (new employees are sent to orientation) and jargon (calling the orientation "the program").

Coupled with his telling you a story about his orientation, your boss passed along cultural elements to you. When you meet the other new employees at the orientation it is likely that you will talk about your experiences as new employees, what you think of your respective bosses and the organization, and how you are evaluating your experiences at the orientation. These conversations function to pass along additional cultural elements and to help you identify and interpret cultural patterns. Once you have completed the new employee orientation and are in the position of explaining it to subsequent new employees, you will reinforce, or question and revise some aspects of these cultural elements. In turn, the norms, jargon, and stories about new employee orientation will be affirmed or reconstituted.

In a second example, dialogue among organizational members at the Pacifica Radio Foundation's Board of Directors Meeting (http://pacifica.org/board/transcripts/min9709.html) demonstrates the process through which symbols, messages, and meanings are derived from the existing organizational culture and the way in which challenges sustain cultural elements or allow for the potential creation of new ones. These processes are revealed as meeting participants discuss procedures for installing new board members.

Chairwoman Berry:	Well, for purposes of moving the meeting along, since I would assume that there is no objection to her [a new representative] being here, if you want to vote on it, you can. I'm assuming everybody would vote that it's fine. [Pause] But it is my understanding that she does not have to be voted on unless somebody—and somebody needs to look at this language. And I don't know who the somebody is. When I say "somebody," who is the somebody I'm talking about that will look at this language and clarify it.
Ms. Brooks:	The attorney has looked at it and felt that it needed clarification, and that was appropriate in this bylaw change. And if we don't adopt this bylaw change, we do need to incorporate that.
Chairwoman Berry:	The attorney has already looked at it and made that recommendation to us as simply saying that it was unclear.

Ms. Makela:	Regardless of whether we need to or not, I would like to recommend that we elect our newest representative since everyone else in my five-year experience has been elected to the Board.
Chairwoman Berry:	Well, would you be willing to change your motion to say, without regard to whether or not it is a required procedure, for the time being you would like to move the following?
Ms. Makela:	Yes.

The words spoken, and the nonverbals that are not captured as part of the written transcript, are the symbols used to create messages in this meeting. In this case, the statement, "The attorney has already looked at it and made that recommendation to us as simply saying that it was unclear," is a message. Its meaning depends on the messages before and after it, who delivers and receives this particular message and the other messages, and the organizational values and assumption against which the messages are interpreted.

Taken out of context, it is difficult to understand these interactions. But upon locating the interaction within the organization's culture— such as informal expectations about meeting behavior or formalized meeting procedures or rules—meanings become clearer. The interactions of organizational members are interpreted within the organization's past, its present, and its future. The message, "Regardless of whether we need to or not, I would like to recommend that we elect our newest representative since everyone else in my five-year experience has been elected to the Board," reflects a norm of this organization. This statement reaffirms the norm, and presents a recommendation for action in the present at the meeting. The present action proposed appears to be consistent with the board's past actions, and would likely confirm the precedence that such actions be handled this way in the future. Thus, the cycle of drawing on past cultural elements, passing them along in interaction, affirming patterns of behavior, and augmenting the belief system about electing new board representatives happens very quickly.

In both of these examples, organizational members are simultaneously responding to and creating the social and symbolic reality of the organizations' cultures. From the social and symbolic realities of all organizational members, an organizational culture emerges. Thus, organizational culture is communicatively constructed. It is both the process of interacting and the product of those interactions. This position recognizes that any particular message or meaning does not come with a predetermined interpretation. All organizational members create messages and meanings in concert with one another (Bantz, 1993). The strategic and spontaneous, intentional and unintentional, formal and informal, and verbal and nonverbal interactions of organizational members create an organization's culture.

Figure 2.1 provides a visual explanation of the fluid relationship between communication and culture, demonstrates the continuous cycle, and identifies the links among the past, present, and future. Culture can morph and change as employees move in and out of the organizational system, and as the organization addresses new opportunities or threats from its environment. This creates opportunities for new practices to emerge, to become patterned, and to be accepted as part of the culture.

Such a model acknowledges organizational culture scholars' assumptions about communication in an organization and its relationship to organizational culture (Eisenberg, Murphy, & Andrews, 1998). That is:

1. Communication creates and recreates organizational reality.

2. Meaning is constructed in local, social, and historical contexts—that is, meanings can be different for different organizational members, they are located in the public dialogue among organizational members, and are influenced by past meanings.

3. Different groups and individuals in organizations construct their view of the organization and its activities differently. Each of these alternative interpretations is an ongoing negotiation of those realities; and all interpretations are valid for the organizational members who hold them.

4. Communication in an organization is constrained by the prior reality and also shapes the existing reality.

Sensemaking

As an organizational member at any hierarchical level, you contribute to the organizing process of the organization and the creation of

Figure 2.1   The process of organizational culture

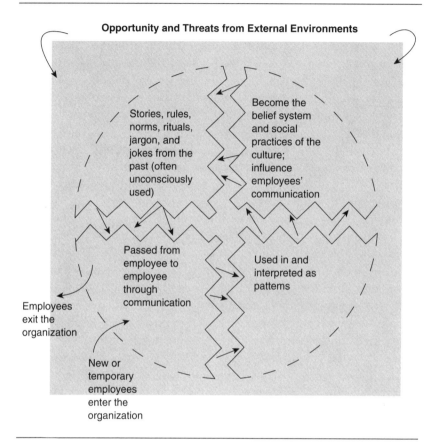

the organization's culture by making sense of your work environment, work activities, and the people you work with. For each salient event, you need to make sense of it—structuring what is unknown into the known. Weick's (1995) concept of sensemaking explains how individuals make plausible, coherent, and reasonable accounts of what happens in the work environment. Oftentimes these accounts result in stories that reveal the meanings made from our organizational experiences (Brown, 1990). Although sensemaking is an individual activity, the accounts we create are developed in a social setting. In organizations, that social setting is the organizational culture.

Although we typically talk about making sense of particular events, sensemaking never really starts—because it never really stops.

Sensemaking is ongoing. For example, something happens in the organization. Then you draw on all that you know about the situation to make sense of it. Aware of what other organizational members have said and aware of the values the organization promotes, this social activity constrains how you make sense of the event. Of course, the sensemaking of this event occurs in the stream of sensemaking in which you are already engaged. And, what happened in this event and how you make sense of it may, in fact, alter a meaning created earlier. Sensemaking is never complete.

Think about all of the events that happened where you worked last. Although some may stand out as more salient, each event that was prominent enough to capture any of your attention required that you make sense of it. What causes some events to stand out? First, as information load—the quantity, variety, and ambiguity of information you process in the organization—increases, you take steps to punctuate it into manageable chunks. You might forget some of the information, file some, or filter other information out. However you punctuate the information flow that is part of your organizational experience, some of it will become more salient than others. Second, the greater the complexity—the greater number of different elements interacting in increasingly interdependent ways—the more it will influence what you notice and what you do not notice. The more complex the information you deal with, the more likely it is that you will create habits or routines for handling it. While those habits or routines may work in many instances, there will be some in which the routine fails—forcing you to take notice. Third, a highly turbulent environment is one in which there is instability or a high frequency of change coupled with randomness— either in frequency or in the direction of change. As turbulence increases, there are more occasions for sensemaking.

When information load, complexity, and turbulence exist—as they do in most organizational environments—ambiguous and uncertain situations are created. Ambiguity exists when there are numerous cues that allow for any number of interpretations. Uncertainty exists when there are not enough cues to create any interpretation. Thus, you engage in sensemaking to create order particularly when something happens that was not expected, or when something that was expected to occur does not.

In some cases, sensemaking occurs in the presence of others who are also trying to make sense of what happened, for example at a meeting. Other times, your sensemaking is influenced because you are aware that you will have to give your explanation of what happened to others who will act upon your explanation. Thus, sensemaking is a social process. It is never solitary. How you make sense internally is contingent on others. That is not to say that your sensemaking will always match the sensemaking of others. Recall that organizational cultures are often better described as a set of subcultures. Individuals in different subcultures may create equivalent, different, or overlapping views. Thus, organizational members can participate in the same event and produce different meanings. How can that be? Sensemaking is not driven by accuracy; it is driven by plausibility. If you believe that the meaning created is likely or acceptable, then it is real for you and you will act on that meaning. Thus, meanings cannot be dictated or controlled. All meanings are possible if they are plausible, coherent, and serve a practical or functional need—that is, through sensemaking you create an account that you believe to be socially acceptable and credible in the work environment.

Murphy's (2001) study of flight attendants demonstrates how organizational members perform sensemaking. As Murphy explains, air travel for flight attendants is a cultural performance; that is, organizational members "participate in a co-construction of meaning that is historically and politically constrained" (p. 37). Although passengers think of air travel as routine, Murphy's descriptions of air travel—its normal routines and its emergencies—make it clear that air travel is anything but routine. For example, water landings are not described as crashing into the ocean, and passengers are encouraged to sit back and relax even while zooming through the air at 30,000 feet. To help passengers manage their performance of routine air travel, flight attendants are required to manage the tensions between reassurance and safety, and accommodation and authority. For example, Murphy describes one flight attendant as smiling and assuring passengers even when flying through turbulent weather; and another who must deal with a passenger who mistakenly believes that "landing in Salt Lake" actually meant landing in a lake.

So, how do flight attendants make sense, or plausible, coherent, and reasonable accounts of ambiguous and uncertain situations? As Murphy explains, flight attendants in their organizational role must make sense of anything that is non-routine or presented as an emergency. There is no checklist or organization-prescribed procedure to follow. Based upon their organization and occupation specific training and their interactions with other flight attendants (both on this flight and on earlier flights), flight attendants must make sense of whatever event is presented when their ongoing cultural performance is interrupted. They may rely on organizational values and norms learned in training and prescribed in procedures and reintegrate the interruption back into the dominant routine (e.g., smiling and saying everything is okay), or they may rely on other, more informal sets of values and norms embraced as stereotypes of what flight attendants should say and do. Regardless, to the passenger, the flight attendant is a representative of the organization, and, in essence, routinely performing that organization's culture for passengers.

The process of sensemaking is central to the study of organizational culture and often revealed in the stories organizational members tell about their organizational experiences (Boje, 1995). If you take the perspective that sensemaking is emergent and dynamic, then the meanings that are created can become codified as values, norms, or beliefs that emerge from the stories and interactions of organizational members. Simply, the process of identifying what is the organization's culture is the process of sensemaking.

Talking About Culture

Although organizational culture emerges from its members' interactions, organizational members generally do not talk directly about what the culture is, how to affirm it, or even how to change it. Indeed, if you asked your friend what the culture was like where she worked you would likely get an "I don't know, you'd just have to work here" type of response. Or, perhaps her response would be "Oh, it's a good [horrible] place to work. The work is easy [difficult] and the people, well, they're okay [pitiful]." Despite being involved in its creation, most employees have a difficult time describing their organization's culture in detail. When asked, many employees report a general positive or negative evaluation of their work environment—much like you would report, "It's a pretty day" when the sun is shining brightly in a blue sky with fluffy clouds while the temperature is at 80 degrees with low humidity, and a light wind from the SSE. While these details create the *pretty day* and are available to you if you seek out a weather report, we tend to reduce the specifics into a generalization. This is especially true when organizational members try to describe the organization's culture to outsiders.

Even organizational executives, who some believe are responsible for an organization's culture, speak about their culture in general terms. For example, Blair Contratto, CEO of Little Company of Mary Hospital has reportedly stated:

> We are currently engaged in a refocusing of our culture on service. That includes service to our patients and their families, service to the doctors who choose to admit their patients to one of our 30 facilities, as well as the service and support employees provide to each other. (Kaufman, 2003, p. xx)

From this description, we know that the organization is refocusing its culture on service, and to whom that service is directed. But what did the CEO actually reveal about the organization's values and assumptions about service? What is service? What constitutes *good* or *bad* service in this organization?

Revisit the meeting interaction of the Pacifica Radio Foundation's Board of Directors Meeting earlier in this section. Notice that the directors are not talking directly about their organization's culture. The content of their discussion is about the procedures for installing new representatives as members of the board. However, the culture *is* being talked about. Norms are being identified, challenged, and then confirmed. Values about board membership and consensus decision-making are evident in the interaction. Board members are expressing their organizational culture through their interactions. And, through their interactions, board members come to know and understand their organizational culture even without their direct awareness of this happening.

The point here is simple. Although organizational culture emerges from organizational members' communication with one another, it can be difficult to identify and describe a culture. Being in an organizational culture as a customer or other external observer is one way to gain a perspective on it. But being a member of the organization is the best way for knowing what the culture is and understanding it. Despite that intimacy with the culture, it can be difficult for organizational insiders to describe the culture to others, or understand the ramifications of organizational culture on their communication performances. One explanation for this is since an organization's culture is ever changing, it is difficult to isolate its characteristics. In addition, since there may be multiple, and potentially competing patterns of assumptions and values in any culture, organizational members may or may not be aware of—or be able to articulate—these integrative or competing systems. These difficulties in talking about culture explain why organizations and their members rely on artifacts to communicate about culture.

Organizational Culture as a Symbolic Communication Process

Communication relies on the use of symbols. We create symbols to name, identify, and distinguish people, things, and situations. Without symbols we could not create meanings or share our experiences with others. For example, the alphabet is a series of symbols that can be combined into words and phrases that also act as symbols. Symbols are powerful physical indicators of organizational life, and the foundation from which organizational members draw meanings for and under- standings of artifacts, values, and assumptions. Symbols "are not simply by-products of organization; rather, symbols are elements that structure members' active construction of sense, knowledge, and behavior. . . . that stand for the ideas that compose the organization" (Rafaeli & Worline, 2000, pp. 72–73). Symbols, in their various forms, can carry an incredible amount of information about an organization, and, as a result, can be meaningful shorthand devices for both internal and external constituencies.

Organizational symbols are abundant. Symbols can be found in almost any form of artifact deemed meaningful by organizational members. Even sounds or a series of behaviors can be used in this way. Across the great variety of things that can be construed as meaningful symbols there are four functions of symbols in organizational culture (Rafaeli & Worline, 2000).

The first function of symbols is to reflect organizational culture, as they represent and reveal what is tacitly known but difficult for an organizational member to communicate. Symbols, as tangible and sensory objects, integrate feelings, thoughts, and actions into a shared meaning. Recall, the description of the University of Kansas Jayhawk in Section 1. In this case, the symbol identified as the Jayhawk is an arti- fact of the university's culture. Its bright vibrant blue, red, and yellow colors configured into the unmistakable shape of the Jayhawk mascot cannot be missed. The Jayhawk is emblazoned across center court in the field house and is featured prominently on letterhead and business cards. The KU Jayhawk is so prominent on campus that someone wearing a jacket or sweatshirt from any other school clearly stands out. Many students and alumni wear the Jayhawk on clothing to represent their university loyalty and adherence to university traditions.

The second function of symbols is to influence behavior by triggering internalized values and norms. Organizations can use artifacts to help guide people's appropriate selection of behavior. For example, you work as a quality inspector on the shop floor. The bright fluorescent lights make it seem like day regardless of which shift you work. As you and your coworkers walk out of the changing facility and onto the shop floor, the volume and pace of conversations pick up to rise above the continuous drone of machinery. You see a red light atop your desk to indicate that a phone message is waiting for you. With a special device to help you hear the message over the noisy shop environment, you learn that the quality control engineers want you to attend their meeting and provide feedback on a design issue. You exit the shop floor by taking the elevator to the floor above. When you step out of the elevator, you pause to adjust to your surroundings—deep-pile carpet beneath your feet, dark wood paneling, dim spot lighting, and background music creates a distinctively different aesthetic from your normal work environment. You move more slowly, and when you walk into the conference room, you adjust your speaking volume to a more normal conversational tone. In the plush office, the norms include talking quietly and respectfully and listening carefully to others (and demonstrating this nonverbally). The physical symbols and the norms of communicating in this environment trigger an inter-nalized value that intellectual work is important and that employees should have the opportunity to carefully deliberate and reflect before making decisions. Contrast this to the shop floor in which noisy machines make even a simple telephone call difficult. The pace is also faster, as employees unconsciously match their activity level to that of the machines. The symbols in this physical environment trigger internalized values that physical work should be completed quickly, efficiently, and with a minimum of interaction among employees. By alternating between the two environments, it is clear to see how the different artifacts of the physical environment carry different meanings and influence your behavior.

The third function of symbols is to facilitate organizational members' communication about their organizational experiences. Organizations rely on logos to identify what is information from or about those organizations. The same logo appears on the letterhead, report covers, the internal phone book, the information directory on each floor, your paycheck, the windbreaker you were given for being an employee of the company for five years, and the company newsletter. Communication that is marked by this artifact sends the signal that this communication is *official* and *real*. Here, symbol use is meant to create an organizational identity and to help you identify with that identity.

The Lawrence (Kansas) Chamber of Commerce recently changed its logo of 17 years. Although conversations about the utility of the logo had been ongoing for several years, the momentum for changing occurred when the chamber acquired a new CEO. Urging his staff to think differently about the chamber and its relationship to the convention and visitor's bureau, he encouraged the two organizations, both of which represent Lawrence, to create one logo that, first, better represented Lawrence, and, second, acknowledged the relationship between the two organizations that had always shared office space. The new logo features a wheat staff, a symbol commonly associated with Kansas. However, "a new logo is only as good as your commitment to make it good," said one staff member. In other words, logos can only be meaningful symbols when organizational members use them in symbolic ways. The consistent use of a logo frames what is and is not connected with an organization, and implicitly provides instruction on how to treat information from those sources. Artifacts, like logos, provide a tangible representation of values and beliefs that can be abstract or ambiguous but critical or central to the organization.

The fourth function of a symbol is to integrate organizational systems of meaning. In most organizations, an ambiguously stated value can foster the notion that everyone has the same view when many different interpretations are actually present. Such strategic use of ambiguity promotes a unified diversity that creates the perception of commonality despite multiple views. In this case, organizational symbols function "at a level of abstraction at which agreement *can* occur" (Eisenberg, 1984, p. 231). The KU Jayhawk is a good example. This symbol can carry several different, equally valid, interpretations—basketball excellence and democratic values—that contribute simultaneously to unique, yet socially meaningful, interpretations of the University of Kansas culture.

Despite their powerful presence, exercise caution when interpreting an organization's culture through symbols. First, artifacts can be superficial (Hofstede, 2001). They can easily be replaced with new ones (recall the change in logo for the chamber of commerce described above). Symbols can also be copied by and from other cultural groups. The slogan, *Quality is Job 1*, often associated with Ford Motor Company, has been copied directly and in similar forms by other organizations. Second, because symbols can be easily identified and meanings easily inferred, it is easy to presume that the interpretation you infer is the interpretation others would give. Symbols can be individually and differently interpreted; thus, it is crucial to discover how organizational members view them.

But cultural artifacts can also reveal deep structures even from innocuous artifacts of work life. For example, Trujillo (1992) examined how tickets, promotional items, and a baseball park were interpreted by ballpark employees, and how those symbols structured their organizational experiences. For some ushers and ticket takers, the symbolic artifacts, their coworkers, and the fans they encountered in their work activities helped to create their romanticized interpretation of the ballpark. Despite working for little pay every summer, these employees described the fun they were having in their ballpark jobs, and the meaningfulness of the relationships they created with other summer-only employees. Thus, organizational symbols can have powerful and deep expressions of the values and assumptions that organizational members create, maintain, and share through communication.

THE STRUCTURE OF ORGANIZATIONAL CULTURE

A Consensus View of Organizational Culture

A consensus view of organizational culture is based on the congruence of artifacts, values, and assumptions jointly held or shared by organizational members. The more unity there is among members, the more consensual the view of organizational culture. From an integration perspective, mutually consistent interpretations are abundant (Martin, 2002) and so deeply held that little variation occurs (Schein, 1985). Generally, a charismatic or otherwise strong leader shapes this integration by initially generating the value and beliefs and then uses strategies to publicize and propagate them.

Sometimes this phenomenon is referred to as a powerful culture or strong culture. Research suggests that some organizations do have powerful cultures—and, generally, this is the mostly widely held popular view of organizational culture. The U.S. Marine Corps is a good example of culture viewed from an integrative perspective. Other organizations that promote themselves as having consensual cultures are Microsoft and Mary Kay. While that may be true for these organizations, it is also possible that when an organization appears to have a strong, unified, and shared culture what is shared may be superficial and not deeply held by all organizational members. Or, the direction of the mutually consistent interpretations may be more negative than positive.

Studies that argue that a strong culture exists in an organization are often narrowly focused on one organizational issue to the exclusion of other issues. Organizational members may share values and assumptions about a particular cultural element. But that is not necessarily an indication that organizational members share values and assumptions about all cultural elements. Even when a congruent view of an organization's culture is held, the influence of this characteristic may not be as strong or powerful as assumed (Isaac & Pitt, 2001). And, of course, promotion of a strong consensual culture by leaders and executives does not guarantee that such a culture exists.

Managers often prefer a culture in which values are shared, believing that widely held values will lead to organizational harmony, and, thus, organizational effectiveness will be enhanced. The benefits of a consensual culture are thought to include job satisfaction, commitment, and lengthy employee tenure—elements that should improve organizational functioning. Employees also can benefit from a consensual culture. When values are homogeneous it is easier for organizational members to make assumptions that will be similar to the assumptions made by others (Stackman, Pinder, & Connor, 2000).

Kunda's (1992) ethnography of a high-tech firm discovered three ways in which its managers controlled the organization to produce a strong culture. First, managers developed, articulated, and disseminated the organization's ideology. Using relentless repetition and a variety of techniques to disseminate consistent information, managers promoted a collective view of its goals and history to encourage employees to become family members in an organization with a moral purpose. Doing so emphasized the social attributes of the company and specified employee roles. These consistent and unambiguous messages persuaded employees to internalize the beliefs and emotions prescribed by management, and to follow their behavioral prescriptions. Second, the ideological principles embraced by management were designed to minimize the use of traditional bureaucratic controls, such as hierarchical and functional differentiation, and pay-motivated control structures. Rather, managers designed the organizational structure so that it was an informal flexible relationship-based network allowing employees to be involved in formal and informal work practices. This structural design maximized employees' sense of ownership and security, and, in turn, heightened their commitment to the organization. Third, rituals were a central part of daily work life. Slogans such as "We are like a football team" reinforced the notions that employees should work hard and have fun. These themes were repeated in rituals—presentations by top management, orientation sessions called *bootcamps*, career seminars, work group meetings, *timeouts* or parties, and organization Olympics. Whether large or small scale, rituals confirmed and promoted the roles employees were to fulfill. The rituals encouraged all employees to become control agents prescribing how employees should complete their work. Through these mechanisms, management was able to create a pervasive and comprehensive, or strong, culture that also demanded a great deal from employees.

However, organizational members' consensual view of their organization's culture can have detrimental effects. When organizational members work in a culture that values consistency, consensus, and clarity, there can be less value placed on innovation, creativity, and questioning—characteristics that have been demonstrated as important to success in complex and turbulent business conditions (Sorensen, 2002). A more unified culture facilitates routine, and thereby reliable, performance in stable environments. The "established way of understanding the world" (p. 88) continues to work, because the business environment is perceived as unchanging. However in a volatile or rapidly changing business environment, a unified culture is less likely to allow organizational members to explore and discover, making it difficult for individuals and the organization to adapt.

Moreover, a strong culture can be situated on the wrong values— ways that are not appropriate or not conducive to growth (Deetz, Tracy, & Simpson, 2000). There can also be a dampening affect on individual rights and freedoms that is particularly alarming when management purposely manipulates employee value and belief structures (Stackman, Pinder, & Connor, 2000). Worker autonomy can be threatened, causing employees to have conflicting ideals of loyalty and allegiance. Do they honor the company or themselves? When employees choose to submit to the premise of an organization's culture, the authenticity of that position can be questioned (Kunda, 1992).

In a study of emotional labor at a nursing home, Sass (2000) points out that viewing culture from an integration or consensual perspective can obscure issues. His investigation revealed that spirituality was a unifying value of the organization. It was expressed in three ways:

(a) alignment between the mission statement representing management and the personal values of staff members, (b) as a context that fostered expression of personal spirituality, and (c) in organizational practices based on relationships rather than bureaucracy. Despite the centrality of spirituality as a core cultural value in the nursing home work environment, not all employees regarded it positively. This raises the question of how much consensus is required and in what ways consensus must be displayed or practiced to be salient for organizational members.

Creating a consensual view of organizational culture may be perceived as being ideal, but it is also likely to be difficult to achieve. Six factors limit the degree to which a consensual view of culture can be achieved (Isaac & Pitt, 2001). First, employees are often members of occupational or professional communities and bring preexisting shared values and practices into the workplace. Second, employees belong to specific functions (e.g., manufacturing, human resources, engineering, sales) or work groups in the organization. Within each of these, employees are likely to develop shared values and beliefs that differ from employees in other functions and in other work groups. Third, organizational members are also structured by the organization's hierarchy. Managers are likely to develop shared values and normative practices that differ from employees in non-management positions. Hierarchical groups of employees differ in the amount and type of responsibility and authority they have, resulting in different core assumptions about work and their workplace. Fourth, other subcultures can develop. For example, working mothers, employees who are continuing their education, or employees who work the third shift are likely to create values and beliefs that support a subculture. The interpersonal relationships that develop among groups of people who share similarities encourage subcultures to develop that are distinct and enduring. Fifth, whatever groups exist in an organization are likely to distinguish themselves from members of other groups. This in-group/out-group distinction often results in intergroup conflict that strengthens the differentiation between groups and the subculture of each group. Sixth, all employees have individual value systems, and core values are often difficult to change.

Thus, while a strong, unified, and shared culture is often the goal of management and perceived to be the ideal organizational culture, creating such a culture is very difficult and may be detrimental to the organization. While some cultural elements may be shared, it is likely that others are not.

A DIVIDED VIEW OF ORGANIZATIONAL CULTURE

The alternative view is that different groups, or subcultures, are created as organizational members interact in their daily work routines. To the extent that different sets of artifacts, values, and assumptions develop in those groups, an organization's culture is said to have subcultures. In essence, the way in which the subcultures coexist creates the culture (Schein, 1992). Subcultures can develop in several ways and can have various relationships to one another. Subgroup distinctions often occur along functional or occupational roles; geographical locations; product, market, or technology distinctions; and hierarchical levels. In addition, subcultures can develop and be sustained when two or more organizations merge or work together in a joint venture or strategic alliance. In ways less connected to organizational structure or functioning, subcultures can also develop along age, gender, racial, ethnic, sexual orientation, physical ability, and family status distinctions among employees. Employees who seek out others with similar characteristics and interests can create informal subgroups to address mutual work-life issues. Friendships among employees can also develop and create a subculture.

Most commonly, subgroups develop along functional lines. It is not uncommon for a subculture to develop when an organization employs many individuals in the same profession or occupation—especially when these individuals are working together or performing a function central to the goals of the organization. Professors in a university, social workers in a government agency, and customer service representatives at a call center are good examples of organizational situations in which groups of individuals with similar jobs are likely to create a subculture. Because the work of these groups is central to the organizational mission, these individuals are likely to bond together as they work to control their collective destiny in the organization (Bloor & Dawson, 1994).

For example, the merger of a home healthcare services company and a medical supply company highlighted the differences between two functional groups (Rosenfeld, Richman, & May, 2004). The social workers and nurses who provided healthcare services to patients in their homes viewed the merged organization very differently than the clerical and administrative personnel who ran the healthcare supply business from the central office. The office workers wanted more information from the company about its policies and objectives, yet the social workers and nurses viewed the organization's culture as placing greater emphasis on planning, efficiency, and other task-oriented elements. Members of the two groups reported different information needs and viewed the type of information and the way it was disseminated in distinct ways. It was not the case that the groups needed more information, but that each group had unique information needs from the organization relative to their specific job functions.

Geography is another common identifier of subgroups in organization. Many organizations even organize themselves this way and use geographical identifiers. For example, Meeks, a chain of lumberyards, is organized into Western and Midwestern Divisions. The Midwestern Division is comprised of 29 stores with a general office in Springfield, Missouri; the Western Division is comprised of 14 stores with a general office in Sacramento, California. Even though the products and services offered are not likely to differ greatly, two subcultures anchored around the Springfield and Sacramento general offices will develop as the stores are clustered around Missouri and Arkansas, and California and Nevada—two distinct geographic locations. Additionally, each store is likely to develop its own culture, as each store pulls employees from the local labor pool and responds to local customer demands. Then, of course, subcultures along functional and occupational distinctions are likely to develop within each store.

Hierarchy can also create subcultures. Organizational members at the same level will share similar organizational treatment, thus subcultures develop. Some organizations make broad hierarchical distinctions, such as salaried and hourly, professional and staff, or managers and associates. Other organizations carefully create similar levels of hierarchy within each organizational function creating a group of vice presidents, a bigger group of assistant vice presidents, and a still larger group of managers. Each group has specific roles, responsibilities, and rights, and as a result, will have more in common with one another than individuals above or below them in the hierarchy. Some organizations even hold executive retreats and staff meetings—further enhancing hierarchical distinctions. And, in some organizations, different sets of employee benefits make hierarchical distinctions even more salient.

Another way of thinking about subcultures focuses on the language use of organizational members as they segment themselves into *us* and *them* (Parker, 2000). Across organizations, three *us* and *them* claims persist: spatial or functional, generational, and occupational or professional. A spatial or functional segmentation of culture occurs based on location of work units, which often represents functional distinctions as well. Clerks who process paperwork work in the office; technicians who manufacture chemicals work in the plant. The two spaces support two different organizational functions, and, as a result, create different communication environments resulting in different language communities.

A generational segmentation of organizational culture is based on who is old and new, or who is perceived old and new to the organization. At a cardboard box manufacturing facility, technicians with 20 or more years of seniority divided themselves from recently graduated engineers with only months of tenure with the company. Implicit in the technicians' complaints about the engineers was the following: "They couldn't possibly understand how these machines work. I've worked on this machine, or one like it, for over 20 years. I know how it runs. I know what it needs. Some wet-behind-the ears kid can't tell me how to make a better box." Alternately, the new engineers explained, "We've got new techniques . . . and they [the technicians] fight us every step in making any change." The generational segmentation underscores the way in which organizational history shapes the present. The occupational or professional segmentation, like that between doctors and nurses in a hospital, is based on expertise or specialized knowledge sets. One claims to know something that the other group does not (or cannot or should not) know. Although this type of segmentation is most often noticed at the professional level, occupational divides can exist at all levels of the organization. At a retail store, a clerk ringing up my order proclaimed, "I'm not in customer service. That's his [pointing to the clerk standing next to him] job."

For each organizational member, identifying the *us* and *them* segments of an organization's culture signals who understands the culture like he or she does and who does not. Each segmentation underscores what is going on, whose job it is, and whose it is not from a unique perspective. Organizational members use language to segment and identify themselves in these ways. Interestingly, the three subcultural forms—spatial or functional, generational, and occupational or professional—can be used singly or in a combination of ways. Moreover, using a spatial identification and distinction in one setting does not preclude the same employee from invoking a generational identification and distinction in another. From Parker's (2000) perspective, a culture is comprised of a variety of contested *us* and *them* claims.

In another example, employees of the investment banking arm of a multinational banking corporation were divided into numerous functional subgroups (Huang, Newell, Galliers, & Pan, 2003). Initially, the employees appeared to identify with and against other organizational members based on their use of technology. Further examination of their first-person reports on their work, work roles, and relationships to other work functions revealed, however, that within those subculture distinctions, additional powerful distinctions (e.g., based on status, glamour of task assignment, permanent or temporary staff) existed. The subculture distinctions could be represented in this way:

- Multinational banking corporation
  - Investment banking unit
    o Business division culture
      ■ Front office trader subculture
      ■ Back office manager and administrator subculture
    o Technology division culture
      ■ Front office technologist subculture
        ♦ Permanent staff sub-subculture
        ♦ Contractor sub-subculture
      ■ Back office technologist subculture
      ■ Central and regional supporting manager and administrator culture

Forms of Cultural Division

In contrast to the clear consensus of an integrated view of organizational culture, there are two configurations for examining the relationship of subcultures to one another in the divided view.

Differentiation

In the first configuration, organizational members may differentiate into subgroups relative to their inconsistent interpretations (Martin, 2002). Typical differentiated patterns are often along the lines of salaried managers and hourly employees, home office employees and field office employees, or any of the dimensions along which organizational members identify and organize themselves into language communities. This type of segmentation reveals oppositional thinking (i.e., us versus them) with each subculture concerned about the power they hold relative to the other subculture.

In most cases, these distinctions will result in multiple subcultures. For example, Helms and Stern (2001) found evidence of multiple subculture patterns. Organizational values were different among organizational units, by hierarchical level, and by age group, ethnicity, and gender. Within each subculture, there is consistency and clarity that makes each subculture distinct from others. Yet, organizational members are likely to belong to more than one subculture. When multiple subcultures exist simultaneously, they are not neatly divided nor neatly aligned. To which subculture does a 30-year-old female African American manager in purchasing belong: the subculture distinction based on function, hierarchy, age, ethnicity, or gender? She belongs to each of these and all of these at the same time, and the artifacts, values, and assumptions central to each subculture may conflict with the artifacts, values, and assumptions of other subcultures.

Subculture distinctions can also be based on the inconsistencies between espoused values and enacted values. An espoused value is one presented to others as a core value, or promoted as central to the organization's mission or treatment of employees. Yet, there is often a gap between what an organization espouses and what an organization does. Organizational members indicate that something is highly valued, but their actions or communication indicate otherwise. For example, an organization says it values diversity and implements marketing campaigns targeted to specific groups of minority customers. Despite preaching this concept in team meetings and in the organization's advertising, employees are beginning to wonder when the organization's value of diversity will filter into the leadership ranks. Despite the push for *customer* diversity, employees are well aware that all mid- and top-level managers in their retail organization are White males. Here the differentiated subcultures are based on the difference between an organizational idea and organizational reality.

A careful analysis of most any organizational culture will expose espoused values that are not enacted. A study of work-family policies (Kirby & Krone, 2002) demonstrates the incongruence between the values espoused and enacted in a regulatory agency's culture. According to organizational policy, employees could take annual leave for personal use, sick leave, family and medical leave, and leave without pay. Employees also had two options for flexible scheduling. All of the policies were available on the agency's website and in a written Employee Benefits Summary. Thus, formally, all employees had equal access to any of the policies that fit their specific circumstances.

However, the way in which employees took advantage of the policies and the way in which their work was supervised led to discrepancies and contradictions. For example, one employee explained that while the agency touted the policies as benefits, she complained that because she was single she could not take advantage of the policies, which in effect gave employees with family members more time off from work than she enjoyed. Of those employees who did benefit from the work-family policies, some were reluctant to take advantage of them, as their colleagues complained about completing their unfinished work. At the macro-level from the organization's perspective, the work- family policies were a benefit to help employees balance their work and family lives. Yet, at the micro-level of the organization, conversations among employees influenced the way in which employees used the policies, or felt about, or acted toward those who did. Thus the espoused value of work and family balance was never realized.

Subcultures have various types of relationships to the primary organizational culture (Bloor & Dawson, 1994; Parker, 2000). These can be characterized in five ways. A subculture might enhance the primary organizational culture by supporting the core values and norms of the organization. Alternately, a subculture could dissent from the core values and norms by developing alternative methods to achieve organizational goals. Third, a subculture could be seen as a counterculture, which rejects the organization's core goals causing it to conflict with the primary culture system. Fourth, a subculture could be orthogonal in that it supports norms and values in addition to, or independent of, those in the core organizational culture. Fifth, a subculture could be deferential by yielding to or not resisting a more dominant subculture. Of course, if the organization employs members of numerous professional and occupational groups, many subcultures could exist and have different types of relationships to the primary organizational culture. In all cases, however, there is recognition of an overall organizational culture that acts as a background against which the subculture or subcultures are viewed.

The cultural differences and inconsistencies revealed from a differentiation perspective are viewed as being inescapable, and often desirable (Martin, 2002). Moreover, the inconsistencies between or among subcultures are usually clear. Recognize, however, that all subculture differences are not necessarily conflicting. Subcultures can exist together in harmony, conflict, or indifference.

Fragmentation

The second divided perspective for viewing organizational culture is fragmentation (Martin, 2002). In this case, ambiguity reigns; there is neither clear consistency nor clear inconsistency. While the clear opposites or dichotomies provide some clarity from a differentiation view of culture, a fragmentation perspective will reveal that the organization is not so neatly divided. From this perspective, organizational members are part of shifting coalitions, forming and reforming based on shared identities, issues, and circumstances. Subcultures appear briefly, but with boundaries that are permeable and fluctuating making it difficult for a subculture to sustain itself for any length of time. In this case, tensions are irreconcilable, and are often described as ironies, paradoxes, or contradictions, as employees may belong to subcultures that are in agreement on some issues and simultaneously belong to other subcultures that are not. From this perspective, organizational members have multiple, overlapping identities making it difficult to create organization-wide consensus.

The fragmentation perspective acknowledges that organizational ambiguities exist. Although ambiguity is traditionally viewed as problematic, ambiguity is viewed as a normal organizing condition within the fragmentation perspective. Thus, *no clear way* is often the hallmark of the multiple realities revealed through fragmentation analysis. So many interpretations and views exist that consensus cannot be achieved throughout the organization or within subgroups.

Despite an organization's best attempts to create a cohesive or unitary view of organizational values and policies, employees can fail to uphold or respect values and policies for a variety of reasons—in turn, creating a culture of ambiguity. For example, in response to several sexual harassment charges, including some that were high profile, a municipality sought to win the trust of employees on this issue by promoting a zero tolerance sexual harassment policy (see Keyton, Ferguson, & Rhodes, 2001). The zero tolerance policy was promoted in the organization's newsletter and was the topic of specialized training—actions taken by management to demonstrate to employees this *new way of doing business.* Because the issue was sexual harassment, management expected that men and women would see the issue differently, but no one expected the various ways in which employees actually responded to it. Ambiguity about the policy and its effect on the organization's culture was created as men not women perceived higher levels of sexual conduct in the organization. At the same time, targets of sexual harassment in the organization, which were more likely to be women, perceived higher levels of sexual conduct. Further complicating the perceived influence of the policy, employees who scored higher on the post-training evaluation did not support the organization's zero-tolerance policy to a greater extent than employees whose scores were lower. Thus, employees' beliefs about sexual conduct in the organization and the influence of the zero tolerance policy were not neatly divided along the lines of men and women. Rather, employees' responses indicated that many perceptions about sexual conduct and the new policy existed simultaneously—creating ambiguity rather than managing it.

CULTURAL CONSENSUS AND DIVISION

Martin (2002) argues, and many others offer evidence, that viewing an organization from a viewpoint of consensus or division is limiting. By focusing on one or the other, we may miss the way in which organizational members construct and enact their culture through communication. All three perspectives—integration, differentiation, and fragmentation—must be allowed for, as it is likely that in any organizational culture:

> some aspects of the culture will be shared by most members, producing consistent, clear interpretations . . . other aspects of the culture will be interpreted differently by different groups, creating subcultures that overlap and nest with each other in relationships of harmony, interdependence, and/or conflict . . . some aspects of the culture will be interpreted ambiguously, with irony, paradox, and irreconcilable tensions. (Martin, 2002, p. 120)

Using all three perspectives allows consensus, consistency, and ambiguity to be revealed as they actually exist in an organization's culture, and avoids the potential blind spots of each perspective when used alone. That is, an integration perspective would not reveal ambiguity, while the differentiation and fragmentation perspectives would not reveal what aspects of organizational culture members share (Martin, 2002).

Together, the three perspectives encourage three distinct revelations about organizational culture. It is not that one perspective is more correct than another. Rather, each perspective offers an incomplete view of an organization's culture. All three perspectives are needed to offer a multifocal view of organizational culture. For example, organizations require some shared cultural elements to survive. Yet, why would we expect any organization to share interpretations of all aspects of its culture? Knowing how organizational members interpret things differently *and* similarly will reveal the most complete view of organizational culture (Martin, 2002). Two examples demonstrate the way in which the three perspectives reveal a multiperspective view of organizational culture.

First, in a study of employees in a federal agency, Hylmö and Buzzanell's (2002) use of integration, differentiation, and fragmentation perspectives revealed a paradox. Through the integration lens, the agency was portrayed as coherent, innovative, and employee-centered. The differentiation lens revealed four subgroups arranged on two dimensions: promotable and non-promotable, and whether work was completed through telecommuting or on-site. The fragmentation lens revealed ambiguity resulting from a recent reorganization attempt and a surge in agency growth.

> Standards and expectations were no longer clearly stated or understood. Rules and operating procedures appear unclear and ambiguous while, at the same time, they were constructed as resolvable and decipherable, if only employees could uncover enough clues. In other words, the way things were supposed to happen and the ways they seemed to occur were rendered mysterious in members' discourses. (pp. 342–343)

Using all three perspectives helped explain why employees could describe their culture as mysterious and confusing while experiencing joy and opportunity.

The second example is drawn from an examination of a 25-member committee charged with identifying candidates and selecting one as their university's provost (Eisenberg, Murphy, & Andrews, 1998). Over one year, the committee, representing a variety of university groups, met to develop the job announcement, review applications, check references, select a short list of applicants for further evaluation, conduct interviews and campus visits, and make a final recommendation. Early on in the committee's activities, the research team was "struck by the differences in perspectives, the large discrepancies in perceptions of the search process." While committee members agreed on what events and activities committee members participated in, members brought different frameworks for understanding and interacting in the search process. "No single narrative captured 'what actually happened' during the search; instead, multiple stories were invented and gained favor in line with individual biases and beliefs" (p. 7).

Eisenberg, Murphy, and Andrews (1998) found that all three perspectives—integration, differentiation, and fragmentation—were revealed by committee members in their descriptions and explanations of the work of the committee. Committee members were not neatly divided into different perspectives with some using only an integration lens while others used only a differentiation or fragmentation lens to explain the committee's actions. Rather, committee members presented a far more complex view of the committee's work, as some used more than one perspective to explain what the committee was doing. The integration perspective revealed that committee members were ordered and disciplined in their meeting activities, and presented their decisions to others as shared by all committee members. However, the differentiation perspective revealed that controversy about a candidate that was not addressed in the public meetings was a topic of concern for some committee members later. The fragmentation perspective revealed that committee members had so many different views about the criteria for evaluating candidates that ambiguity over this central issue influenced their discussions and decisions.

In this case, the committee members treated their narrative interpretations from the three perspectives as rhetorical choices; that is, committee members chose the perspective that suited a particular audience and communication situation. While the narrative explanations were used independently as strategic devices, communication among the committee members created a nexus, or a connection or link, across the three perspectives allowing a variety of cultural influences to come together within permeable and arbitrary boundaries (Martin, 2002). Together, the narratives from the three perspectives created a richer explanation of how committee members interpreted the search process.

A nexus approach to the study of organizational culture acknowledges internal and external influences; such an approach also distinguishes what is unique in an organizational culture from what is not. As Martin (2002) explains, some external influences—such as the influences from an industry, profession, national culture, or racial or socioeconomic group—are not unique to any organization. Similar organizations have the potential to be similarly influenced by the same external forces. These external forces, however, do interact with influences internal to an organization to create a unique mix. This mix of influences is not contained in an organizational structure that is rigid and fixed. Rather, this mix of internal and external influences is part of an organizational structure comprised of moveable, fluctuating, permeable, and blurred subcultural boundaries. Thus, it is more accurate to think of any organizational culture as being many cultures that are blurred, overlapped, and nested to create an organizational multiculture.

As Alvesson (2002) argues, "organizational cultures are then best understood not as unitary wholes or as stable sets of subcultures but as mixtures of cultural manifestations of different levels and kinds" (pp. 190–191). Even in what appear at first glance to be homogeneous and stable organizations, cultural configurations—influenced by both internal and external conditions—are likely to be multiple, complex, and shifting.

Martin (2002) argues that the way in which subcultures relate to one another *is* the organization's culture. Martin uses the metaphor of the organizational culture terrain. Two subcultures are differentiated; their views are inconsistent with one another and possibly conflict. Or, from a fragmentation perspective, the organizational culture is in such flux that ambiguity is normal. In this case, subcultures cannot be clearly distinguished because consensus does not develop within any collective. Although from an integration perspective there are no subcultures, as all organizational members are integrated and consensus is common. While it is tempting (and easier) to select one of these three perspectives to interpret organizational culture, Martin advocates that we view an organization's culture from all three. Each subculture perspective provides a different lens or perspective for interpreting an organization's culture. Using all three provides a more robust interpretation of the relationships among cultural manifestations, the organization's orientation to consensus, and its treatment of ambiguity.

> Each perspective has conceptual blind spots that the combination of the three does not. For example, the integration view is blind to ambiguities, and the fragmentation and differentiation views are blind to that which most cultural members share. In this sense, the three perspectives combine well with each other, offering a conceptual sweep that no one of these perspectives can encompass. (pp. 120–121)

One way to grasp Martin's perspective is to think of a kaleidoscope— a tube-shaped optical instrument that when put to your eye can be rotated to produce an infinite succession of brightly colored symmetrical designs. Just as the kaleidoscope creates a unique image based on the interplay of light, reflection, and color, each of Martin's perspectives illuminates unique aspects of an organization's culture. For the most complete view of a culture, each perspective must be applied and then interpreted relative to the others.

For Parker (2002) however, using the term *subculture* even from Martin's perspective does not allow us to recognize the nested, embedded, or overlapping character of organizational culture. He asks, "Can a sub-subculture exist?" Rather than focusing on subcultures, he would have us identify the way in which organizational members use language to identify the multicultures that exist. Parker argues that focusing on the identification of subcultures implies a search for unity where unity might not exist. Thus, the more recent conceptualization of subcultures relative to organizational culture is a multi-perspective view that allows for all structural possibilities to exist. Looking for the ways in which organizational members organize their language is likely to be the best representation of the symbolic practices of an organization. Some level of sharedness must exist for organizational members to coordinate their actions toward the organization's superordinate goal. But within that unity, multiple lines of fracture will exist and employees may not agree on the pattern of fractures (Parker, 2000).

Still, identifying the subcultures of an organization is a convenient method for making distinctions about different groups of organizational members. From Parker's perspective, however, you should allow for the possibility of one person belonging to many subcultures simultaneously. Not only should you look for ways in which organizational members organize themselves to understand an organization's culture, you should also consider the relationship between the values organizational members say they favor and the values they act out.

WHAT ORGANIZATIONAL CULTURE IS NOT

Arguably, organizational culture can be a difficult concept to define and study. Organizational culture was previously defined as the set(s) of artifacts, values, and assumptions that emerge from the interactions of organizational members. Using that definition as a basis, we can explore what organizational culture is not.

Organizational culture is not any one value, belief, or assumption. It is the combination or configuration of the multiple artifacts, values, and assumptions that create an organization's culture. It is neither a simple or single phenomenon (Morgan, 1997).

Organizational culture is not what someone says it is. All members of the organization socially construct its culture. Culture is often believed to be management driven; yet employees also influence it by accepting, rejecting, resisting, or subverting management efforts. Culture can be facilitated, but it cannot be dictated.

Organizational culture is not just the habits and practices of an organization. Although habits and practices are typically observed, they are the manifest activity of underlying or latent norms, values, beliefs and assumptions that are often taken for granted by organizational members.

Organizational culture is not the social structure of the organization. Although organizations are comprised of social structures of organizational members, the two are not the same. Social structures are the tangible and specific ways in which organizational members create relationships through their interactions with one another. Organizational culture is the patterns of artifacts, values, and assumptions that are created in those interactions. But, an organization's social structure does not necessarily mirror the organization's system of assumptions, values, and beliefs (Trice & Beyer, 1993).

Organizational culture is not an organization's trademark symbol or phrase. Any one thing—a symbol, a saying—may be a physical or outward representation of an organization's culture, but it is not the culture. Organizational members interacting with one another create meanings for symbols and sayings. Organizational culture emerges from these meanings.

Organizational culture is not a professional culture. The specialized training of professionals—such as nurses, journalists, and engineers—creates a professional or occupational culture. Professionals learn the culture of their occupation as they are educated, and later enact cultural beliefs and values as they perform the practices and ceremonies of their occupation (Bloor & Dawson, 1994). Professional culture is also endorsed and encouraged by the professional associations (e.g., American Association of Neuroscience Nurses, Society of Professional Journalists, American Institute of Chemical Engineers) that certify, endorse, or provide further professional training. Professional culture establishes the norms, standards, and operating practices of a profession, which in turn shapes how individuals enact their profession.

Although professional cultures dictate many norms and operating procedures, individual professionals vary in their adherence to these in completing their work. It is a rare organization that employs only one type of professional. More commonly, many types of professionals are employees of an organization, and those many professionals are just part of the organization's total employee base. As a result of these two factors, a professional culture seldom becomes an organization's culture. However, if the number of one type of professional is large or if powerful organizational members belong to one profession, a professional culture may form and exist simultaneously with the organization's culture.

Organizational culture is not equivalent to industry characteristics. Organizations in the same industry are likely to use similar resources for accomplishing their work. As a result, tasks across organizations in an industry are likely to be similar. While technology is considered one of the most salient similarities across organizations in the same industry, industry-wide standards and government regulations are also likely to impact organizations in a similar way (Chatman & Jehn, 1994). Despite these similarities, culture can vary across organizations in the same industry. Why? Organizations compete for workers. Once hired, each employee contributes differently to the organization's culture.

Organizational culture is not static. Rather, organizational culture is dynamic because it emerges from the interactions of organizational members and the meanings they create from these interactions.

Organizational Culture or Organizational Climate

In the communication literature, organizational culture and climate are typically different constructs: in the management literature, these two are often seen with a high degree of similarity; the popular and business press often use the two terms synonymously. As a result of this conceptual confusion (or integration), it is important for you to be able to distinguish which construct is being addressed.

Scholars (Alvesson & Berg, 1991; Denison, 1996; Eisenberg & Riley, 2001; Glisson & James, 2002; Hofstede, 2001; Isaac & Pitt, 2001; Trice & Beyer, 1993) argue that over time culture and climate have become recognized as conceptually distinct phenomena. That is, culture is the set of enduring deep values, beliefs, and assumptions that are produced through the symbolic interactions of organizational members. Alternately, climate is based on individual perceptions of the work environment and is one surface-level manifestation of an organization's culture, making it temporary and subjective to direct control. Thus, culture focuses on the underlying context of assumptions and values while climate focuses on the surface features of organizational context.

McMurray's (2003) study of culture and climate in a university setting reinforces this view, as aggregated work unit climate scores could be used to estimate the congruence of specific work unit values. The culture-climate relationship is fundamental to the study of organizations. For example:

> creating a climate of teamwork and openness is a common goal nowadays, but it is the rare company that figures out how cultural assumptions about individualism, about managerial prerogatives, and about respect for authority based on past success may make teamwork and openness virtually impossible. (Schein, 2000, pp. xxiii–xxiv)

Martin (2002) argues that the central dispute between the two claims is one of consistency of interpretation. Climate tends to be measured quantitatively focusing on one or just a handful of cultural manifestations. Indeed, from a management perspective, "only when there is perceptual agreement does an organizational climate objectively exist" (Dickson, Smith, Grojean, & Ehrhart, 2001, p. 199). Alternately, culture tends to be measured qualitatively and allows for inconsistency in interpretations to exist. But, the distinction between culture and climate is really not one of methodology.

Historically, communication scholars focused on communication-related dimensions—such as supportiveness, trust, openness, participation, decision making—and the concept of *communication climate* became well established (Eisenberg & Riley, 2001). On the other hand, management scholars included other dimensions to evaluate, for example, marketing climate and ethical climate, as well as climatic dimensions relative to safety, innovation, justice, and fairness. More commonly, climate (regardless of what type of climatic characteristic is examined) is conceptualized as a subset of culture.

Thus, the question about the distinctions between culture and climate remain. As Denison (1996) suggests, culture and climate are more likely differences in interpretation than differences in phenomenon. Both address the social context and environment of organizational life. This position is slightly different from Martin's (2002) position about the way in which the two constructs allow for inconsistencies of interpretation. But the point is well taken. Studies of organizational climate rarely, if ever, examine the whole of the organization's climate, nor do they examine the way in which climatic dimensions are independent or interdependent. Nor do climate studies examine the values and assumptions that result in a particular climate or organizational environment. Finally, climate studies do not address political and ideological consequences of organizations (Denison, 1996). Cultural studies, however, are more likely to address or reveal these issues.

Ideally, studies of organizational culture do pursue a holistic assessment and do look for the ways in which cultural artifacts, values, and assumptions are related—consensual or conflicted. In climate studies, the assumption is that climatic conditions are consistent with one another—that they fit together. Thus, a climatic interpretation would focus on the elements as comprising a whole. Cultural studies from a communicative perspective are not likely to adopt the position that assumptions, values, beliefs, and norms are always consistent with one another. Therein, the richness lies.

MYTHS ABOUT ORGANIZATIONAL CULTURE

Just as it is useful to explore organizational culture by distinguishing what it is from what it is not, it is also useful to explore popular myths about organizational culture. Anytime a concept becomes popularized, it often becomes so simplified that it loses its vitality and complexity. Such is the case with organizational culture. Exploring the myths of organizational culture can help you appreciate it in its fullest regard.

Myth: What works as culture in one organization will work in another.

Reality: Organizational culture cannot be replicated. Each organization is unique with different sets of employees, business challenges and opportunities, goals and resources. Organizational culture is constructed locally, socially, and historically.

Myth: Organizational culture is the responsibility of top management.

Reality: The CEO, president, founder, or the top management team cannot dictate all aspects of an organization's culture. No one person or team is that omnipotent. No one person or team can control the communication activity of all organizational members. Groups and individuals can construct and communicate their view of the organization differently, and all views are legitimate. As a result, culture is self-organizing and always evolving—being shaped and reshaped, but never in an absolute way.

Myth: Organizational culture is the key to success.

Reality: Not necessarily. An organizational culture that is successful at one point in time may fail in the future; an organizational culture that is successful for one organization will fail at another. Despite the promises from the popular business literature, no one set of cultural elements has been identified and linked to organizational success.

Myth: Talking about changes to the culture will change the culture.

Reality: Espoused values cannot create a culture; only enacted values can.

Myth: Everyone needs to see the culture similarly for a sense of unity to exist.

Reality: Differences and dissonance among organizational members can exist. Acknowledgment of those differences can be the unifying glue that allows two or more groups to work together.

Myth: Organizational culture is real.

Reality: Organizational culture is a symbolic representation created through communication.

Myth: Organizational culture does not matter. Employees are motivated by money; pay them well enough and they will be productive.

Reality: Money is not the only motivator. People have choices about where and how they work.

Myth: It is easy to see all aspects of an organization's culture.

Reality: No one person can see all aspects of the culture. From any one person's perspective, some aspects of the culture are unknown or unimportant, and thus, out of their awareness.

Myth: It is easy to see or know the culture of an organization.

Reality: Cultural values become embedded in the communicative practices of organizational members and are often not easily detectable. Many times, employees cannot describe the culture they work in.

Myth: All aspects or elements of organizational culture are positive.

Reality: While managers like to point to the aspects of their organizational culture that are effective, productive, efficient, or beneficial to employees, virtually all organizational cultures have negative elements—aspects that cause uncertainty and conflict, take advantage of or demean employees, or limit organizational innovation.

SUMMARY

There are five core characteristics of organizational culture. Organizational culture is (a) inextricably linked to organizational members, (b) dynamic, not static, (c) comprised of competing assumptions and values, (d) emotionally charged, and (e) both foreground and background for an organization's communication. Organizational cultures are symbolic performances, as organizational members are simultaneously responding to and creating a social and symbolic reality from which the organizational culture emerges. Thus, organizational culture is communicatively constructed. It is both the process of interacting and the product of those interactions.

Through their communication, organizational members are simultaneously responding to and creating the social and symbolic reality of the organization's culture. Thus, organizational culture is communicatively constructed by all organizational members. It is both the process of interacting and the product of those interactions. Thus, culture can morph and change as employees move in and out of the organizational system, and as the organization addresses new opportunities or threats from its environment. This creates opportunities for new practices to emerge, to become patterned, and to be accepted as part of the culture. Organizational members use the social context of their environment to make sense of the organization's communication. The process of identifying what is the organization's culture is the process of sensemaking.

Organizational cultures can be structured as a consensus or divided into subcultures. A consensus view of organizational culture would find organizational members having highly similar, or integrated, meanings for cultural elements. From an integration perspective, mutually consistent interpretations are so deeply held that little variation occurs. This type of strong and unified culture is often the goal of management and perceived to be the ideal organizational culture.

To the extent that different sets of artifacts, values, and assumptions develop, an organization's culture is said to have subcultures. Using differentiation, organizational members differentiate into subcultures relative to their inconsistent interpretations, especially along functional or occupational roles; geographical locations; product, market, or technology distinctions; and hierarchical level. From a fragmentation perspective, ambiguity reigns; there is neither clear consistency nor clear inconsistency making it difficult to see clear subcultural divisions. From this perspective, organizational members are part of shifting coalitions, forming and reforming based on shared identities, issues, and circumstances. Subcultures appear briefly, but with boundaries that are permeable and fluctuating. Viewed this way, organizational members have multiple, overlapping identities making it difficult to create organization-wide consensus.

All three perspectives—integration, differentiation, and fragmentation—should be used in the exploration of organizational culture, as some cultural elements will be shared by members while other elements will be interpreted differently by various subcultures. Using all three perspectives allows consensus, consistency, and ambiguity to be revealed, and helps avoid the potential blind spots of each perspective when used alone. Together, the three perspectives encourage three distinct revelations about organizational culture. It is not that one perspective is more correct than another. Rather, each perspective offers an incomplete view of an organization's culture. All three perspectives are needed to offer a multifocal view of organizational culture.

Over time, organizational culture has been conceptualized practically and academically in a variety of ways. By distinguishing organizational culture from other organizational concepts, a clearer picture of organizational culture emerges and the realities of organizational culture can be separated from common myths.

3

Lenses for Understanding Organizational Culture

Communication in an organization is ubiquitous and complex. Virtually all jobs, occupations, or professions rely on communication with other organizational members. Communication can be formal or informal, verbal or nonverbal, written or electronic, spontaneous or strategic, task or relationally oriented. In any form and at any level, communication is consequential. Communicating is not a neutral act; it does not simply move information from one organizational member to another. It is a complex transaction among organizational members influenced by a number of factors. Simply put, the communication system of an organization influences the people in the organization and its activities. Because this process is not neat or tidy, and because the communication system is difficult to see as a whole, scholars have developed a variety of lenses for identifying and investigating the culture that emanates from organizational communication systems. A brief review of the way in which organizational culture developed as a construct serves as an introduction to these primary lenses.

THE DEVELOPMENT OF THE ORGANIZATIONAL CULTURE CONSTRUCT

Like you, researchers and scholars spend at least a third of each 24 hour day as members of organizations. More of our waking hours are spent in organizations with our colleagues than at home with family and friends. Particularly in the United States, a substantial portion of our identities is connected with the organizational memberships we claim. We are also clients and customers of organizations. For example, we see glimpses of organizations as we stand in line at the grocery store waiting for a clerk to conduct a price check, visit the doctor's office expecting to see the doctor but spending more time with a nurse, and negotiating with a salesperson when purchasing a new car. Organizations are central to our society—in creating a viable economy and in structuring our system of government. As a result, our contact with organizations is nearly constant.

This constant presence of and interaction with organizations has transformed us from a traditional society based on households, families, and agriculture to an organizational society (Morgan, 1997). It is no wonder that scholars who study organizations are intrigued with organizational cultures. Morgan argues that viewing organizations through a cultural lens—rather than simply as bureaucracies or hierarchies—reveals the rich symbolism that exists in all aspects of organizational life. A cultural lens also shifts the more traditional focus in organizational studies from that of managers, leaders, and executives to all organizational members, as cultural elements exist in interactions throughout the organization. Through a cultural perspective, researchers can explore (a) an organization's way of life, (b) how that reality is created, (c) how that reality is interpreted by various organizational stakeholders, and (d) the influence of those interpretations on organizational life and organizational activities. With a better understanding there is the opportunity for individuals to make more informed choices to help organizations be profitable and humane (Martin & Frost, 1996).

The threads and notions of organizational culture began early in the field of management, most notably with Elton Mayo's human relations studies. One of the first to recognize the role of social interaction and its influence on organizations, Mayo can be credited for identifying that (a) informal interactions among organizational members set up expectations and constraints that cannot be explained by other organizational structures, and (b) employees' beliefs, attitudes, and values brought with them into the work setting influence how they view themselves, the organization, and their roles within it (Parker, 2000).

Eisenberg and Riley (2001) place the origin of the concept of organizational culture in Jacques's (1951) book, *The Changing Culture of a Factory: A Study of Authority and Participation in an Industrial Setting* while Parker (2000) identifies the first use of the term in an article by Becker and Geer (1960). By 1969 organizational culture was inextricably linked to organizational change with Bennis (1969) proclaiming that the only way to change an organization was to change its culture.

In the 1970s, communication studies of organizational culture became more prevalent when scholars' use of systems theory "relocated communication as the central process in organizations and equated communicating with organizing" (Eisenberg & Riley, 2001, p. 293). Weick's (1979) book, *The Social Psychology of Organizing*, was particularly influential in moving researchers toward discovering systems or patterns of interpretation in organizations. An explosion of scholarly studies on organizational culture or organizational symbolism appeared in the 1980s. At about the same time, popular business books, such as Peters and Waterman (1982) and Deal and Kennedy (1982) provided case analyses of organizational cultures resulting in prescriptive advice for practitioners. Since that time, scholarly interest in the study of organizational culture has continued to increase.

Communication scholars have been particularly intrigued by the concept of organizational culture because of the way in which messages, meanings, and symbols are central to an organization's existence; and over the years, organizational communication scholars have contributed their expertise in symbolic interaction to the study of organizational culture. More recently, organizational communication scholars have taken an interpretive approach to the study of organizational culture (Putnam, 1983). The interpretive approach focuses on the complexity of meanings in social interaction and emerged directly in opposition to positivist and functional social science beliefs. This approach treats organizations as social constructions of reality with the processes of organizing and communicating being inextricably linked. From this perspective, communication is not something that an organization does; rather, the process of communicating creates the organization.

As Putnam (1983) explains, the interpretive approach supported two traditions: the naturalistic and critical study of organizational communication.

Naturalistic research aims to describe and to understand organizational reality as it is without questioning what it could or should become. It adopts a regulation stance for understanding how the status quo works, irrespective of the power structures that maintain it. . . . Critical research strives for emancipation through a critique of social order. In industrial society critical theorists see bureaucratic hierarchies and practices as creating a false consensus among organizational members. Exposing the pseudo nature of this consensus provides alternatives for changing the status quo. (p. 53)

The hallmark of naturalistic research is its ability to provide findings that (a) describe and interpret organizational messages and meanings, (b) reflect the organization's social reality so that it is recognizable to organizational members, and (c) are informative to those outside the organization (Bantz, 1983). The goal of critical research is social change. Thus, the hallmark of critical research is its ability to uncover practices that constrain communication and develop findings that contribute to free and open communication situations in which societal, organizational, and individual interests can be mutually accomplished (Deetz & Kersten, 1983).

Communication scholars have contributed to the growth and development of the study of organizational culture in five ways (Eisenberg & Riley, 2001). First, a communication perspective has demonstrated the symbolic nature of day-to-day conversations and routine practices, emphasizing that culture is present in all organizational communication. Second, a communication perspective emphasizes the way in which both interpretation and action exist within communication practice. Third, the communication perspective on organizational culture recognizes how societal patterns and norms facilitate or constrain the practices of individuals within a particular organizational culture. In other words, this perspective recognizes that any organizational culture is embedded in a larger culture. Fourth, the communication perspective honors a variety of researcher-organization relationships. The researcher can be within, close to, or more removed from the culture being studied. Finally, the communication perspective acknowledges all motives as legitimate for the study of organizational culture. These five contributions underscore the role of cultural studies in moving the study of organizations and organizational communication from a rational, objective, and abstract perspective, to one that is capable of providing deep, rich, and realistic understandings of organizations and the experiences of people within them (Alvesson, 2002). Greater attention to organizational culture also provided a conceptual bridge between micro- and macro-level views of organizations, by connecting the whole of the organization with everyday experiences (Smircich, 1983).

Accordingly, Deetz (1988) argues that the goals of organizational culture studies should be twofold. The first goal should be to generate insight about cultural processes by understanding how individuals create sense and meaning at a particular time and location, and to demonstrate how our sensemaking of our work lives articulates basic information about cultural processes. The second goal should be to continue to develop and re-form organizational practices acknowledging the complexity of the work environment, the variety of stakeholders, and their competing interests.

In addition to these goals, the investigation of organizational culture has the potential to produce three outcomes (Schein, 1992) vital to our understanding of and practice in organizations. Greater diversity along any dimension will require a deeper understanding of how different groups can integrate their work activities. A deeper understanding of integration is also required as organizations acknowledge diverse groups within the workforce. Second, technology is increasingly being used to enhance the communication and work activities of organizational members. A new technology, or a new use of an existing technology, can substantially alter the work environment and accompanying work practices, as well as mediate interpretations. Third, cultural analysis is necessary to manage organizations across national and ethnic boundaries. On a local level, increasing globalization has created a work environment where some employees communicate with coworkers and clients distributed across time zones and nations. On a broader scale, understanding culture is essential when organizations from two nations merge or when international joint ventures or strategic alliances are created.

Scholars and practitioners view organizational culture differently, and the scholar's perspective is unique. Practitioners can oversimplify what organizational culture is and how culture can be used as a mechanism for improving productivity and performance (Martin & Frost, 1996). Scholars, using multiple theoretical and methodological lenses, can illuminate the complexity (and messiness) of organizational culture—revealing it for what it is rather than what managers want or expect it to be. Scholars' focus on the way in which culture is developed, maintained, or changed can identify frames or scripts that managers can credibly use to bridge the different assumptions held by organizational members. Thus, organizational culture is popular with both scholars and practitioners, and enjoys both academic respectability and practical relevance (Alvesson & Berg, 1991).

Given the history of organizational culture scholarship, and the variety of academic disciplines that have contributed to its development, scholars bring many different perspectives to the study of organizational culture. Each of the perspectives, or lenses, described in the following sections is useful for studying the processes of communicating and organizing that create an organization's culture. Each has merit, and each has shortcomings. No one lens can reveal a complete view of an organization's culture—thus, the necessity of multiple lenses. Lenses can be used singly or in combination. Used together, different lens are likely to reveal different cultural elements, as well as different interpretations of the organization's culture.

THE LENS OF SYMBOLIC PERFORMANCE

Early on scholars argued that organizational culture emerged through the interpretation of symbols. A symbol is an object, word, or action that stands for something else or something more than the object, word, or action itself (Cohen, 1974). From the symbolic perspective, the everyday conversations among organizational members were considered, well, ordinary and everyday. Rather, the focus was on symbolic devices, as when metaphors, stories, jokes, rituals, and myths were used purposely. Because such occurrences were infrequent, great significance could be attached to them when they were used (Eisenberg & Riley, 2001). When interpretations of these symbols were shared, culture became a mechanism for regulating organizational behavior (Allaire & Firsirotu, 1984).

Although important information can be learned about an organization's culture by examining its unique and highly visible symbolic elements, this approach sacrifices the complexity and depth that come from studying the organization's communication system as a whole. Thus, this limited view was replaced by the view that all types of communication—including the mundane and everyday—were responsible for the creation, maintenance, and transformation of organizational reality (Eisenberg & Riley, 2001). Rather than focusing on one type of symbol or a set of symbols, this perspective moved to acknowledge that a system of symbols—including the everyday and the unique—is responsible for creating complexity, and sometimes contradictions, in the totality of organizational communication and the organization's resulting culture (Carbaugh, 1988b). Thus, this view of organizational culture seeks to examine the way in which communication brings culture into being. Rather than simply identifying artifacts, values, and assumptions as cultural displays or symbolic representations of organizational culture, the symbolic performance perspective examines the way in which organizational performances reveal cultural meaning as well as how the performance itself is developed, maintained, and changed.

Characteristics of Organizational Performances

The organizational performances that reveal organizational culture have four core characteristics (Pacanowsky & O'Donnell-Trujillo, 1982, 1983). First, organizational performances are interactive. Organizational members create and participate in them together. No organizational role or function is independent from others. When people enact their organizational roles, these role enactments acknowledge the roles of others. In a sales presentation, the sales agent role is enacted with the role of customer. In a team meeting, coworker roles are enacted as the team chooses a new team leader.

Second, organizational performances are contextual. They happen in a particular organization within a larger set of organizational events. The situational and temporal embeddedness of an organizational performance allows specialized and localized meanings to develop. For example, team members choosing a new team leader know what activities are the responsibilities of the team leader and choose a team leader based on the information unique to this team. In doing so, they reinforce the role of team members and team leader, the relationship between those two roles, and the activities of people within those roles. This performance is grounded in the team's history (and perhaps the organization's history of teamwork), and provides a map to future behavior.

Third, organizational performances are episodic. Having a beginning and end, organizational members can tell one performance from another. Much of organizational life is driven by events: formalized events such as work shifts, Monday morning meetings, budget cycles, and annual performance appraisals; and informal events such as coming to agreement that *it's time* for lunch, a lunch hour that stretches regularly to 90 minutes, and coffee breaks. Whether formal or informal, these events—or episodes—create regularity and a routine for the flow of work, as well as a framework for interpretation. Monday morning meetings, which are supposed to start at 8 a.m., really start when the division manager signals that it is time to start. Thus, the interaction up to, within, and coming from the episode can be interpreted as typical ("We never start on time"), unusual ("I wonder why he's late today"), or uncertain ("Can we just decide on a meeting time and stick with it?").

Fourth, organizational performances are improvisational. While an organization's culture can provide some structure for a performance, a performance is never fully scripted. Moreover, organizational members can alter the script or completely ignore it. New employee orientation may cover the same material for each new orientation session. But each session is also unique as employees ask questions requiring the trainer to move through some material quickly to allow adequate time to focus on the particular material that is unclear or unfamiliar. While the trainer is ready to answer any question, the number and topic of the questions creates a different performance in each new orientation session. While the trainer may have expectations about her organizational performance, she cannot know if she will be able to follow those expectations until she interacts with the new employees. Some of the questions asked may allow her to fall back on her expectations and training outline; other questions may require that she improvise or create an answer on the spot.

Types of Organizational Performance Processes

Despite the diversity of organizational performances, there are types of organizational performances that can generally be found in organizations: ritual, passion, social codes or practices, politics, and enculturation (Pacanowsky & O'Donnell-Trujillo, 1983). Organizational performances are processes through which symbols take on and display meaning. A richer explanation of organizational culture occurs when we can identify what the ritual is, how it came into being, what cultural meanings are enacted or developed in the performance, and why organizational members enact these performances.

The first type of organizational performance is *rituals*—personal, task, social, or organizational performances that occur regularly to punctuate work experiences. For example, Jeff goes to work early to allow himself time to leisurely drink a cup of coffee at his desk (personal ritual) before his work team joins him in his cubicle (task ritual). But before the team moves through its agenda, Jeff knows that Samantha will encourage others to share what they did the night before (social ritual). When Jeff recognizes that everyone has said something, he moves the team quickly through the agenda so that he will not be late for his manager's meeting that immediately follows this one (organizational ritual). Examining this series of rituals, we can discover how team members' view and value meetings, what assumptions provide a background for work in meetings, and what artifacts signal that meetings are ready to begin and end.

A second type of organizational performance is *passion,* or the heightened description of common workplace activities. Most jobs have routine elements. Even the glamour job of being an actor has work activities that most report as tedious or boring: coming in before dawn to the make-up trailer to be fitted with a wig, make-up, prosthetic teeth, and costume to become the character; and waiting for technical adjustments to light and sound equipment between takes. These routine activities are transformed into passions in the form of stories told by actors about the tedium and time-consuming activities of getting into character. In some instances, the *drama* of being transformed into one's character becomes a key part to promoting the movie. The organizational performance of passion is transforming common work activities into heightened and enhanced descriptions of those activities, often in the form of stories.

A third type of organizational performance is the social codes of behavior at work. *Courtesies,* one type of social code, are enacted by flight attendants as they welcome passengers on board, and by a coworker who lets the person making only one copy cut in at the copy machine. *Pleasantries,* another code of behavior, are exemplified when colleagues engage in small talk waiting for others to join the meeting. Seemingly senseless, these activities reveal organizational members' communication and working styles and provide openings for making introductions and creating relationships. Another code of work behavior is *sociability,* a performance that implies familiarity among interactants. Telling an inappropriate joke to the *right* person is a form of sociability—you would not be secure in telling the joke if you did not know that the person you share it with will not take offense. The final code of work behavior is labeled *privacies* and can be exemplified by the way in which one worker momentarily invades a coworker's personal space to whisper something secretive in the other's ear. Privacies are those performances in which sensitive or political information is being communicated, and thus, requires a protocol (e.g., a performance appraisal behind a shut door) to make the activity fit appropriately within the normal work routine.

The fourth type of organizational performance is *politics*. Showing personal abilities, recruiting allies, bargaining, and negotiating are political performances in organizations because they demonstrate power, control, and influence. For example, in your organization salespeople compete with one another for customers as they walk in the door. Some customers had complained to management that they felt bombarded as one salesperson after another asked, "Do you need some help?" To avoid such problems, your manager implemented a procedure for linking customers to salespeople. Based on a rotating schedule, salespeople are "up" to greet and help new customers as each new customer enters the store. Initially, everyone liked the new procedure, and it was used efficiently and effectively. But, soon, the salespeople had conflicting ideas of identifying customers. Some salespeople believed that if it was their turn to be "up," then that customer should be theirs even if they had gone into the storeroom momentarily to retrieve something. Other salespeople believed that a rotation for being "up" was forfeited if a salesperson was not ready to greet customers as they walked through the door. To avoid a potential forfeit, many of your colleagues started to avoid stocking and cleaning tasks that were part of the job. Those who did continue with these chores—and also put themselves at risk for not being available when customers entered—were verbally rewarded by the manager. But those who refused to perform the stocking and cleaning chores were rewarded with increased sales. In this example, a group of salespeople quickly divided into two groups, each trying to recruit the others to join them. One group attempted to positively influence the manager by continuing to perform tasks that would result in praise; the other attempted to demonstrate power by strategically avoiding the stocking and cleaning tasks. This cultural performance demonstrates how organizational members' use of power, control, and influence created a political interpretation of the procedure of being "up."

The final type of organizational performance is *enculturation*. These are the interaction activities by which organizational members acquire knowledge and skills to be considered competent in their work roles. Certainly new employees must be acculturated; but seasoned employees may also be expected to learn new procedures. Nevertheless beyond learning the task skills necessary for the job, employees must also learn how to negotiate organizational realities, such as asking for a raise or time off, positively influencing coworkers when they are not those coworkers' supervisor, and bringing concerns to the attention of the union steward. Each of these activities requires learning the ropes; for other organizational members, these activities require teaching the ropes. Thus, enculturation is the process by which organizational members learn the intricacies of organizational life.

Witmer's (1997) study of the world's largest and most successful Alcoholics Anonymous group, the Friendship Group, demonstrates the processual nature of communication, and the role of symbolic performances in creating an organization's culture. Using a variety of methodologies—field observation, interviews, unobtrusive methods—Witmer discovered how the Friendship Group's founder created, and its members continued to enact, a culture distinct from other A.A. meeting groups. The founder, a dynamic and powerful leader, brought his own (and more rigid and intense) interpretation of A.A. into this organization. Claiming that acting better made him feel better, the founder's behaviors soon became cultural performances for his followers in the group as well. The Friendship Group ritualized and continued to practice for over 30 years greeting people at meetings with a formal reception line, repeatedly using specific phrases (e.g., "it is an honor and a privilege") to address the group, and adhering to a dress code that set the tone of disciplined behavior for the group. Members were organized into activities to keep active and away from events where alcohol was likely to be served. Although no longer formally the group's leader, the founder's informal authority was not disputed. Sponsors of new members taught and reinforced this culture by setting the example of the culture in their one-on-one meetings, group meetings, and Friendship Group activities. The rituals reinforced disciplined behavior and celebrated sobriety, which in turn created an organizational culture that valued action, acceptance, and selflessness as a route to recovery.

Locating and analyzing the communicative performances between and among organizational members within an organization's communication system demonstrates how an organization enacts its culture and creates it symbolic self. This view of organizational culture moves beyond simply identifying the assumptions, values, and artifacts as symbolic representations of culture. Rather the organizational performance perspective reveals how meaning is created from cultural symbols and the way in which these meanings are integrated into a performance.

THE LENS OF NARRATIVE REPRODUCTION

Everyone has stories about their work experience. A narrative is a story, and a common way for people to make sense of their organizational experiences (Boje, 1991; Bormann, 1983). While organizational stories are about particular actors and particular events, they serve as artifacts to provide information about an organization's values, norms, and beliefs (Bruner, 1991; Meyer, 1995). The specifics are the exemplars of the culture the storyteller wants to describe. A story is essentially the unfolding of action that has a beginning, middle, and end. In its telling, the specifics are meaningful only to the whole.

For example, Bill, who works for an insurance company as an adjuster, tells the following story when asked how employees are motivated:

> Okay, you know that we have the *Bestest Awards*. Each quarter, our managers get together and pick the employee from each department that they believe is best—or, it may be the employee they think has made the most improvement. Whatever. Anyway, at the end of the year, the managers get together again and pick the *Best of the Best* out of each division's *Bestest* award winners at the department level. This person—last year it was Georgeanna—gets a cruise to Alaska . . . in August . . . when the rest of us are melting in the heat and humidity. Now think about it. Let's say I won a *Bestest* award at the end of this quarter—that's in March. By the way, the award is a certificate given at the quarterly meeting. And, then let's say that I'm selected as the *Best of the Best* at the end of the year, but I don't get to take my cruise until the following August. I'm getting rewarded 15 months after my supposedly award-winning performance. What kind of motivation is that? [pause.] At any rate, I wanted you to know about the awards here and how they work.

In this story, Bill is describing his organizational experiences. Although he is describing a particular organizational practice (how departmental awards are given), he is also providing information about how the organization values its employees. Notice that his description of the awards is accompanied by his positive evaluation of the award (i.e., an Alaskan cruise when it is hot where he lives), and his negative evaluation of how the award is given (i.e., 15 months after someone's performance is acknowledged). In telling this story, Bill is describing, and in essence evaluating, the organizational culture and its norms for evaluating and rewarding employees.

Notice how the narrative is generated from one person's viewpoint. Also notice how the narrative reproduces the culture and provides insight into what the culture values (Meyer, 1995). A new employee would not have experienced these events. However, listening to Bill's narrative, a new employee would have some information, both objective and subjective, that would undoubtedly influence her expectations about the organization. Indeed, a new employee might even accept this narrative description and evaluation about organizational rewards and tell the story herself until she has direct experience with this practice, at which point she will modify the story to suit her needs and view of the organization (Boje, 1991). If others in the organization tell the same or similar story, the narrative will gain legitimacy and be seen as the way things really are—even though the story varies by its teller. Legitimacy in this case is not located in truth. Rather, legitimacy depends on the narrative's plausibility.

Of course, not all organizational events are story worthy. For an organizational story to be worth telling, there must some event worth telling about. In organizational life, that event is usually something that deviates from normal practice, known as a breach of social order (Bruner, 1991). Although negative deviations are more common, narratives can also be developed when there are positive deviations from organizational norms. In the narrative above, there is a minor and major breach that forms the basis of the story. First, the storyteller reports the minor breach about how employees are selected for the award. Are employees selected because they are the best performers? Or, are employees selected because they have made the most improvement? This may seem like a minor detail, but this aspect of the narrative also alludes to the storyteller's belief that no clear criteria exist for how employees are identified as award recipients. In an organization, lack of objective criteria gives power to managerial subjectivity both in what the award represents and who gets the award. The storyteller reports the major breach as the delay between the employee's performance and taking the cruise, the reward for superior performance. Underlying the narrative is the storyteller's negative evaluation of this practice and his belief that performance and rewards should be more closely linked.

In examining the orientation of the storyteller to the organization, another interpretation of this narrative is possible. Notice how the storyteller reports that Georgeanna won last year's *Best of the Best Award*. Then Bill projects the story into the future by describing the hypothetical situation in which he wins the award. The way in which the story is told suggests that he has not won either the quarterly or the annual award, which is his implicit evaluation of what his manager thinks of him.

Narratives are particularly powerful in passing along organizational culture because they are a natural component of organizational communication. Not only do organizational members purposely tell stories, but they also tell stories as part of their ongoing conversations when working through conflict and solving problems. Thus, storytelling to others and story construction with one another are often used as employees create a logic or rationale for understanding the complexity of what is happening in their organization (Jameson, 2001), as well as creating bonds that hold organizational members together (Coopman & Meidlinger, 2000; Kaufman, 2003).

Controlling Organizational Culture Through Narratives

Long acknowledged for their influence in creating cohesive and productive organizational cultures (Mohan, 1993), stories are never neutral. Each narrative relays more than just information (Taylor & Van Every, 2000), especially the interests of dominant groups (Putnam & Fairhurst, 2001) by indicating what values are accepted and which are rejected (Coopman & Meidlinger, 2000). Because stories reinforce what is and what is not valued, they both produce and reproduce the organization's power structure (Mumby, 1988). In other words, "organizational stories are not innocuous. Rather they are inherently linked to organizational issues of power and hierarchy" (Coopman & Meidlinger, 2000, p. 579).

When multiple organizational members tell (and retell) similar stories, the specifics of the stories accrue and are taken as findings about artifacts, values, and assumptions of an organization's culture (Bruner, 1991). Many managers use stories in public meetings to demonstrate (and reinforce) how organizational objectives should be enacted and to demonstrate what the organization can realize (and what employees should do) when the values of the organization's culture are upheld. And, of course, stories can become powerfully dangerous when management reconstructs the organizational events of a story to serve as a managerial representation that meets their needs.

It is not uncommon for members of an organization to create a set of connected and shared stories about some aspect of organizational life. A manager might tell a newcomer several stories about how the department's employees treat one another to express the family-like atmosphere fostered under his supervision. A CEO might repeatedly tell stories of how her account managers repeatedly go the extra mile in producing results for clients. Stories like these create a general principle about how employees should behave, and in turn, can control employee behavior. Because the principle can be expressed in different sets of specifics, the principle becomes a legitimate part of the organization's culture, and part of its control mechanism.

THE LENS OF TEXTUAL REPRODUCTION

Written texts are widely prominent in organizations, providing a fixed view on organizational culture (Eisenberg & Riley, 2001). Written texts exist as formal communication in the form of newsletters, mission statements, procedures, handbooks, reports, and slogans. Typically these represent managerial perspectives because of their permanence and ability to be controlled.

Gilsdorf's (1998) study found that managerial employees across a wide variety of organizational types and sizes pointed to memos, postings, and newsletters as being more influential than manuals, policies, and handbooks. Not surprisingly, they indicated that management should control most or all communication within an organization. Emphasizing the role of textual reproduction of organizational culture, these managers pointed to instances in which a policy should have been developed to provide guidance about verbal communication, and how when policies or procedures were not followed or enforced, problems occurred.

However, informal texts, such as graffiti, can also portray a view of an organization's culture. Not only is graffiti informal, it is not controlled by an organization's established management structure. Graffiti, often humorous, also serves as a territorial marker implying who has been in the space, as well as their values about the space or the organization that provides it. Because of its informality, spontaneous, and cumulative nature, graffiti writers can express their views of the culture without being identified directly and, at the same time, take a stand against the culture while creating a space for like-minded others to express their views. For example, Scheibel (1994) analyzed the graffiti in the editing rooms in a communication department at a university.

Students' graffiti revealed their alienation toward the conditions of their films (school projects with short time demands, lack of equipment) and the process of filmmaking (long nights, lonely editing sessions), which established the *film school* culture that is interpreted against the background of the film industry. Graffiti disclosed students' perceptions of relationships with other students, faculty, university administration, and the filmmaking industry while portraying themselves in a favorable way. As an example of how students used graffiti to express the relationship between student filmmaker and faculty, one entry read:

You know you've got a good film when _____ hates it!

So what if _____ doesn't like it.

Remember to do what you want—not what _____ wants you to do. (p. 12)

Such comments express students' views of artistic control or ownership over the film product relative to the frequent criticism students received from faculty.

Textual reproductions of organizational culture are especially useful for exploring espoused versus enacted elements of culture. Formal documentation represents the espoused view. Written documents tell what should happen or explain the culture from a managerial perspective. Alternately, informal texts are better representations of the enacted culture. At one manufacturing plant, the company newsletter (the formal espoused view of culture) was regularly ignored by hourly employees. Believing that the newsletter was managerial propaganda, the hourly workers used the newsletter to make paper airplanes, folded them and used them under table legs to keep tables from wobbling, or kept a stack of the newsletters in a box as a door stop. Using the formal textual representation of the organization's culture in these informal ways demonstrated the tension between espoused and enacted values.

THE LENS OF MANAGEMENT

Starting as a topic of academic pursuit in the human relations movement (Parker, 2000), organizational culture quickly found its way into business conversations and the popular press, in part, prompted by the management principles laid out in *In Search of Excellence* (Peters & Waterman, 1982) and *Corporate Cultures* (Deal & Kennedy, 1982). These books responded to practical management needs, such as dealing with increased competition, more turbulent markets, shrinking productivity, increased organizational size, and social changes. Thus, pitching organizational culture as a kind of social glue to hold an organization together was very appealing (Alvesson & Berg, 1991). Executives and managers at all levels sought to instill in their own organizations and units the principles described in these popular business books, which are now considered classic management texts. Soon, executives and managers expected that their organization's culture would be evaluated when organizational development and change experts were consulted in hopes of improving business outcomes. So, it is not surprising that the study of organizational culture took on a managerial perspective.

Clearly, enthusiasm for studying organizational culture and the role of communication in creating and maintaining culture blossomed from the managerial perspective presented in these popular business books. This movement was more prescriptive than descriptive (Parker, 2000). Moreover, explanations that resulted from this movement suffered from a particular attribution bias. "If the organization succeeds, it is because of the vision of the executive and the collective mission of the workforce. If the company fails, the culture is weak, or inappropriately adapted to a changing environment" (p. 25). Either way, the term *organizational culture* became synonymous with everything that was right or wrong with an organization.

Culture as a Control Device

Treating organizational culture as a resource or tool, a managerial perspective of organizational culture can be characterized by a number of elements. First and foremost, from this perspective, organizational culture is developed and directed by managers for the purpose of improving operating efficiencies, enhancing the bottom line, or creating satisfied customers. Thus, organizational culture is seen as an internal process that influences external outcomes. The role of managers from this perspective is to create a culture in which employees are happy and satisfied so that they will follow managerial directives.

This means, essentially, that organizational culture is viewed as a control device. Managers want to create or manufacture a culture that will motivate their employees to work productively. From this perspective, communication is seen as a relatively straightforward instrumental activity under the control of management that can be used to achieve organizational outcomes. Thus, communication is treated as one aspect of the organization that can easily be changed or improved upon (Penman, 2000).

Two examples demonstrate this. The Center for Corporate Culture and Organizational Health—summarizing evidence from literature reviews, database assessments, and interviews with business leaders, human resource professionals and consultants—concludes that "healthier organizational cultures are likely to reduce workforce turnover and stress; improve employee health, productivity, performance, and retention; and lead to significant improvements in business results" (Levey & Levey, 2000a, ¶ 3). Further, leaders are encouraged to "develop organizational cultures with the strong foundation of trust and mutual respect necessary for almost super-fluid communication" (Levey & Levey, 2000b, ¶ 10). From this perspective, organizational culture is produced by managers with the intent of making workers productive.

Other evidence of organizational culture being used as a control device comes from a scholarly investigation of the impact of the organizational cultures of university nursing programs on the scholarly productivity of nursing professors (McNeal, 2000). Improving informational resources, finding ways to promote faculty accomplishments, and periodically reducing workloads were reported as strategies college deans and department chairs could take to change their organizational cultures to improve faculty productivity. While these structural changes might create the expected outcomes and benefit the faculty as well as the university, notice that the recommendations are directed toward administrators—not the nursing professors who must produce scholarship in addition to their teaching and clinical responsibilities. The underlying assumption is that if administrators control the work environment, and hence, change the culture, they can control worker output. Both examples demonstrate why some managers believe that organizational culture can be directly influenced by them to produce enhanced organizational outcomes.

Employee Selection

A second way to characterize organizational culture from a managerial perspective is to view it as a screening device in selecting employees. All organizations must hire employees, and the costs of doing so coupled with the costs of training new employees can be significant. Thus, one goal of organizations is to minimize employee turnover. One way to do this is to hire employees that *fit* with the organization's culture. Such an objective assumes two things: First, that employees in authoritative positions know what its culture is, and second, that these employees can identify these characteristics in new hires. The presumption is that when individuals are a good fit with an organization, there will be congruence between their patterns of values and the organization's patterns of values (Chatman, 1991).

O'Reilly, Chatman, and Caldwell (1991) set out to demonstrate that person-organization fit was achievable and a viable mechanism for reducing turnover. First, the research team created the Organizational Culture Profile, a questionnaire comprised of 54 values across seven dimensions: aggressive, detail oriented, innovative, outcome oriented, respectful, stable, and team oriented. Next, the Profile was used to identify the cultures of organizations in the accounting, consulting, health care, postal service, and transportation industries (Chatman & Jehn, 1994; O'Reilly, Chatman, & Caldwell, 1991; Vandenberghe, 1999). An implicit assumption of such an approach is that a few dimensions are appropriate across a wide variety of organizations. This approach also presumes that the profile will represent what is shared about the culture across all employees in the organization (Chatman & Jehn, 1994).

Once identified, then organizations could screen potential recruits for their individual value profile. Across many organizations, researchers found that when new employees exhibited a values profile similar or close to the values profile of the organization that hired them, new employees expressed higher levels of organizational commitment and job satisfaction, and were more likely to stay longer with the organization. Thus, person-culture fit is often a central part of the interviewing and selection process. Human resource personnel and managers often compose questions ("What would you do . . . ? How would you handle . . . ?") to determine if the applicant fits with the organization's culture.

Goodall (1990) provides a different view of person-organization fit. His ethnographic study of a computer software company reveals how fit was achieved through entering the organization with nonverbal artifacts similar to those valued by organizational members. Rather than person-organization fit being based on personality, fit was achieved because new employees displayed the dress, appearance, and artifacts valued by organizational members. Thus, looking like you can easily play the part is a strategic device new employees can use to fit in to a new organization. Looking like you fit in suggests to others that you value the same things as they do. Indeed, research has demonstrated that a good person-organization fit results in quicker adjustment by new hires, higher levels of individual satisfaction, and longer organizational tenure (Chatman, 1991).

Organizational Culture and Organizational Success

The functional perspective of organizational culture, embraced in the management literature and popular press, often examines how an organization's culture can be managed or changed to influence organizational success. Because managers and executives are primarily responsible (at least from a financial point of view) for the success of an organization, it makes sense then to argue that an organization's culture is the product of its decision making (Schoenberger, 1997), especially the decision making that is done by the managers and executives who steer the course of the organization's activities. Managerial decisions in for-profit organizations are generally future-oriented and strategic in nature with the objective of improving organizational income, net sales, invested capital, income/sales ratio, or income/investment ratio. For example, decisions about market expansion, product or service quality, return on investment, and adoption of new technologies are intended to improve what the organization produces with the expectation that doing so will improve the organization's financial success. This is a key point. From this perspective, organizational success is financial success, even when customer satisfaction is measured. So, how is organizational culture tied to an organization's financial success?

These types of decisions, intended to improve organizational success, are embedded with the cultural values and beliefs of the key decision makers. Once the decisions are made and implemented, the policies and practices that emanate from them function to either enhance or modify the organization's values and beliefs (Denison, 1990). Thus, how decision makers interact in making the decisions, and communicate those decisions to others in the organization, ties organizational culture to organizational effectiveness.

Despite the number of studies that have attempted to demonstrate the link between organizational culture and organizational performance, the evidence is far from convincing (Alvesson, 2002). There may, in fact, be conditions and circumstances in which an organization's culture will predict organizational success, but those conditions and circumstances have not been well identified. Characteristics that are likely to influence this relationship include degree of cultural integration, controllable work situations, degree of cultural adaptability or flexibility, and valuing both internal and external constituencies (Wilderom, Glunk & Maslowski, 2000).

Typically, findings that support the culture-performance link are drawn from studies that operationalize organizational culture simplistically as shared values or values consensus (Eisenberg & Riley, 2001) without considering the likelihood of multiple cultures. As a result, culture-performance studies tend to cast culture broadly using only the most general values and norms and fail to capture the cultural complexity (Alvesson, 2002). Such studies are more likely to take the view that strong cultures enhance organizational performance without considering the way in which strong cultures can negatively impact organizations' capacities for change (Alvesson, 2002). Studies that pursue an organizational culture-performance link are typically cast as cause and effect (Siehl & Martin, 1990). That is, if the culture is of a particular type, strength, or variety, then a specific outcome will be achieved. Such a position de-emphasizes the roles of all organizational members in creating organizational culture, and the many interpretations that can be generated and sustained.

A conceptually stronger argument about the culture-performance link is found in Alvesson's (2002) notion that some elements of culture may be related to other manifestations of culture. For example, feelings of community could lead to reduced turnover. But to claim that an organization's culture as a whole is responsible for organizational success is problematic to conceptualize and study.

When organizational success is the focus, organizational culture becomes a means to that end. The popular press and literature continue to embrace the notion that there are good and bad cultures and that a strong unified culture is best (Morgan, 1997). Some organizations hire trainers and consultants to coach an organization (usually leaders at the executive level) through a cultural change process. Arguably, the belief that what is good for the organization is in the best interest of employees seems reasonable. But when organizational culture is created and managed to entice or provoke employees to accept working harder, there are potential drawbacks and liabilities. Management has always been an ideological practice—promoting attitudes, values, and norms—to control employees (Morgan, 1997). Recently, however, some attempts at culture control to achieve organizational success have included value-engineering practices that employees resist and resent. Subtle manipulations disguised as rewards for employees breed distrust. Morgan clarifies: "There is an important distinction to be drawn between attempts to create networks of shared meaning that link key members of an organization around visions, values, and codes of practice . . . and the use of culture as a manipulative tool" (p. 151).

Using Culture as a Competitive Advantage

Yet another way to characterize organizational culture from the managerial perspective is to view it as the element that distinguishes it from other similar organizations, and, as a result, provides a competitive advantage. Scholars argue that it is the human resources of an organization that provide a sustainable competitive advantage (Ferris, Hochwarter, Buckley, Harrell-Cook, & Frink, 1999). Organizations in the same industry are likely to use the same technology, and have similar access to financial resources. The one thing that is unique for an organization is its mix of employees. As a result, an organization's culture can provide a competitive advantage because competitors would have great difficulty in imitating it.

Executives and managers believe this premise, and it is reinforced by articles written in professional and trade associations (McKenna, 2003; Mitchell, & Yates, 2002). The presumption is that a strong, unified, and coherent culture is the path to excellence or high performance (Alvesson & Berg, 1991). At UPS, for example, organization executives consider its culture as a strategic asset. UPS senior vice president of human resources explains that the UPS culture is based on hiring and retaining the right people, nurturing innovation, and building a customer mindset. UPS, which employs 350,000 worldwide, communicates its values through training and education programs; relies on the business principles developed by its founder (known as the *UPS Policy Book and Code of Business Conduct*); and introduces new employees to its business from the ground up—all UPS employees begin their careers at the loading docks or in package cars (Soupata, 2001).

The Two Sides of Managerial Views

Despite the popular position promoted by many business books—that managers are solely responsible for an organization's culture—management scholarship presents a more varied perspective of organizational culture. Some management scholars adopt a position very similar to that of organizational communication scholars in acknowledging the role of all organizational members in the creation of an organization's culture. Adopting this perspective, a manager would appreciate that employees are as active in the creation of culture as managers and executives. To change some aspect of the culture, a manager would create clear, consistent, and continual messages about the change with that communication positioned within an environment that supports the desired change. By listening to employee concerns and seeking their input and feedback, managers include employees in creating or changing the culture. From this perspective, a manager would also acknowledge that employees may not attend to these cues or perceive them as she intended (Isaac & Pitt, 2001).

The two managerial positions toward organizational culture can be characterized this way. The traditional managerial position is more objective and presumes that an organization's culture resides in the organization as a result of other management controlled resources, such as organizational structure, technology, and managerial strategies. From this view, "a culture is something an organization *has*" (Smircich, 1983, p. 347). The second managerial position, which is more subjective and more similar to communication perspectives on organizational culture, presumes that culture is the essence of the organization. Thus, it would be logical to believe that all members contribute to the creation of that essence. From this view, "a culture is something an organization *is*" (Smircich, 1983, p. 347). It is unclear how practicing managers actually conceptualize organizational culture. However, the first position is the one that the contemporary popular business literature continues to fuel, as its books are directed toward what managers can do to direct or influence their organizational culture.

THE LENS OF POWER AND POLITICS

Power and politics are manifested in many different ways in organizations—four of which are primary to this discussion (Ragins, 1995). First, power can exist in an organizational member's ability, in their perceived ability, or in others' perceptions of that ability. For example, the attorney who wins the most cases, and secures the most fees for his law firm, is perceived by his colleagues as setting the standard for production quality and quantity. Second, power can exist in the interactions among organizational members. Even without having a legitimate or formal role typically associated with rewards and punishments, an individual, through his or her interactions and relationships, can reward and punish others. Acknowledging good performance or excluding a coworker from the discussion are subtle and informal power mechanisms available to employees at all levels. Referential, or charismatic, power is also available to all employees.

Third, power may be structural because it is built into the design of the organization. For example, status attached to certain organizational functions (e.g., international operations, the engineering department) or roles (e.g., special assistant to the president, CFO) is derived from the organization's structure. In these cases, discretionary power over people, information, and resources is legitimized by the organization. Fourth, sociopolitical power—such as racism, sexism, and classism—can be imported from the organization's larger social environment into the organization. The assumptions and values embedded within and between demographic groups from which an organization pulls its employees are likely to be reflected in the organization's culture. As a result of these four types of power, the cultural diversity of an organization may reflect an unequal allocation of power among diverse groups (Ragins, 1995).

Because the ideology of organizational leaders influences the values and assumptions of their organizations (Ragins, 1995) an ethnocentric perspective can emerge and result in unstated and unconscious bias. Thus, a leader's ideology—the biases and perceptions held by that person—can infiltrate what the organization defines as success and who it allows to be successful (i.e., structural power). Both factors contribute to a self-perpetuating cycle reinforcing inequity from both social and individual sources. Sociopolitical and structural power are integrated and built into the day-to-day interactions and influence perceptions of power throughout the organization. The integration of these power sources can result in segregation of certain demographic groups into low-power jobs, functions, or departments with few opportunities for advancement. This integration can also create stressful and unhealthy work environments as organizational members from certain demographic groups are reminded on a daily basis of the value of their work or worth to the organization. Low wages, being denied participation in organizational discussions, or being mistreated by a boss of a dominant demographic group are painful reminders that some groups of employees have power and others do not. It would be impossible for an organization's culture not to carry symbolic meaning about who and what is powerful and who and what is not.

The Political Division of Employees and Managers

Obviously, not all cultural aspects are positive in nature or seen as positive by employees. Employee discrimination, harassment, and emotional abuse—behaviors that can be knowingly or unknowingly endorsed by management—often result in employee dissatisfaction and resistance. Employees experiencing abuse from their superiors can resist by taking personal leave days, focusing their energy on self-preservation rather than completing work goals, or leaving the organization.

Supervisors are charged with the organizational responsibility of evaluating employees and their performance—a practice that creates the potential for abuse to occur (Lutgen-Sandvik, 2003). Thus, it is not surprising that most discriminatory and harassing abuse is carried out by supervisors on their subordinates. How the organization responds when an employee reports abuse from a supervisor is indicative of the organization's (or least management's) values about abuse, the role and nature of supervision in the organization, as well as beliefs about the superior-subordinate relationship—all elements of the organization's culture. For example, an organization can take a variety of positions: take no action, admit that a problem exists but take no action, promise action but do nothing, attribute the problem to a personality conflict, ask the abused employee to change his or her behavior, minimize the complaint but enhance the abuser's organizational status, label the abused employee as a troublemaker, retaliate against the victim, or discipline or terminate the abuser (Lutgen-Sandvik, 2003). Notice that all but the last action demonstrates negative value toward the employee. Although abuse is situated in a specific workplace relationship of unequal power, organizational reaction to the abuse can influence other individuals who are not subject to the initial abuse. If employees believe the workplace is an unjust place, they can resist the cultural norms that support the existence of abuse.

Of course, employees can resist the politics and power embedded in organizations' cultures. In the mid to late 1980s, the television series *Designing Women* had attracted a large viewership and was regularly one of the 10 most watched shows. Part of the show's success was attributed to Delta Burke who played one of the characters, Suzanne. Although the show was a vehicle for an ensemble cast, the basis for the show's setting, its characters, and most of the scripts were attributable to Linda Bloodworth-Thomason, one of the show's co-producers (see Keyton, 1994; Smith & Keyton, 2001). Thus, the culture of Mozark Productions that produced the show could be described as strongly leader-centered (i.e., Bloodworth-Thomason), yet group oriented. Tension between the producer and the actress heightened, as Burke's star status escalated while Bloodworth-Thomason continued to write ensemble-oriented scripts allowing her to control the actresses. In the final episode of the 1989–1990 season a conflict erupted during production of the episode with Burke refusing to a do a scene as written by Bloodworth-Thomason. Her resistance resulted in delay of production and contract negotiations. Eventually, the conflict moved into the public arena as both parties used the media to state their claims. In this case, creative control of the show was equal to reasserting cultural control and Burke's resistance attempt eventually resulted in her leaving the show as well as the show's cancellation.

Organizational Culture and the Critical Perspective

The critical perspective views the communication of an organization as an index of its ideology (Cooren & Taylor, 1997). Thus, critical cultural studies explore forms of organizational domination and control as well as the ways organizational members perpetuate or resist these forms. Deetz (1992) explains that the time spent in organizations and the influence of organizational routines and practices on our everyday lives (as both employees and consumers) ensures that we live under multiple forms of corporate control. Therefore, the critical perspective of organizational culture focuses on the ways in which organizational communication practices negatively influence employees' quality of life.

Two elements are essential to understanding a critical perspective of organizational culture. First, organizations reside in the communication activities of its members. Second, organizations are sites of hierarchy, dominance, and power, and, as a result, organizational members have varying degrees of power and status and varying degrees of control over message creation and message meaning. When powerful organizational members can get others to accept their views about the organization and values about working, as they often do, then powerful organizational members are in a position to create the normative practices of the organization's culture. At first glance this may not seem so bad—after all, someone has to be in charge, and employees are paid to work.

However, powerful organizational members can establish a culture that is more favorable to them and less favorable to the less powerful. And, sometimes that is obvious. But, a favorable-unfavorable imbalance can be created and presented in such a way as to be seen as normal. When that happens, less powerful organizational members accept the views and values of the powerful without question. Two examples of critical cultural studies amplify these issues.

In a case analysis (Barker & Cheney, 1994) of Tech USA, a communications hardware manufacturing company was changing from a traditional hierarchical structure to self-managing teams. Under the previous structure, supervisors would provide directives and orders; under the new self-managing structure, the teams were to develop mechanisms to regulate worker attendance. The vision for the self-managing team structure was laid out in a statement by management that included values, such as personal initiative, responsibility, commitment to the team, and quality of individual and team contributions. As the teams worked, team members began to "establish value-laden premises that they expected each other to identify with and to apply" (p. 34). Thus, discipline that earlier had been established and practiced by management was now transferred to and willingly accepted by team members. These values were embedded in their interactions; moreover, the values were embraced by everyone, resulting in few attendance problems.

Several years later, after an influx of new employees, attendance problems became significant obstacles to work completion. Now, the seasoned team members who identified strongly with the teamwork values talked directly about the need to be on time. The subject was brought up at team meetings, team members began to monitor others' attendance, and peer pressure was used to acknowledge and remedy the problem. Teams began to develop attendance policies, give reprimands and warnings, and report violations to management so attendance infractions could be entered on personnel records. Over a period of time, the teams had embraced the teamwork values with such passion that this attendance discourse was a regular part of their interactions. Not surprisingly, through collaborative efforts the teams developed an attendance policy that was "eerily reminiscent of the old, supervisory system" (Barker & Cheney, 1994, p. 36). Although employees had the opportunity to enact the self-managing team structure in many potential ways, they eventually chose, embraced, and codified a stance toward attendance that was essentially the same as the previous system—emphasizing the power of organizational norms and its power when employees willingly monitor their own performance on behalf of the organization.

As a second example, Zoller's (2003) study of an automobile manufacturing plant revealed the way in which employees, called *associates*, consented to work conditions that were, in essence, hazardous to their health. By self-identifying as a *good associate*, employees used several mechanisms to manage the contradictions between acknowledging the health risks of their work activities and supporting and protecting their employer. Some employees tolerated the increasing production pace, and its accompanying physical risks, by emphasizing that a fast pace masked the amount of time spent on the line; others argued they preferred to be in an active job rather than sitting behind a desk. Employees also acknowledged that being a good associate meant being able to *take* the hard work. Further, they emphasized the level of fitness required for the job instead of emphasizing the physical demands of the work that could be potentially unsafe. The level of physicality and the pace of work were accepted by employees because they believed that they were paid well (relative to other work available in their area).

In these ways, employees were trading their physical safety for the organization's production goals and, as a result of this trade-off, embracing the organization's view that valued quick-paced physical labor without complaints from employees. Thus, the culture shifted the responsibility of safety from the organization to the employees. Employees consented to this value shift despite experiencing numbness in their hands, injuring their teeth, and experiencing other injuries while working the line. Employees further embraced this shift by seeing their personal physicians rather than reporting injuries as OSHA incidents, and by maintaining their physical strength by working out on their personal time. In this culture, the shift for the responsibility of safety was structured by management in part because the company doctor refused to classify injuries as work-related and in part by the organization's provision of a recreation center as a *benefit* to employees.

Organizational Culture and Concertive Control

Organizational power often comes in the form of concertive control, especially when organizations are motivated to pursue ongoing change through popular management frameworks, programs, or strategies that emphasize employee participation. Concertive control occurs when employees adopt management's interpretation of values and objectives in support of the organization's mission (Tompkins & Cheney, 1985). The irony is that while change programs espouse that using their particular framework will allow the organization and its employees to be more flexible and adapt to environmental uncertainty, the change programs are often enacted as top-down strategies to control and dominate employees and their work environments (Zorn, Page, & Cheney, 2000). Although employee flexibility and autonomy can exist in a concertive organization, employees are guided in their decision making based on their identification with the values that serve the organization's interests.

Such control can be established through three mechanisms (Zorn, Page, & Cheney, 2000). First, goals and values can be communicated through employee newsletters and annual reports; seeing these in print solidifies them as being real. Often presented in short phrases (e.g., "Focus on the customer," "Lean and mean," "More in 2004"), goals and values become repeatable slogans that can be adapted to any of the organization's work settings. Second, managers can communicate goals and values orally, framing them within the advantages and virtues of the change program to create a vision of the future.

For example, a study of employees in a large retail organization revealed that their perceptions about employee morale predicted their identification with the organization (Schrodt, 2002). Their responses to items from the Organizational Culture Survey (Glaser, Zamanou & Hacker, 1987), such as *The organization motivates me to put out my best efforts* and *Working here feels like being part of a family,* better predicted their organizational identification than items capturing their perceptions about teamwork, information flow, involvement, supervision, and the use of meetings in the organization. The values of trust and respect adopted and endorsed by the organization as part of its culture created a positive, but controlling, relationship between employees and the organization. Employees who reported identifying with the organization were more motivated in performing their organizational roles.

Third, managers can use active participation strategies in which employees help create the methods and strategies by which they (and the organization) will achieve the stated vision. As a form of control, concertive control can be effective and received positively by employees (e.g., Sobo & Sadler, 2002). At the outset, such change programs are touted as empowering for employees, and such a premise can encourage employees to accept the program. Ironically, however, "control is masked by high-flying talk about mission, values, and ethics . . . precisely the kind of case in which control is most subtle . . . where it masks its own mechanisms and diverts the gaze of participants from the recognition of power" (Zorn, Page, & Cheney, 2000, p. 558). Employees—although enthusiastic about the organizational changes—were being influenced to work harder and more hours; some were asked to work unpaid weekends while others in the organization had lost their jobs. Although the efficiencies and gains in effectiveness that can be achieved through such change programs are laudable goals, the possibility does exist for employees to be disadvantaged, as they are less aware of the way in which the change program controls them.

Organizational Culture and Gender and Race

Demographic trends are evidence that organizations will experience greater gender and racial diversity in the workforce. Many organizations have programs (e.g., day care, flexible work hours, and hiring and recruiting more people of color) or policies (e.g., sexual harassment and antidiscrimination policies) purportedly designed to address some diversity issues. The absence or presence of such policies and programs are artifacts of the values and assumptions implicit in organizations' cultures relative to gender and racial diversity. Yet even when such programs or policies are in place, most organizations have not developed innovative strategies for increasing the acceptance and support of diverse employees (Corsini & Fogliasso, 1997).

Gender

Because assumptions and values that are communicated create a culture, and because gender is socially constructed, workplaces are intersections of both organizational and societal cultures imbued with notions about gender. As a result, organizational cultures generally are male dominated and reinforce those gender stereotypes, beliefs, and assumptions (Alvesson, 2002). It is important to acknowledge that a male-dominated organization does not simply mean that males are favored and women are disfavored. Rather, both men and women can subscribe to masculine values and assumptions in an organization because organizations and society are based on male models. This masculine orientation is embedded within structure (e.g., organizational hierarchy), activity (e.g., the organization sponsors golf tournaments for its executives), and language (e.g., sales *contests, competitive* strategies, price *wars*), and it becomes and is perceived by employees as the *normal* or *natural* manner in which organizations function, even as women internalize this orientation that devalues their own (Ashcraft & Pacanowsky, 1996).

For example, Ashcraft and Pacanowsky (1996) describe and analyze the culture of Office Inc., a commercial office furniture organization, which was founded by and is largely staffed by women. Most of the company's 32 employees are women; only 9 men work at Office, Inc. Employees were quick to point out that their organization was different due to the large number of female employees. Yet, they were hesitant to label their organization or its culture as feminine even though they identified their focus on relational concerns—including emotions, feelings, and a dislike of direct approaches for managing conflict—as characteristic of the Office, Inc. culture. Complicating employees' view of their organization's culture was their acknowledgement of the pettiness and jealousy that allowed a destructive cycle of indirect competition to also characterize the culture. As a result, getting ahead was achieved at the expense of someone else. One female employee described her disappointment at joining an organization largely composed of women only to find the other women divided into impenetrable cliques. While female employees "embraced a 'female' concern for human relationships in business affairs, they simultaneously revered the gendered values of conventional business practices, including the supremacy of objectivity and a limited conception of rationality as rigidly task-centered, strictly linear, and non-emotional" (p. 233). Many women voiced their difficulties in balancing the contributions that being female provided with the normalized masculine characteristics of the business world.

In another example, Dougherty (2001) examined how sexual harassment functions within a regional comprehensive health care center. Male employees argued that the emotional nature of their work created stress, and that engaging in sexual communication and behavior was one way to reduce the stress. Their cultural assumption was: This workplace behavior serves important stress reducing functions, therefore it is not sexual harassment. On the other hand, female employees did not view sexual behavior as functional or appropriate, but they did view it as the norm in their organization. In this organization, organizational norms and assumptions about the same behaviors were differentiated by gender.

While a masculine orientation to organizing "traps people in all respects from occupational choice to acceptance/rejection of tasks in every day working life" (Alvesson, 2002, p. 134), women are more likely to suffer physically, psychologically, economically, and socially from an organization's masculine orientation. The stories of Frances Conley (1998), who resigned her position as professor of neurosurgery at Stanford University medical school due to overt gender discrimination, and Lois Jenson (Bingham & Gansler, 2002), who initiated the class action sexual harassment suit against Eveleth Mines, demonstrate the embedded ways in which organizational cultures can uphold masculine values as normative while devaluing the workplace contributions of females. Both stories underscore the way organizational cultures can be differentiated into male and female subcultures with the female subculture being subordinated to the male subculture.

In reporting her experiences, Conley (1998) describes performing brain surgery with a junior male resident observing and assisting when one of her male colleagues burst into the operating room and asked, "How's it going, honey?" (p. 65). Lois Jenson worked in an organizational culture in which the following sign (Bingham & Gansler, 2002, p. 132) was posted on the company's locked bulletin board along with work schedules and assignments, and company job postings:

Sexual harassment in this area will not be reported

However, it will be graded

Both examples reveal the normative acceptance of the masculine orientation in these organizational cultures, as both communication behaviors were public and common.

As another example of gender domination in organization cultures, Murphy's (1998) examination of flight attendants explores the way in which the gender-stereotyped profession is enacted in one airline's culture. She explains that although no longer legal, the airline's written policies and procedures present a feminine construction of airline attendant as caretaker, mother, subordinate, and sexual object. Although both women and men are now employed as flight attendants, the profession is still predominantly staffed by women and the profession is still feminized by airline organizations and the flying public. For example, one written airline rule dictated that flight attendants should "assure that all pilots have sufficient beverages before taxi and during cruise to avoid dehydration" (p. 512). Flight attendants, she observed, resented the airline's rule that flight attendants must take care of, or serve, pilots when they are busy with boarding, safety, and other passenger service activities. In addition to the internal organizational value that subordinated flight attendants to pilots, Murphy (1998) explains that flight attendants were also subjected to public, or external, value preferences. For example, passengers regularly made negative comments about flight attendants' appearances in spite of having positive service experiences. Flight attendants, in their role as public representatives of the airline, work in organizational cultures in which societal influences help drive internal organizational values.

Race

Organizational cultures are also sites in which organizational values about race intersect with employees' assumptions and values about race brought by them into the organizational environment. Just as gender is socially constructed, race is socially constructed, as we choose to interpret race in particular ways. The values and assumptions relative to race and racial differences that are negotiated in society are also negotiated in organizations.

While it is true that the United States is becoming a more culturally diverse workforce, it is also true that "people of color persistently and disproportionately occupy menial service-sector jobs" (Ashcraft & Allen, 2003, p. 5). Just as organizations are predominantly masculine, they also predominantly support values and ideals of Whites, Caucasians, or European Americans. As a result, organizational cultural diversity can result in tension, conflict, and discrimination as dominant values intersect with values held by groups of minority employees. At a surface level, some employees have more organizational power based simply on their cultural background—most often when employees' cultural background is similar to that of the legitimate power holders in the organization.

As an example, in a study of a large organization (Meares, Oetzel, Torres, Derkacs, & Ginossar, 2004), interviews with employees revealed the way in which different cultural groups perceived mistreatment in their organization. Narratives of European Americans indicated that they perceived themselves as having the agency to confront and rectify mistreatment within the organizational structure. For example, a European American male in his 50s said, "I'm a White male, so I'm not used to it. I'm not preconditioned, so I wouldn't let it [mistreatment] pass" (p. 13). Conversely, organizational members from minority cultural groups indicated that they had little confidence that they would be able resolve or eliminate mistreatment on their own. For example, a 40-year-old Hispanic woman said:

> I'd try to resolve with the person, but often it goes nowhere. If you go higher up you get on the shit list of troublemakers, which affects promotion and appraisal, and managers say you are not a team player. I feel that there's no effort to institute fairness. . . . Everything can't be fair, but an effort should be made, an attempt. (p. 15)

The narratives of organizational members from different cultural groups revealed that mistreatment was culturally based. The narratives also revealed the different assumptions different groups of organizational members held about mistreatment and what they could do about it. Undoubtedly, in this organization the intersection of organizational and cultural values created differentiated subcultures.

Using a much smaller health care facility in a small town that employed 49 African Americans and 471 White-Americans, Corsini and Fogliasso (1997) found that African American employees adjusted their communication style to that of the majority when answering phones or when interacting in formal organizational meetings. This examination underscores the additional burden placed on African Americans during these adaptations. Not only did they adapt their communication style to that of the organization's culture, they also had to adapt their communication style to that of the majority or White culture. In comparison, White employees' adaptation to the style of the organization is easier in that they are familiar with the majority culture style having grown up in it. The assumptions one carries about what constitutes an appropriate or effective communication style are influenced by our race and social interpretations of others. Carried into the workplace these assumptions can influence our evaluations of other workplace behaviors and motives.

While gender and cultural diversity can be beneficial to the workplace, the domination of masculine and White values often results in harassment and discrimination. Subtle value differences can become manifest in the behaviors of majority group organizational members such that minority group members face systemic and organizational barriers by having less opportunity to (a) advance or be promoted, (b) take on or be given challenging assignments, and (c) be treated equally with respect to salary and other organizational benefits. In addition, an organizational culture that unknowingly or knowingly supports discriminatory practices can also result in informal barriers, such as daily and ongoing interaction that is rude, disrespectful, and prejudicial (Cox, 1993). Thus, the powerful (based on their ethnicity, race, or gender) enact organizational values that disadvantage the powerless (based on their ethnicity, race, or gender).

THE LENS OF TECHNOLOGY

Unless you work in an IT (information technology) job, you are probably like me. I like to learn and use new computer applications to help me be more efficient and effective in my job—but I do not know how the technology works (and I really do not care; I just want it to work).

As technology is applied to jobs, two types of expertise are created. First, there is the content expertise—employees who work on the machines that produce cardboard boxes are a good example. At one of these companies, many employees have been manufacturing boxes for more than 20 years. They are experts. They can identify a good box from a bad one. But as technology has developed, box making has become less industrial and more computerized, which requires the second type of expertise—process expertise. The large and complex machines now used in box making require employees with engineering, computer, and technical expertise, in addition to context expertise. With the new equipment, the box makers still make the call on whether the boxes are good or bad, and they understand how the machinery works. In fact, they are often the ones who fix the equipment or identify for the engineers or computer technicians what is wrong with the machinery. But, they do not make the machinery, nor do they program it, or write the programming code. As work processes become more reliant on more complicated technologies, other types of expertise are needed in the organization.

Think about how technology has changed organizations. If your primary work tool is a pencil, three things can happen: it needs to be sharpened, it snaps in two, or you lose it. The solution is simple: sharpen the pencil or get a new one. However, if your primary work tool is a personal computer, many different malfunctions can happen. The power can be disrupted. The hardware can fail to function properly. The software can become infected with a virus. And, most workers cannot fix these things, as they are not electricians, computer techs, or software experts. Rather, they are experts in processing medical insurance claims, experts at scheduling airline flights, and experts in designing traffic flow. In this sense, improved technology distinguishes the process of work from the content of the work, and, in turn, requires organizations to employ cadres of employees or consultants who can get something fixed so we can get back to work.

Schein (1992) points to the irony that this situation has created. Many IT workers can be characterized as being intolerant of ambiguity, precise and accurate, and preferring logical rules and procedures. These characteristics are useful in creating electronic and computer systems and devices to help others accomplish their work. But frequently the order that technology provides is layered on a job that is best handled by an employee who can deal effectively with an ambiguous and imprecise work environment, and who can see the uniqueness in each situation and person. Thus, technology has heightened different approaches to work styles and their accompanying values.

A study of 18 government and for-profit organizations demonstrates the reciprocal relationship between organizational culture and technological implementation (Harper & Utley, 2001). When employees reported that their organizational cultures valued autonomy, trust, teamwork, flexibility, and the sharing of information, implementation of information technology systems was more successful. On the other hand, when employees reported that their organizational cultures valued a strong or rigid rule orientation and compliance to managers' orientations, and could be characterized as careful, precise, or predictable, implementation of information technology systems was less successful. Thus, having technology is not enough. Having a culture that supports organizational members in their use of technology is also required.

The way in which technology structures work activities influences organizational members' work roles and work relationships as well. Thus, the relationship between technology and organizational culture is inherent. Too frequently, the expense associated with technology causes it to be viewed as a universal organizational improvement without considering the ways in which different groups of employees might view or use it. As Huang, Newell, Galliers, and Pan (2003) found, subculture groups have different technology needs as well as different relationships to the organization. As a result, different groups place different demands on the use of technology.

Technological Monitoring of Employees

A second impact technology has had on organizational culture is the opportunity technology provides to control and monitor employees (Schein, 1992). Companies routinely monitor employees' email and web use; phone calls are recorded; and entrance and exit to one's workspace is documented. The practice is widespread. The American Management Association (2000) reports that as many as 75% of large companies electronically monitor their employees in some way. In many organizations security is tied to technology.

Ostensibly, the action of swiping your organizational identification card to release the locked door to the building is for your safety. Yet, such devices also track your whereabouts and notify your supervisor when you are available for work. In one pharmaceutical company, pharmacy techs service customers around the country by phone on a rotating 24/7 schedule. Pharmacy techs are required to slide their identification cards through a card reader when they enter and exit the building, and when they take time for a scheduled break or lunch in the organization's lunchroom. This type of monitoring allows management to shift calls from one tech to another by simply looking at a computer monitoring employees' whereabouts. So rather than having a break between calls, techs found their phones ringing almost immediately as they completed the previous call. Techs who took longer-than-allowed breaks were reminded with a printout of their rules violations.

This type of managerial monitoring and control is arguably put into place to increase productivity, improve quality of service, and reduce costs (Alder, 2001). Yet, these systems can dampen employee enthusiasm and motivation, increase work stress, diminish employee health, and encourage employees to subvert and create ways around the system. Alternatively, employee performance monitoring systems have been reported to increase employee satisfaction and morale because they resulted in more objective performance appraisals and improved performance feedback. Still, assumptions about employee responsibility (and rights) are being challenged. As one tech said, "I work for them, but they don't own me." This type of monitoring and control emphasizes values than can hamper innovation and teamwork. "I'm here, I do my job; that's it."

As you might suspect, organizational culture influences employee attitudes and reactions to employee performance monitoring systems, especially employee reactions of fairness and trust. Members of supportive organizational cultures are more likely to have negative reactions as the practice of monitoring conflicts with a culture that values openness and support. Alder (2001) claims, however, that employees may respond more favorably to monitoring if organizations focus on monitoring task-related activities that are directly related to employee performance. Such a premise presents a conundrum, as not all monitoring devices can determine if your email, phone call, web activity, or break time is personal or work related. Electronic monitoring of employee activities is central to employees' sense of fairness and trust, both of which will influence employees' view of organizational culture.

THE LENS OF GLOBALIZATION

Many organizations have expanded beyond their national borders by entering global markets, working with foreign subsidiaries, creating international alliances, and engaging in multinational joint ventures. As such, these global organizations "are at the intersection of diverse communicative, cultural, and social practices" (Stohl, 2001, p. 325). This type of organizational global expansion has occurred due to the creation of international trade alliances (e.g., NAFTA, the European Union), and greater reliance on innovation that requires foreign labor and material resources, and in hopes of saturating new markets and securing more sales. With these expansion efforts, global organizations are (a) becoming structurally flatter and more team oriented, (b) increasingly relying on communication technology, (c) becoming geographically more scattered, and (d) becoming more culturally diverse. Despite the financial and market incentives for organizations to create international and multinational organizations, many suffer and fail due to cultural differences (Pothukuchi, Damanpour, Choi, Chen, & Park, 2002).

Traditionally, organizations are believed to be embedded in the larger society in which they exist. For example, national cultures vary along dimensions of orientation to time, authority or power, communication, community, formality, goal-orientation, performance orientation, space, structure—all dimensions that would influence business practices, how an organization is configured, how work is structured and coordinated, and career and occupational expectations (Dickson, Aditya, & Chhokar, 2000; Hofstede, 2001; Stohl, 2001; Triandis, 1983). Despite the admission that cultural variability exists within any nation, national or societal culture is still assumed to coincide with the geographical boundaries of nation-states (Child, 1981). With the globalization of organizations, new questions about the relationship between national culture and organizational culture are being debated.

One of the most distinguishing features between nations and cultures is language. Even when two countries such as the United States and Great Britain speak the same language, nuances, patterns of speech, favored expressions, and idioms demonstrate differences between the two cultures. Language reveals what is valued by a nation and how society is structured. A language system is embedded within a nation's historical, political, legal, and economic systems. Together these influence how organizations organize and how organizations and employees express organizational roles.

Because of these inherent national differences, communication competence is believed to be culture specific. Managers from one country who take work assignments in another often lack awareness of the foreign culture, and are often deficient in language skills as well. In particular, many U.S. citizens are more likely to be monolingual, relying entirely on their English language skills, as compared with citizens of other nations who are educated to be bilingual or multilingual.

Even when language skills are satisfactory and cultural awareness is heightened, it is still possible for organizational members to commit national cultural transgressions in organizational settings. One common cultural transgression is the overreliance on negative cultural stereotypes. Phrases such as "All Germans are . . ." or "All Mexicans are . . ." demonstrate an individual's failure to see other organizational members as individuals with overgeneralizations based on group membership rather than individual employees' work competencies or contributions. Another common transgression occurs when one national group is structurally positioned vis-à-vis other national groups. For example, phrases like "Americans think they need to lead this effort" or "German engineers are better" use cultural stereotypes to position one group as being organizationally superior (or deficient) to another.

The prevailing business practices, norms, and values of an organization are, to a large extent, aligned with the nation's culture (Katz, Swanson, & Nelson, 2001; Lindsley, 1999). For example, the U.S. culture supports the work values of salary equity, job independence, and compensation for initiative and performance. While widely supported as ideal values, these values are not always enacted; when enacted these values take on divergent forms; and alternative organizing structures support other sets of values. Thus, the alignment between a national culture and an organization's culture is not always similar or isomorphic. Indeed, across 64 cultures and 800 organizations, Dickson, Aditya, and Chhokar (2000) discovered no consistent correspondence across cultural dimensions between organizations and societies. A pattern simply did not exist. National culture shifts over time and subcultural differences do exist within a nation's larger cultural framework. Still, national cultural tendencies can and do surface in organizations.

Greater cultural complexity occurs when organizational members from many national cultures work together. For example, in studying U.S.-owned assembly plants in Mexico, organizations known as *maquiladoras,* Lindsley (1999) found that managers from the United States used communication behaviors that reflected an independent view of self with the result of violating Mexican communication behaviors that reflected an interdependent identity. Although managers from both groups shared an organizational identity, their national identities regularly conflicted. Thus, individuals drew on values from both their national culture and their organizational association that provided a layered interpretation of their experiences in the maquiladoras.

How do different cultural expectations influence business success? In the study of joint ventures, Pothukuchi, Damanpour, Choi, Chen, and Park (2002) discovered that differences in national and organizational culture influenced organizational outcomes differently. When the joint venture included organizations with different national cultures, the differences had the potential to positively or negatively influence efficiency and competitiveness of the joint venture. Thus, the direction of the influence depended on the ways in which the national cultures differed and the ways in which those differences were perceived by the international partners—as either conflicts and barriers, or as challenges and opportunities. When the joint venture included organizations with more similar organizational cultures—particularly around how the organizations shared information, the difference positively influenced employee satisfaction with the joint venture. Thus, while national cultural differences could generate positive or negative effects, differences in organizational culture were more likely to generate negatives ones. These findings suggest that how organizational members view national cultural differences is key. If national cultural differences are perceived to be part of an international or multinational organizational culture and embraced positively, they can in turn create a challenging and stimulating work environment with organizational members developing an organizational culture to accommodate and bridge national cultural differences.

Some of these national culture issues are evident in the 1999 merger of Chrysler Corporation and Daimler Benz. This merger required that organizational members from two national cultures become integrated into one company, DaimlerChrysler AG. The companies had distinctive personalities and cultures. On one hand, Chrysler, an American company, valued innovation and flexibility in a highly focused business strategy; on the other hand, Daimler Benz, a German maker of luxury cars, valued rigid structure and managerial hierarchy. While Chrysler had little international success, Daimler Benz had operations throughout Europe, South America, and India causing industry experts to see the merger of the two companies as a logical fit.

Fitzgibbon and Seeger's (2002) analysis of the metaphors used as strategic devices during the merger eventually revealed the extent to which these companies were different and the way in which national culture influenced those differences. Initially, the merger was announced accompanied by Daimler Benz CEO Jurgen Schrempp's pronouncement that the companies complemented one another and created the perfect fit of two market leaders. He went so far as to indicate that the companies shared a common corporate culture and mission. Throughout the merger process, three metaphors—a single global entity, a good fit, and a marriage of equals—were repeated frequently by executives of both companies. Early in the merger process, Chrysler's Integration Team identified that the expected "good fit" of markets and products must be accompanied by a cultural fit, and suggested cross-cultural training, and a shared and defined code of conduct. A few months later, a Chrysler management group revealed that one risk was that Chrysler's identity and culture would be incorporated not into, but under Daimler's way of doing business. Despite the projected values for the merged company, it did not result in a good cultural fit. Merging the American innovation and informality with German structure and bureaucratic form produced a confusion of American and German values, creating organizational inconsistencies with little synergy.

Obviously, the DaimlerChrysler AG merger involved organizational members at the highest executive and professional levels. If national cultures influence organizational culture at those levels where psychological rewards and material benefits from work are great, in what way are employees at lower hierarchical levels affected? Cruise line employees participated in a study that compared their national cultures with their organizational cultures, particularly examining the way in which national-organizational culture fit influenced their ratings of job satisfaction. Results revealed that lower level employees were more likely to have lower job satisfaction ratings when their organizational culture did not fit their national culture values. Given that lower level employees generally experience less job satisfaction than those in managerial ranks, these findings suggest the importance of greater national and organizational culture awareness among companies that employ workers from many cultures (Testa, Mueller, & Thomas, 2003).

These cases highlight the way in which international and multinational forms of organizing must address issues of cultural convergence and cultural divergence (Stohl, 2001). Cultural convergence emphasizes one best way—predominantly capitalism—of conducting business regardless of the cultural identities of the organizations involved. Convergence assumes that the marketplace has created organizations so similarly structured that multinational organizations can be organized in such a way as to bear no national allegiance. These supposedly culture-free multinational organizations can emerge because common market characteristics demand a common business language. Under the convergence frame, communication is viewed as functioning similarly across cultures. Cultural divergence, on the other hand, focuses on how business is conducted differently in different countries and highlights rather than dismisses national values and traditions. Divergence acknowledges that cultural differences do make a difference in how people interact in the conduct of business. However, organizations do not simply choose between cultural convergence and divergence. Rather, "the environmental and technological pressures on contemporary organizations to become more and more similar clash with the proprietary pull of cultural identifications, traditional values, and conventional practices of social life" (Stohl, 2001, p. 36). Despite being profit driven to build global markets, organizations cannot resist the influences of the political, legal, and social constraints of national culture. The interactions of organizational members are laden with values drawn from these systems. Thus, when individuals from two or more national cultures interact within an organizational culture, the convergence-divergence dichotomy fails to leave room for cultural variation or practical contingencies created by the individuals in that organizational situation (Nelson & Gopalan, 2003; Ogbor, 2000).

Any exploration of organizational culture in multinational corporations must consider all potential cultural influences on organizational members. Obviously, national culture comparisons will be made. However, a simple U.S. versus Japanese cultural comparison, for example, will miss the variability within each culture—particularly on dimensions of gender, profession, ethnicity, and religion that produce powerful influences on organizational culture. This simple either/or comparison will also miss the cultural influences of each of the organizations or of each of the units within the organization, as well as regional, national, and industry influences (Sackmann, 1997). In a multinational organization, or any joint venture, "all of these potential cultural identities may simultaneously influence the cultural context of an organization" (p. 2).

This discussion reinforces the notion that organizations are facing a new business environment—one that integrates business strategy, innovation, strategic planning, technological change, organizational vision and mission with issues of organizational culture (Ulijn, O'Hair, Weggeman, Ledlow, & Hall, 2000). Expanding into global markets to create and sell innovative products is one way for organizations to remain competitive, as well as to attract and retain skilled workers. Generally, global organizations are faced with a number of communication challenges, as they find it necessary to make decision making more participative, rely more heavily on cross-functional teams and communication technology, and improve systems of organizational learning. Thus, communication within global organizations becomes increasingly more complex, as does communication with external constituents. As a result, organizational culture is challenged to both satisfy and represent the multiple perspectives evident in global organizations.

SUMMARY

Communication in an organization is ubiquitous and complex, and it is not neutral. Because the process of creating organizational culture is not neat or tidy, and because the communication system of an organization is difficult to see as a whole, scholars use a variety of ways of identifying and investigating organizational culture.

The symbolic performance perspective acknowledges that a system of symbols—including the everyday and the unique—is responsible for creating complexity, and sometimes contradictions, in the totality of organizational communication and the organization's resulting culture. This view of organizational culture seeks to examine the way in which communication brings culture into being.

Organizational culture as narrative reproduction examines stories as artifacts to understand an organization's values, norms, and beliefs. From the storyteller's perspective, the specifics of the story are the cultural elements that are salient to the storyteller. Organizational culture as textual reproductions examines the formal and informal written texts from organizations and their members. Textual reproductions of organizational culture are useful for exploring espoused versus enacted elements of culture. Formal documentation more frequently represents the managerial and espoused view of organizational culture while informal texts are better representations of the enacted culture.

From a managerial lens, organizational culture is viewed as prescriptive and treated as a resource or tool. From this perspective, organizational culture is developed and directed by managers for the purpose of improving operating efficiencies, enhancing the bottom line, or creating satisfied customers. Thus, a managerial lens views organizational culture as a control device, and as a screening device in selecting employees to achieve good person-organization fit. A managerial lens also views organization culture for how it can be managed or changed to influence organizational success or as a competitive advantage in the marketplace or in attracting new employees.

Power and politics are manifested in many different ways in organizations. This lens highlights those struggles in organizational culture from both functional and structural viewpoints, as well as from the critical perspectives. The critical perspective views the communication of an organization as an index of its ideology or culture. Thus, critical studies explore the ways in which organizational members resist domination and other forms of corporate control in the organization's culture. Organizational cultures are also sites of concertive control—when employees adopt management's interpretation of values and objectives in support of the organization's mission. The values and assumptions relative to gender and race that are negotiated in society are also negotiated in organizations. Organizational cultures often replicate societal power and domination as organizations are often constructed based on masculine and White values resulting in harassment and discrimination. Thus, viewing organizational culture from a gendered and racial viewpoint can illuminate how organizational power is created and maintained in an organization's culture.

Technology and globalization are other external forces that influence organizational cultures. Technology structures the work of organizations, and as a result, influences organizational culture, work activities, organizational members' work roles, and their work relationships. Too frequently, the expense associated with technology causes it to be viewed as a universal organizational improvement without considering the ways in which different groups of employees might view or use it. Electronic monitoring is another form of organizational technology use that influences organizational culture. Many organizations are being influenced by globalization as they have expanded beyond their national borders by entering global markets, working with foreign subsidiaries, creating international alliances, and engaging in multinational joint ventures. This new business environment creates an intersection of diverse communicative, cultural, and social practices that raises new questions about the appropriateness of the traditional cultural convergence and cultural divergence dichotomy.

4

Developing, Managing, and Changing Organizational Culture

I t is likely that in your working experiences you will be charged with the responsibility, or you will need to take the initiative, for developing the culture for your organization or work unit. Even in acknowledging that organizational culture emerges from the interactions of all organizational members, managers and other key personnel, including informal leaders, are regularly assigned or take on the task of evaluating or changing the organizational culture. In some organizations this happens at a local level as self-directed work teams and other self-managed operating units are responsible for creating and maintaining the culture of their particular team or unit. And, of course, in some organizations, employees work to create a culture that is in opposition to managerial preferences, or work to create and manage a culture when their manager is unable or unmotivated to do so. What processes can you engage in to create a change in your organization's culture?

CULTURE FORMATION

Culture forms when organizational members accept solutions that provide an acceptable conclusion to a problem (Gagliardi, 1986; Schein,

1983). Such solutions might be developed from problem-solving interactions designed to tackle a problem, emerge from an amalgamation of individuals' previous experiences in dealing with the issue, or be initiated by the formal or informal leader. If the solution works over a series of experiences with a degree of success accepted by organizational members, then the group (ranging from the organization to a small work unit) starts to adopt the practice and its associated values. Over time, the group accepts the practice and its values as normative and will teach it to newcomers. In this way, elements of culture are formed when practices are accepted as *the way we do things around here* (Isaac & Pitt, 2001). Thus, organizational culture is formed through an interactive process of learning and teaching that embeds the practice into the organizational system.

Note that such an informal process does not ensure that the best practice will become part of the culture. Organizational members can and regularly do adopt practices that simply satisfice by meeting the minimum rather than the optimum requirements. For example, a work crew at a recently-opened fast food restaurant is told to figure out among themselves how to accomplish three tasks during their late night shift. They are to (a) take customer orders at the drive-up window, (b) prepare and deliver food, and (c) clean the restaurant to prepare it for opening the next morning. Crewmembers do not get paid for time spent in the restaurant after it is closed to customers so they want to figure out how to simultaneously accomplish all three tasks.

The five-member crew tries different approaches. Some are not so successful. For example, when all but one crewmember focused on cleaning, drive-up customers complained that it took too long to receive their food after ordering it. While this strategy got the crew out within minutes of the restaurant closing, complaints to the manager were so numerous that he started to stay with the crew until closing. With the manager in his office, the crew goes back to an effective, but not acceptable, approach with two members taking orders and preparing and delivering food while the other three clean the restaurant. But this division of labor causes the work team to stay at least 30 minutes after the restaurant closes. Working this approach for several weeks does, however, win the confidence of the manager and he no longer comes in to check on them.

Again, the crew tries different approaches. Now the strategy is to have the two employees who cook food and serve customers start to clean their work areas while serving customers. This leaves the other three to clean the inside dining area and restrooms—areas always inspected by the morning manager. Over a period of time, members rotate through the different jobs and figure out that they can leave immediately after the restaurant closes if everyone starts to take short-cuts in cleaning. Figuring that it will be "no big deal" if they cut corners, the crew is able to complete the cleaning tasks that *need to be done* rather than *what should be done*. Leaving on time is seen as justifiable given that they are not paid for time spent in the restaurant after closing. In the short term, the morning manager does not notice the cleaning cutbacks. But over time, grease and grime start to build up and the new morning manager stops by one night to investigate. Much to her surprise, the crew describes their actions as routine practice, endorsed because the previous manager did not complain. Accepting their explanation, but conflicted between asking employees to stay to clean without being paid and believing that such sloppy practices are unacceptable, she quits! The crew continues its work habits and looks for other ways to cut corners during their shift. Feeling justified in cutting corners becomes a value of this crew and part of the organizational culture.

CULTURAL MAINTENANCE

Just as managers are interested in creating a culture that promotes their views of organizational effectiveness, they are also interested in maintaining such a culture when it is established. Reinforcement of an organization's culture is achieved when an organization has a strong and effective internal communication system with built in redundancies. For example, organizational symbols and slogans appear consistently across a host of different platforms—letterhead, reports, internal and external signage, jackets, hats, and paychecks. Rites, rituals, and ceremonies are regularly promoted and practiced. These elements must be integrated and anchored toward similar themes.

Cultural maintenance is an integral part of a manager's day-to-day activities (Alvesson, 2002). Managers maintain or reproduce culture by consistently enacting assumptions and values, and by encouraging acceptance and use of particular cultural meanings. Managers who support organizational and departmental identity by focusing employees on core values are attempting to maintain the coherence of the culture. And, managers who help employees control and manage their professional, occupational, or organizational image to external stakeholders are maintaining culture.

Maintaining a culture also requires the socialization of new employees. Both recruitment and selection processes can be tailored to promote the organization's culture with the hope of attracting applicants whose beliefs and values are in line with the organization. Selection interviews have long been used to provide a preview of what an applicant could expect upon joining the organization. Sometimes applicants seek organizational information before going for an interview; in other cases the organization is proactive in supplying that information. Either way, preinterview information can create applicant expectations about the culture of their potential employer. Yet, one study (Cable, Aiman-Smith, Mulvey, & Edwards, 2000) suggested that cultural knowledge is not so simply transferred in this way. Results demonstrated that firms overstate desired values to applicants (e.g., risk taking) while understating undesired values (e.g., rules orientation of the organization). Other socialization activities that help an organization maintain its existing culture include orientation programs that introduce new employees to the organization, their departments, and their jobs; formal and informal mentoring programs; and opportunities for social and interpersonal interaction with other organizational members.

Despite attempts to maintain it, organizational culture is always morphing—sometimes so slowly that it appears to be stagnant. Nevertheless, some change will always occur as new practices or norms are adopted or as individuals join or leave the organization. Thinking about organizational culture from a hologram perspective helps us to remember that by changing even one element of an organization, its culture will shift. Thus, when managers try to maintain culture they really are trying to stem cultural drift—keeping the organizational culture from changing faster than they can manage it.

CULTURAL CHANGE IN ORGANIZATIONS

Cultural change in organizations is a fundamental aspect of organizing. Employees come and go, new policies and procedures are implemented and new products and services are offered. Each of these creates an opportunity for an organization's culture to change as well. Just as organizational culture is directly tied to the interaction of organizational members, so is the organizational change process. Some organizational cultures change subtly, or evolve, over a period of time; others change more dramatically (Gagliardi, 1986).

What factors will affect cultural change? The change cycle depends in part on how the culture is structured. The more consensual the culture, the more likely change will be slower because the change has to be introduced to and accepted by all organizational members. When cultures are divided into subcultures, change may spread more quickly, but within a subculture's boundaries.

Hierarchical level will also influence cultural change. For example, executives pronounce that cultural changes are going to happen, as they initiate new goals and philosophies for doing business. At this level, values appear to change to create alignment with these new goals and philosophies. But at the lower levels, changes in work activities are minute and barely affect day-to-day work practices. Thus, at one level, cultural change appears to be occurring rapidly with one value system replacing another. At another level, changes will appear more slowly as the new goals, philosophies, and values trickle down to affect the work environment.

The number of new members relative to existing members can also influence the speed of organizational change. When an organization hires enough new employees to staff a previously nonexistent third shift, these employees have the potential to create significant change in the culture. Initially, the socialization attempts by the organization and its supervisors coupled with the newness of the situation for the employees will keep the culture from shifting too greatly. But, as these employees learn more about their jobs and the organization, they will have considerable potential to work within existing cultural practices to invoke change, particularly if existing cultural norms are weak and not well accepted.

Understanding the Existing
Culture to Achieve Organizational Change

To be most effective, managers must get to know—really know—their organization's culture before embarking on any type of formal change program (Michela & Burke, 2000). So, the first step to understanding the existing culture is to not assume (a) that all organizational members have the same view of the organization, and (b) that the view you hold is the view of others. Indeed, a study of accounting firms demonstrated that managers held considerably different views than those of nonmanagerial employees. In these firms, top-level managers viewed their organizational cultures as people-oriented, whereas employees did not. Missing such a difference in cultural interpretation would obviously be detrimental to formulating and enacting cultural change. Because it can be difficult for managers to see interpretations and perspectives other than their own, leaders often hire consultants or direct their human resource departments to assess the organization.

Organizational leaders can also use surveys or questionnaires to identify their culture, despite their inability to really reveal cultural assumptions (Schein, 1999). Creating a survey dictates that you know what to ask. How, then, can a survey reveal a value or assumption that is hidden to you? There are surveys available that purport to examine organizational culture. The disadvantage is that commercially-available surveys can only measure the values or assumptions commonly associated with many organizations; and all organizations are unlikely to promote the same values and assumptions. Thus, such surveys may be better indicators of organizational climate, or used as an initial step in a more thorough investigation.

More effective is to use processes that help you identify what the culture is—from your perspective and that of other organizational members. Because organizational members are often not aware of cultural assumptions, the following process can be used to reveal them. Schein (1999) recommends using this process with small groups—first with a small group of your colleagues, and then with groups of employees across other levels and functions:

1. Define an organizational problem—something that can be fixed or something that could work better.

2. Identify the artifacts (e.g., dress codes, level of formality, how decisions are made, rituals) that characterize the organization; ask new employees what they noticed when they joined the organization.

3. Identify the espoused values of the organization. Look at the organization's vision or mission statement as a place to start.

4. Compare the espoused values with the list of artifacts. If teamwork is highly valued, identify the cultural artifacts that support teamwork.

5. Identify any inconsistencies or conflicts between values and artifacts; dig deeper to discover what is driving the overt behavior associated with artifacts that are consistent with the espoused values.

When the data collection is completed, the next step is to identify the shared basic assumptions and examine them for the ways in which they facilitate or constrain the goal set out in Step 1 above. Because change is difficult, pay particular attention to assumptions that support the change that is desired. Are there cultural assumptions that will be positive attributes in the change process? If assumptions are exposed that will constrain or inhibit acceptance of the desired change, then these cultural elements should also be considered in the change process. Taking steps to become familiar with the culture and acknowledging that different views of culture exist in the organization is essential to cultural change attempts. If you do not understand how subcultures are related within the overall culture and cannot acknowledge cultural views different from your own, you are more likely to be limited to superficial approaches to cultural change (Goodman, Zammuto, & Gifford, 2001).

Another key to understanding an organization's culture is to identify and acknowledge who is influencing it. Frequently, managers approach such a task by looking at the influences of executive and other top-level managers. And, this may be the case for assumptions and values shared widely throughout the organization. However, studies have documented that nonmanagerial employees in both key formal and informal positions can exert considerable influence over the way work is performed and how performance is regarded—both of which influence culture in departments and smaller work units (Jones, 2000).

Intentional Cultural Change

Intentional cultural change programs often start at the top of the organization. With a specific goal in mind, organizational leaders want to lead or direct the organization to a new way of doing business or valuing things or people. Communication is key to all change processes. For example, Suzuki's (1997) study provides direct evidence of the role of communication in the transmission of culture. Of three types of employee communication network links, task-general (communication about broader issues beyond the immediate task) and nontask (communication about issues not directly related to work) communication links were better predictors of cultural transmission than task-specific (communication required to accomplish work) communication links. Thinking about the pervasiveness of culture in an organization, such a finding makes sense. Value-laden information carried in the task-general and nontask links could be useful and applicable to more employees, as well as create additional opportunities for employee sensemaking about cultural change. Thus, one way to accomplish cultural change is to create opportunities for employees to have nontask and task-general conversations.

As previously noted, when managers believe they want to make changes or are making cultural changes, they are often really addressing organizational climate. Because climate is an artifact of culture, climate can only be changed when the desired climate change is congruent with the underlying cultural assumptions. "One cannot create, for example, a climate of teamwork and cooperation if the underlying assumptions in the culture are individual and competitive" (Schein, 2000, p. xxix). Thus, change programs often fail because the underlying cultural assumptions are not addressed.

Too frequently, executives try to change their organization (and presumably their cultures) using management techniques and strategies promoted by management gurus. Recently, these have included benchmarking, knowledge management, reengineering, Six Sigma, TQM (total quality management), and strategic management. Executives select techniques and strategies like these to enhance financial success, especially when there is market or economic uncertainty. Despite their popularity with executives and managers, employees often described these techniques and strategies as fads or a "program of the month." While most of these techniques are primarily aimed at improving organizational efficiency (to improve profit), many executives and managers believe that such programs can also help them change their organization's culture.

Realistically, however, cultural change is hard to facilitate. Executives responding to a survey reported using 16 tools on average. "Managers can't keep rebuilding their companies around each successive tool. . . . tools come and go, but corporate cultures last" (Rigby, 2003, p. 8). Cultural change is also hard to facilitate because often the use of managerial tools creates a more controlling management ideology, and as a result, a more controlled work environment. Less-controlling ideologies should produce more flexible and adaptable organizational cultures, which in turn, should help organizational members become more accepting of changes and innovations. Simply stated, for cultural change there is no magic bullet (Zammuto, Gifford, & Goodman, 2000).

No matter how well you think out or plan for cultural change or what strategies to employ, cultural change is very difficult to implement for two reasons. First, cultural change cannot be forced because cultures are symbolically constructed. Taking the position that organizational culture emerges from the interactions of organizational members requires that change efforts be facilitated rather than driven from the top-down. Cultural change is more complex than simply changing a procedure or laying a management tool across all organizational practices. Values, norms, and artifacts change over time. Values cannot be dictated. Individuals can stimulate the acceptance of a new value, but a change in values, for example, is only realized when a core group of organizational members identifies the value as their own and create norms and artifacts to support that value.

Second, intentional changes in organizational culture are usually management driven, but not necessarily followed. As the point has been made, managers are not in complete control of culture. Many intentional change attempts fail because organizational leaders find "themselves in the awkward position of pushing an ideological stance that is at odds with the already established local culture" (Eisenberg & Riley, 2001, p. 310). Because the process of organizing is always present in organizations, culture is also changing and not well suited for overt managing—especially when managers seek a supposedly strong culture of shared values. Sensemaking is always occurring and values can be regenerated or recharacterized. Indeed, "everyone involved in a culture remakes meaning daily, thus opportunities for change are ever present, as is change itself" (Hatch, 2000, p. 259).

Cultural Evolution

Cultural evolution occurs as new values and assumption are introduced and accepted in a way that integrates them with existing values and assumptions. This process is subtle with cultural values and practices being constructed, reconstructed, adjusted, and reinforced on an ongoing basis as organizational members process the change (Kuhn & Corman, 2003). Viewing cultural change from an evolutionary perspective also provides more opportunities to identify the intentional as well as unintentional outcomes, and the ways in which change creates consensus and conflict over practices and values.

Alvesson (2002) labels such a cultural transformation as an organic social movement. In this case, there is no strong unifying push from the top. Rather, groups of people throughout the organization revise their thinking based on internal or external conditions. A good example of this is the way in which some universities and colleges have adopted the customer-orientation of retail and service organizations. It is highly unlikely that students or faculty specifically requested such a change. But recently there has been a change in the general business orientation in this society to include a stronger customer focus. Organizations do not want simply to meet customer needs, they want to satisfy or delight customers with their products and services. Some organizations have even reframed the internal structure of their organizations by specifying that some departments are internal customers of other departments. This shift, made prominent by our consumer economy and greater competition, influenced the ways in which university administrators viewed their institutions. Today, many universities and colleges offer customer service training to employees who have job responsibilities for recruiting students and for employees who work in providing direct student services. For example, many university libraries have adopted a customer focus, basing their services on the needs and desires of students (e.g., putting coffee shops in libraries where previously all food and drink were prohibited). Thus, the customer orientation movement generalized throughout our economy filtered in to organizations that previously had not taken such an orientation. From the organic social movement perspective there is no clear management objective and no plan for change.

Cultural Revolution

Alternately, cultural revolution occurs when main cultural elements are abandoned as new ones replace them. In this case, it is believed that culture is static or frozen, and that it can be unfrozen and changed only to be refrozen once again (Lewin, 1951). Thus, culture moves from being relatively stable through a period of disarray and back to being relatively stable with the change process causing the temporary disarray.

Ultimately, most organizations are seeking to create alignment among culture, strategy, and structure (Semler, 1997). Several strategies have been identified as successful in creating that alignment (Alvesson, 2002; Michela & Burke, 2000). First, training can introduce and help orient organizational members toward desired values and behaviors. The more directly relevant the value-associated behavior is to an employee's work situation, the more effective the training. Second, what an organization chooses to measure and reward can influence cultural change if what is chosen for measurement is relative to the cultural change desired, and if there is a tight link between what is measured and what is rewarded. Third, selectively promoting those employees who are visible champions of management's prescribed cultural values creates a public acknowledgment of the culture and places these individuals in positions of influence. Fourth, in some organizational change efforts, members of top management become more public and more visible to employees to affirm the organization's cultural direction. For example, some executives hold coffee talks, respond directly to email inquiries, are interviewed in company newsletters about the change, or even hold press conferences to announce the organization's new direction. And, fifth, new uses of organizational symbols herald a change in organizational culture. A new slogan, logo, or vision appears on widely distributed printed materials. All employees receive a wallet card with the company's new guiding principles. Meetings end with a discussion of how the decisions made there reflect the organizational mission. From this perspective, "culture change is a project emerging from and run from above" (Alvesson, 2002, p. 178).

Complementary Change Processes

Neither revolutionary nor evolutionary, the third type of organizational culture change is *everyday reframing* (Alvesson, 2002). In this case, there is no overt management objective for change, nor does the change emanate from some broad trends in society. Everyday reframing is guided by a few senior employees, incremental, and more informal than formal. As an example, the vice provost for information services at the University of Kansas created collaborative task groups across university stakeholders (i.e., faculty, students, and administrators) to provide guidance in how the university could make more effective use of its technology and information resources. Given the charge of creating new models of service within one semester, the three task forces were given the latitude to do whatever they felt was necessary to collect information from the university's constituencies, vendors, and other universities to develop their recommendations. Labeling the project as High Velocity Change for High Volume Collaboration (shortened to HVC2), task force members were encouraged to think differently about how the university could use its technology. Task force members, of course, sought the input of their colleagues and coworkers that resulted in their informally spreading current technology capacities to individuals who were unaware of them and creating a buzz about the university's technological future.

The caution with this approach, however, is that its influence on culture can be weak because all organizational authorities are not part of the change process. Often, too, such plans have limited resources or lack formal power to implement change. Thus, organizational change from this perspective will likely fail if it does not resonate with other organizational members and develop enough interest to sustain itself. Alternately, everyday reframing is powerful in that it is anchored in the interactions of organizational members and, therefore, culture change is more realistically connected to existing day-to-day activities. In the case of HVC2, task force members found that developing ideas for change called on their creativity and challenged their own assumptions and values, forcing them to acknowledge the multiple interpretations that existed in the university's culture about technology use.

Alvesson (2002) argues that different types of culture change are not necessarily contradictory; indeed they can be complementary. New ideas in the organization's environment can create the opportunity for cultural change as organizational members become aware of these through interactions with external stakeholders. Top management can draw on perceived internal problems or opportunities as a motivation for cultural change whereas organizational culture reframing occurs when organizational members sense both change in the external environment and willingness from top management to pursue changes.

Across the three organizational culture change processes, Alvesson (2002) describes five principles for consideration. First, tying organizational culture to specific events, situations, actions, and processes helps individuals identify with cultural artifacts, values, and assumptions more clearly. Second, consider the organizational culture as a network in which meanings are created and maintained rather than presuming that meaning can be driven downward in the organization. Organizational culture change is more likely to take hold when it is internally rather than externally driven. Third, through the change process, view meanings in the network as processual and situated rather than fixed, allowing meanings to float and be flexible to reveal the multiplicities that employees face in their organizational activities. For example, an organizational member's role can be viewed differently in different organizational situations: Is a university librarian in a role that serves students, serves faculty, conducts his or her own research, or all four? Fourth, be open to variation, and the potential contradictions that variation can bring. It is unlikely that all organizational members will create the same interpretation for any one cultural element. Finally, be aware of the way in which organizational power creates dominant meanings and influences asymmetric social relationships among organizational members.

Creating Successful Change

Taking the position that an organization's culture cannot be directly changed, Eisenberg and Riley (2001) argue that "certain patterns of behavior can be encouraged and cultivated" (p. 310) particularly when cultural change is jointly considered with the organization's business strategy (Deetz, Tracy, & Simpson, 2000). A positive work culture can stimulate potential in employees if the business strategy and culture embrace the same goals and values. Building employee commitment, enhancing employees' identification with the company, and creating a positive organizational spirit are three steps leaders can take to facilitate organizational change.

> When employees are highly committed to an organizational mission, they are more likely to go forward with actions that are consistent with company goals, even when these actions may not necessarily be in line with their individual or departmental priorities. (Deetz, Tracy, & Simpson, 2000, p. 32)

Another way to realize successful change is to empower employees to participate in the process. A study of a hospital gridlocked under ineffective leadership (Bate, Khan, & Pye, 2000) demonstrates that giving employees the opportunity to simultaneously work through changes in organizational structure and organizational culture can be effective. Using a process-driven rather than top-down approach, organizational members first met to identify their cultural foundations and their visions for the future of the organization. These discussions acknowledged their common vocabulary and created a public record of their work together. This step also identified the assumptions and values on which they wanted to build their work structures. Next, employees met to negotiate new ground rules for working together. As new rules, procedures, and working structures were developed, they were tested—everyone agreed that new ways of working should be tried out before being adopted. Small projects were set up for employees to explore these new working arrangements. Feedback from employees in these projects led to changes before the new work routines were arranged in a new organizational structure. Because employees and management had committed to negotiation and compromise as a way of working out conflicts, problems of interpretation and implementation were overcome. In the final stage of the culture and structure change, employees monitored traditional business indicators as well as engaged in discussions to facilitate their sensemaking of the new work structures and ways of working. By using a change process that was inclusive, tentative, and based on values employees identified as being important, employees took ownership for change and making it work effectively.

Two Levels for Addressing Cultural Change

A hologram is a good metaphor for an organization's culture (Czarniawska-Joerges, 1992; Morgan, 1997). Look at the hologram on your credit card. Although it is a flat image, it really is a three-dimensional picture that contains information about the size, shape, brightness, and contrast of the object. This information is stored in a very microscopic and complex pattern. When you shine a light on the hologram, the stored information is recreated to reflect the object. As you vary the light source, your eyes and brain perceive different (and often moving) views of the object.

Now imagine that all of an organization's members are crowded together to create a snapshot of the organization. Each organizational member is representative of the organization's culture, and, at the same time, uniquely reflects the organization's culture. Thus, each member could tell you something about the culture, but not everything. By going from person to person (just as if you would vary the light source on a hologram), you would hear and see different aspects and views of the culture.

Of course, people are different from holograms. While the hologram on your credit card is fixed, organizational members are dynamic. When I look at the hologram on my credit card I always see one of multiple views of the same bird flying. The flying bird cannot morph into a flying squirrel. However, if I were to talk to different members of an organization over time, their views of the culture are likely to change. In the beginning of their association with the organization, individuals are likely to be attracted to the organization's positive features. But after settling into a work routine, issues that were tolerable initially can become annoying, procedures that helped you initially organize your activities are now seen as unnecessary, leadership that was viewed as charismatic is now viewed as controlling. Alternately, procedures that were initially overwhelming now make your workday breeze by, and practices that were initially confusing now make sense. Not only will the perceptions of culture that individuals reflect be different from one another, they will also change over time.

One of the inherent problems in examining an organization's culture is deciding which level of observation to use. Do you choose the level of individual organizational members? In doing so, you are likely to get rich detail, but detail that is biased from a particular individual's perspective. Thus, you might not capture the complexity or the totality of the organizational culture. If you choose the organizational level of observation it is possible to miss the undercurrents that reflect the organization's subcultures. When we address communication at the organizational level, there is a tendency to view the organization and its culture as a consensus—being the same for everyone. A more complete picture of an organization's culture is developed when you draw information from a variety of organizational members—members at a variety of locations, in a variety of functions, and with differing tenure. This allows you to identify subcultures and examine their relationships to one another.

CREATING A VISION OF THE ORGANIZATION AND ITS CULTURE

"Organizations do not form accidentally or spontaneously" (Schein, 1992, p. 212). The only way for an organization to form is for people to create it. These people—the organizational founders—are goal oriented. Literally, then, every organization begins with a vision. Its founders have a spark of an idea that is refined through contemplation and conversation. The ideas start to crystallize encouraging founders to believe that this organization is unique and viable as an economic entity. Over a period of time and a series of interactions, a vision of the organization—a statement that describes the value of what is to be achieved—is turned into the organization's mission—where specifically the organization wants to go. Typically, these are accompanied by a strategic plan that details in the short-term how the organization will achieve its mission (Deetz, Tracy, & Simpson, 2000). The role of an organizational vision, mission statement, and strategic plan are central to how an organization operates. "The beliefs and ideas that organizations hold about who they are, what they are trying to do, and what their environment is like have a much greater tendency to realize themselves than is usually believed" (Morgan, 1997, p. 149). Although, organizations start with a vision, mission statement, and strategic plan developed by the organization's founding members, most organizations regularly revisit these to fine-tune their organizational activities to their current organizational environment.

A vision creates a realistic long-term path for the organization. To be effective it should describe a future for the organization that is recognized as achievable, powerful enough to generate commitment, coherent enough to provide coordination, and stated in such a way that all organizational members can accept it as their own. For example, Sutter Health, a not-for-profit network of community-based health care providers in Northern California (http://www.sutterhealth.org/), defines its vision as:

> Sutter Health will be a recognized leader in transforming health care to meet the needs of the 21st Century. At both the local and regional levels we will be:
>
> - The preferred provider to our patients and customers
> - The best place to work and practice
> - A role model of community citizenship

How might you set out to develop a vision? First, vision development is a group activity. When organizational members are involved in setting the vision, it becomes meaningful to them, increasing their ownership in the organization's activities. Depending on the size and history of the organization, the group that develops the vision may be a small task force of employees across organizational functions, the 5 to 20 members of the top management team (usually vice presidents and other organizational members who report directly to the CEO, president, or executive director), or executives—such as the CEO, CIO, CFO, President—and the organization's board. Regardless of which group develops the vision, the vision must be communicated clearly and consistently to all organizational members.

Visions that have the following five characteristics are more likely to be meaningful (Deetz, Tracy, & Simpson, 2000). First, vision statements should provide a sense of direction for the organization. Where is the organization headed? What is it trying to accomplish? Based on the values of the organization (or the values the founders want a new organization to support), a vision statement should be worded in such a way that three objectives are accomplished: (a) The future of the organization is clear and attainable; (b) employees are energized and excited about the future orientation of the organization, and (c) regardless of their organizational role, all employees can connect their work activities to the vision. The second characteristic of a good vision is that it provides an appropriate and effective context for decision making. As opportunities and challenges are presented to the organization, decision makers at all levels should be able to use the organizational vision to decide what actions to take. For example, the first point in the Sutter Health vision statement indicates that the organization wants to become the preferred provider of its patients and customers. When presented with a dilemma, decision makers can use that point as a litmus test for their decisions.

Third, a vision must reflect the values and culture of the organization. Even if a shift in vision is being articulated, the vision must be developed from the organization's current circumstances. Thus, a vision often incrementally pushes the organization forward into new markets, new products, new principles, and new technologies—but remains grounded in or relevant to the existing organizational purpose. Fourth, a strong vision recognizes and responds to a pressing need. Shrinking profits, higher customer expectations, increased regulation, adoption of new technology, and a higher patient-to-provider ratio plague the health industry. Sutter Health's vision articulates that need by setting the organization on a path toward transforming health care. Finally, a strong vision creates a future by acting in the present. This means that a vision, despite its future orientation, must be integrated into the daily activities and routines of organizational members. Once developed, the vision should be assessed for the way it impacts all roles and each function of all roles in the organization. Because a vision typically cannot be applied in the same way across or within functions, it is important for leaders and managers to help organizational members discover ways in which the vision can be relevant to their jobs. Some organizations use only a vision statement or mission statement. But when these are distinct, visions tend to be more future oriented while mission statements tend to be more present-oriented.

Mission statements state the goal or objective of the organization, and often dictate the organization's salient relationships with stakeholder groups: employees, investors, suppliers, community, and customers.

As founders create their organizational mission, conversations become debates—forcing a confrontation of the underlying assumptions. When consensus is found and formalized as the mission statement, it provides a foundation for the organization's culture. Thus, mission statements are laden with underlying assumptions and overt values that shape organizational practices and the behaviors and interactions of organizational members. Mission statements that are timeless, general, and applicable to all functions of the organization are powerful in creating a foundation of assumptions and values for organizational members. Sutter Health's mission statement is:

> We enhance the health and well-being of people in the communities we serve, through a not-for-profit commitment to compassion and excellence in health care services. (http://www.sutterhealth .org/)

Yet a vision of the organization and a mission statement are not enough to create and sustain a culture. Nor is revision of the vision or mission sufficient for changing the culture. Organizational members must own the vision and mission. Not only must leaders clearly communicate the vision and mission, it must be consistent with and integrated into organizational norms (Deetz, Tracy, & Simpson, 2000). In this way, leaders help to create relevance among artifacts, values, and assumptions and supporting cultural practices emerge.

SOCIALIZING NEW EMPLOYEES TO THE CULTURE

Socializing or assimilating new employees is the process by which new employees are integrated into the organization's culture. Employees who are acculturated are likely to be more satisfied with their jobs, less likely to leave the organization, and have higher identification with the organization. More important, employees across different industries report that being acculturated was distinct from being familiar with their supervisors, being recognized for doing a good job, feeling as if they were involved in the organization, feeling competent on the job, and being able to negotiate aspects of their work (Myers & Oetzel, 2003).

In most cases, newcomers are essentially unfamiliar with the organization. Despite interviews and information collected from current employees and others, most newcomers have only superficial information about the organization (Jablin, 2001). However, there are cases in which the newcomers do have preemployment information that helps them to socialize more quickly and with less effort. Gibson and Papa (2000) describe the organizational entry of manufacturing employees whose family members or friends worked at the plant or who had worked at the plant previously. Thus, this group of new employees had substantial and intimate knowledge about the company, its work, and the work environment. Based on their second- and third-generation knowledge of the organization, most were favorably predisposed to the occupation and the organization. Organizational osmosis, or the seemingly effortless adoption of values and organizational culture, created a different assimilation path for these employees. One employee reported, "I fit in pretty good because I knew what to do and when to do it, and because I had my relatives looking out for me." Employees understood the work and expectations of the organization allowing them to assimilate into their work groups—often populated by family members and friends, or people who knew their family members and friends. In turn this eased their metamorphosis of becoming an accepted and participating organizational member, and facilitated their adoption of organizational norms. Gibson and Papa's findings underscore the blurring of an organization's internal and external boundaries, as organizational and occupational values and norms were communicated to these employees when they were adolescents. "To some degree, these workers have already been 'indoctrinated' into the organization, and their identification has been forged long before entering the organization" (pp. 84–85).

For other employees, however, being socialized into a new organizational culture really begins on the first day of work. To help acculturate employees, many organizations require that new employees attend orientations on the first day at the organization. One employee described her experience this way:

First they showed us a 10-minute video about the company, divisions, products, history, and so on. Next they talked a little bit about payroll, timesheets, and direct deposit. We had to fill out our W-2 forms. Then on to benefits. We covered health insurance, the stock purchase plan, our 401K, and dental insurance. Then we took a tour of the building—where to find the copy room, the mail room, the loading dock, and the cafeteria. There was a discussion about security—building security and confidential documents. We also received our security badges. Then we had a computer presentation to learn the organization's email, calendar, conference room scheduling and employee information systems. Next, someone provided a brief presentation on community relations like United Way and volunteer programs.

Employees like to have "What will the company do for me?" answered early in their association with an organization. Doing so helps to establish a relationship between the employee and the organization. The orientation described above may accomplish some of that as salary and other benefits were described. But this employee's description of her new employee orientation does not directly address whether she was directly introduced to organizational assumptions and values. Perhaps she inferred what the organization valued from the orientation, but the onslaught of practical details provided that first day was likely overwhelming—and results in her attributing a value to the organization's culture that may not be valid.

This type of face-to-face orientation, however, will introduce the organization's culture to a new employee more effectively than handing them a handbook with all of the policies, procedures, and regulations outlined. Imagine yourself a new employee and being handed a three-inch thick notebook and your supervisor saying, "The most important ones for you to know are flagged," and then being left on your own to figure everything out. As a new employee, what would you assume about the company values?

From a managerial perspective, the first day of work is the most critical day of employment. A manager at a television station explains:

> This day is a tool to validate all of the previous communication from the initial interview, the hiring process communication, and the follow up communication. The first day confirms the company culture by reinforcing or confirming what you have already told the employee and what you think you need the employee to know and feel in the future. It's the "launching pad" for the rest of the employee's career. Little things such as the dress code, and the specific tasks are communicated, but also the foundation is laid for "painting the picture of the company's growth." Expectations are set on this day.

Thus, socializing new employees is an important step in acculturating new organizational members. But, the orientation process cannot be completed on the first day, in the first week, or even in the first month. New employees continue to learn about the organization, their job, and their work unit throughout their first year of employment. As their level of assimilation increases, their understanding of the organization's culture changes as well.

LEADERSHIP AND ORGANIZATIONAL CULTURE

"The only thing of real importance that leaders do is to create and manage culture . . . the unique talent of leaders is their ability to understand and work with culture" (Schein, 1991, p. 5). This dramatic statement underscores the relationship of leadership to organizational culture. Schein argues that an organization's leaders create its culture, and that they also determine which other organizational members can be leaders. True. But leading an organization through the lens of organizational culture is a reframing of leadership itself. When leaders ask:

- What impact am I having on the social construction of reality in my organization?
- What can I do to have a different and more positive impact? (Morgan, 1997, p. 148)

they are viewing their role in the organization differently than a leader in a bureaucracy. The focus on function, control, and authority is replaced by an awareness of the roles of all organizational members in creating and sustaining the organization. The view that a leader has a monopoly on employees and other stakeholders is replaced by a view of leadership that is more organic, emergent, and reflective—it is a complex social process, not a mechanistic portrayal of leaders acting and subordinates responding. In this way, leadership is a culture-influence activity as well as a cultural manifestation itself (Alvesson, 2002).

Effective leaders facilitate, rather than impose, a vision that will inspire and empower (Mohan, 1993). For example, local United Way organizations are being urged by United Way of America to reframe their way of doing business (United Way of America, 2004). Thus, local board presidents and executive directors are being encouraged to shift the vision of United Way from a federation of agencies for which the local United Way organizations are primarily fundraisers and fund allocators to organizations that create meaningful and tangible impact in their communities. Rather than focusing solely on the number of dollars raised and agencies served, local United Way organizations are being encouraged to focus on community impacts—that is, how are lives changed and how are communities shaped.

This new symbolic vision is a reframing, or qualitatively new template (Bartunek, 1988), of the manner in which local United Way organizations operate. In their leadership positions, local board presidents and executive directors would have great difficulty imposing this shift in perspective. They will be more effective in persuading board members and agency stakeholders that this new vision can be both compelling and productive by including organizational members in determining if, and how, the new vision can be manifested in their communities. By working within the culture rather than *on* the culture, leaders are closer to the cultural elements that are preconditions for changing culture. That is, a leader will be more effective in influencing assumptions, values, and norms if he or she understands what artifacts, values, and assumptions exist and how they currently influence organizational practice (Alvesson, 2002).

Arguably leaders have other responsibilities—that is, as managers, they control organizations through financial, strategic, and coordinating activities. Individuals who are leader-managers influence culture in different ways depending on which role is primary.

Leaders often take a future orientation, providing a vision for the organization that ultimately shapes the organization's culture. To be successful with new visions, leaders must understand the values organizational members currently hold, and if possible, incorporate those values in the transition to the new vision. Managers are more present oriented and often try to manage culture by shaping the tangible, artifactual levels of culture. If these changes are not coherent or relevant to organizational members, or if changes are forced upon members, then they are likely to result in greater cultural fragmentation. Most effectively, leader and manager roles converge so that there is some balance between flexibility and control, future and present, inspiration and guidance (Mohan, 1993).

While leaders are important to establishing or changing organizational culture, so are organizational members. They are "not passive receptacles, but imaginative consumers of leaders' visions and of manipulated cultural artifacts" (Bryman, 1996, p. 286). Sure, leaders articulate cultural messages and these value frames do constrain how organizational members think and communicate in the organizational setting. Yet, leaders cannot force organizational members to accept these cultural-framing attempts.

Leadership behavior, especially role modeling, is the most important tool for achieving change in organizational culture (Schein, 1983). In this case, leaders must *walk the talk* to reinforce new cultural values and assumptions. In other words, espoused values must also be enacted values. For example, management in a research and development organization wanted to respond to the history of mistreatment—the systematic or procedural abuse at both the interpersonal and institutional levels—that had plagued their organization (Meares, Oetzel, Torres, Derkacs, & Ginossar, 2004). They developed and clearly stated their objective—eliminate the mistreatment of employees—and frequently publicized this goal. Despite these steps, however, they did not take any specific actions to eliminate mistreatment nor did they develop procedures for employees to follow if they were mistreated. Moreover, employees were confused about what constituted mistreatment, as management did not provide a definition of the very thing they were trying to eliminate! While management was sincere about wanting to change the culture, their actions did not provide a path for new values and norms to develop.

Despite the energy, intensity, or resources leaders use to invoke a cultural change, they cannot change the culture by themselves. But leaders can create the opportunity and space for cultural change to occur by interacting with employees, embracing new values and assumptions, listening to employee comments about the new values and assumptions, and listening and watching for their resistance to cultural change (Kouzes & Posner, 1995).

Formal Leadership Influences on Culture

How do leaders convince others to adopt their vision of the organization and the assumptions and values embedded in its mission statement? Leaders control the resources of the organization. They decide where attention is directed, what gets measured, and how rewards are handed out. These formal management mechanisms reinforce their assumptions and values and set in motion a series of procedures and practices that get other organizational members to do the same. The importance of founder values during organizational formation cannot be dismissed as Shockley-Zalabak and Morley (1994) found that the organizational rules that emerged were drawn directly from founders' values.

Some leaders make it a practice to *manage by walking around*— getting outside of their offices to interact with employees, seeing how operations are working, and asking questions and giving encouragement. Other leaders use their legitimate status as leader to create opportunities to talk directly with employees in meetings, or less directly through videos or newsletters. One four-star general in the U.S. Air Force held weekly meetings with high ranking officers to distill the values he believed would increase efficiency and effectiveness. Officers were invited back repeatedly for "tutorials" until he was sure their understanding of command values replicated his. This kind of leader-directed coaching and teaching can be powerful and effective in establishing strong consensual cultures.

Leaders have direct and formal influence over organizational culture by the ways in which work is designed through systems and procedures, resources are allocated, and rewards are structured. Value shifts are revealed to employees when leaders devote considerable resources in terms of money and time toward new initiatives. For example, one CEO budgeted $100,000 for a task force to study the technology needs of the company in order to create a powerful indication that all routine work should be handled with technology. These monies were in addition to the budget to purchase and implement any technological changes. The task force, initially suspect of their charge—to deliver a model of technological improvement in 120 days—were convinced that the CEO was serious when he described the monies that were set aside to assist the task force, and that an extension to the project would not be granted. He encouraged them to survey employees, visit other organizations to discover best practices, and hire whatever expertise they needed to create an innovative and rapid change in how the organization used technology. Knowing that money was tight and having been encouraged to spend money to create the plan for a new technological work environment convinced members of the task force and the organization that the CEO was serious about both goals. In turn, not only did they perceive a higher value for technology, they also recognized the shift toward a different and faster way of doing business. Previously technology was viewed as only a tool in this organization with departments differing in their technology, use and applications. Moreover, previous change efforts had dragged on for years. This new project signaled a change in values on two dimensions.

Another direct influence leaders can have on the culture is through what they choose to endorse as a rite or a ritual. For some companies, this is the annual sales award dinner; for others it is the company picnic where the leader and her family cook and serve barbecue to all of the employees as guests. The more engaged the leader is in these activities, and the sincerity with which he or she interacts with employees, provide signals as to what is valued.

At one company, two different but related meetings were ritualized. The first meeting was held at a nice restaurant or country club to announce the year's sales contest. A grand prize of a 2-week vacation to an exotic location was announced at the meeting. Salespeople and their partners were invited to the dinner meeting, but did not know the theme. At the door, the president would meet them dressed as a character from the location of the vacation. At one dinner meeting, he was dressed as a warrior from the Roman Empire; at another he greeted them as a South Sea Islander. This was quite a departure for someone whom employees only saw in a dark blue suit. Each party would be elaborately decorated, transforming the location into the locale of the grand prize. After dinner, the details of the sales contest would be announced and goals set. The second ritualized meeting occurred when the sales winner returned from the exotic vacation. This time the employee and his or her partner were the hosts. The president would ensure that the exotic location was replicated from the kickoff dinner. And, the president ensured that the winner was given enough spending money to bring back a gift for each employee. These two ritualized meetings focused on several organizational values. One was to have fun. The salespeople sold steel wire—not a very glamorous business. Hyping the sales contest and planning the themes for the two meetings around the location of the prize vacation reminded employees that selling steel wire could be competitive and fun. Although there was only one winner of the exotic vacation, the ritual of the winner bringing back gifts for everyone also reinforced the value that no one works alone.

Stories like the following are common in the business press and demonstrate the different ways in which leaders can influence their organization's culture. CEO Steven H. Temares and cofounders Warren Eisenberg and Leonard Feinstein of Bed Bath & Beyond, Inc. are described as quirky and low key (Byrnes, 2004). Unlike leaders of other big corporations, Temares, Eisenberg, and Feinstein rarely give interviews, pose for pictures, speak at conferences, or accept awards. Also atypical is the headquarters of this home-furnishings retailer, which is marked only by a small sign. Partly by letting its 569 managers select stock based on local tastes, Bed Bath & Beyond became one of the top 50 performing companies in 2003. Temares, a self-critical, quick-talking lawyer with no retail experience initially joined the chain after six interviews, and then only to help the company with its real estate transactions. His leadership style follows closely that of Eisenberg and Feinstein, who started Bed Bath & Beyond in 1971 with two stores. In the beginning Eisenberg focused on merchandising and Feinstein focused on everything else, creating a culture of mutual respect— no one can ever remember seeing the two fight. Acknowledging that the company is managed today as it was when it started, managers are always promoted from within, and even experienced managers start on the floor so they can learn the culture.

Indirect Leadership Influences on Culture

Besides the formal and direct mechanisms that are traditionally part of leadership roles, leaders can also use indirect processes to influence organizational members' acceptance of values and assumptions. For example, a vice president and branch manager of a brokerage firm was dismayed that the office kitchen space was untidy and unclean. One weekend he walked into the office, threw away all of the paper and plastic dishes in the kitchen, cleaned it, and then restocked the kitchen with brightly colored dishes, glassware, and accessories. Monday morning, employees were startled that *their* kitchen was cleaned. The office was all abuzz as employees tried to figure out what happened and who did it. The vice president kept silent. Over time, but not as quickly, the kitchen once again became cluttered and dirty. Again, he came in over the weekend and transformed the kitchen. Monday morning, employees were less startled that the kitchen had been cleaned, but more curious that someone among them had tidied it up. Again, but over a longer period of time, the kitchen would become messy; however, now employees were taking responsibility for cleaning it up. When they did, the vice president would come in early on Monday morning and put fresh baked goods and flowers in the kitchen. If something needed restocking, he did that as well. Every time the employees took responsibility for cleaning the kitchen, some treat or new kitchen accessory would appear on Monday. At a regularly scheduled office meeting, the vice president complimented the group, noting that the kitchen was cleaner and less cluttered. Proudly, employees boasted of their efforts to keep the kitchen area clean and tidy. The vice president then complimented them on the way the reference library and storage closet had been reorganized, and the way in which employees had decluttered their desks. He never revealed to them that he was the one who started cleaning the kitchen.

Why did he take this approach to influencing employee behavior? In explaining himself, the vice president indicated that he believed that the brokerage's clients would view the organization and its stockbrokers more favorably if the environment were neat and orderly. He also believed that employees were more likely to clean up their workspaces if they felt valued and respected. He explained that cleaning the kitchen area was something he could do to set a pattern in motion; and when he first cleaned the kitchen the employees knew that someone had done it *for* them. Rather than repeatedly telling employees to clean their workspaces, and employees complying because they were given a directive, he wanted them to value clean workspaces and create an organizational environment that imbued values in line with client expectations; and it worked.

There is one final point about the relationship between leadership and organizational culture. Organizational culture influences who will be selected as leaders and how leadership roles should be enacted (Alvesson, 2002). Leadership does not arise magically from a neutral sociopolitical environment. Rather, leadership develops from organizational culture, from within an existing pattern of artifacts, values, and assumptions. Those who embrace the organization's (i.e., senior management's view) of the culture are more likely to be selected to be leaders. Thus, organizational culture shapes an organization's leadership, and organizational leaders shape the organization's culture.

PERSONAL, PROFESSIONAL, AND ORGANIZATIONAL ETHICS

The personal and professional ethics of high profile organizational leaders have recently been subjected to a great deal of scrutiny. While the ethical issues encountered at lower levels in the organization seldom are reported publicly, ethical issues do exist at all levels of all organizations. Personal ethics results from our upbringing, education, and experiences. Professional ethics can be a set of principles, like the oaths that attorneys, realtors, doctors, and nurses take to achieve certification, licensure, or entry into a professional association. Or, professional ethics can result from how a society, community, or organization views a particular occupational role.

Ethics are based on values. While typically we think of having ethics as being favorable, there are instances in which personal and organizational ethics result in unfortunate and negative outcomes. In the best of situations, our ethics are socially responsible, similar to, and supported by the values of our organizations. In other cases, personal and professional ethics can conflict with organizational values. And, of course, it is possible that one's personal and professional values and the values of one's organization result in socially undesirable outcomes.

Cultural Elements Conducive
to Unethical Behavior

Organizational cultures can have a dramatic impact on the way in which we enact our personal and professional ethics, and the way in which we act on the organization's ethics. Organizational members tend to behave consistently with organizational values about ethical issues when those values are known. However, if an organizational member does not understand the organization's ethical values, then he or she will consider other options for making ethical choices (Douglas, Davidson, & Schwartz, 2001).

In particular, six elements of culture can be conducive to unethical behavior (Deetz, Tracy, & Simpson, 2000). First, whenever an organization becomes fearful of external influences, leery of external inquiries, and promotes an overly-cohesive environment, organizational members may begin to act unethically. This type of highly cohesive isolation allows organizational members to act in a vacuum and not fully consider the impact or outcomes of their decisions. Known as groupthink (Janis, 1982), members overestimate their power and invulnerability and, as a result, make faulty decisions because maintaining harmony is valued over critical thinking. The demise of Enron is a good example of how groupthink can become pervasive in an organization's culture and result in dramatic and negative outcomes. Enron's "winner-take-all culture" created intense pressure on Enron executives to take greater risks with investments and accounting procedures. Also labeled as a "pressure-cooker culture," Enron insisted on results from employees and expected employees to protect the practice of inflating revenues while hiding growing debts. Because employees wanted to be seen positively by those in the power circle, employees reported undermining their personal ethics to stay within the powerful subculture at Enron.

Even when they did not understand the accounting practices, employees were too fearful of losing their jobs (and the monetary benefits that a successful Enron could provide them) to ask critical questions (Stephens & Behr, 2002).

A second aspect of culture that can create unethical behavior is when organizations have vague or contradictory vision statements. If an organization's vision or mission is vague, then employees can rationalize that their potentially illegal or unethical behavior will be supported by the organization. For example, the U.S. Cooperative Extension System created a task force to assess and report on the Extension's future. Based on input from hearings, the task force identified prominent themes that could be drafted into the organization's vision. However, the task force report also revealed contradictions and paradoxes (Quinn, 1988). In some themes, the Extension advocated an open issues orientation aimed at cross-program and interdisciplinary work. In other themes, the task force advocated that the Extension serve specific clientele with a narrow program focus—a future clearly inconsistent with a cross-program interdisciplinary approach. With these types of contradicting themes in the Extension's vision statement, it would be easy for those making decisions aligned with one aspect of the vision to question the ethics of those making decisions aligned with the other aspect of the vision.

A third cultural element that leads to unethical behavior is organizational segmentation and specialization. Although all organizations are structured into departments or units to accomplish work more effectively, excessive organizational segmentation can make it easier for unethical activities to take place. An organizational structure that lacks internal checks and balances creates a culture in which dishonesty can flourish. Recording star Toni Braxton revealed on *The Oprah Winfrey Show* how her business manager spent all of her money forcing her to file bankruptcy for herself and three of her companies and move back in with her family—two activities she believed were humiliating. Although the business manager-client relationship was built on trust, the story reveals that the business manager used a different definition of trust than the client. The star argued that the business manager was the expert, and, therefore, she trusted him to make the right decisions. Unfortunately, they were decisions that favored him, not her, and resulted in financial hardship for her personally and professionally.

Incentive programs are the fourth feature that can create a culture conducive to unethical behavior. Particularly in sales jobs, companies implement incentive programs to motivate their salespeople (Stevens, 1983), but often such programs have divisive and unethical outcomes. Salespeople believe it is unethical when their organizations reward high sales one year with a higher quota the following year. Such a practice implies this organizational value: Despite how hard you worked, it was not enough. Another unethical practice regarding incentives occurs when a sales manager counts sales as his own, rather than acknowledging the role of the salesperson in developing the relationship and closing the deal. The implied value is: As your manager, I can take what I want. Your effort results in a reward for me.

Fifth, unethical behavior is more likely to be condoned when organizational practices discriminate against certain groups of people in the organization. For example, Shirley, a vice president of human resources of a hotel chain, made a point to be in her office just before lunchtime. That way, she was *available* when the other vice presidents—all male— gathered in the hall to make their lunch plans. It was harder for them to ignore her if she was in her office with her office door open. She believed it was important to have lunch with the other vice presidents, as these informal lunches were the site of planning and decision making, and because their decisions impacted hiring and evaluation processes that she administered. Despite her efforts to be included and contribute to the top management team, the president unconsciously perpetuated her exclusion by taking the top management team for a week's *working* retreat to a hunting lodge. When the invitation was extended to all members of the team, Shirley enthusiastically accepted and asked for suggestions for where she could practice shooting before the trip. The president chimed in with a smile on his face, "Shirley, that won't be necessary. The lodge doesn't have accommodations for women. We're staying in one big cabin in the wilds of Canada. Where would you sleep?" Not surprisingly after their return, the male vice presidents started to exclude Shirley from the working lunch meetings even when she was in her office with the door open. Discriminatory organizational practices like these can exist at all levels of the organization. Systematic discrimination—intended or not, formal or informal— is unethical. These practices underscore what and who is valued in the organization.

Finally, when organizational members adopt a code of silence, unethical behavior will go unchecked. As was finally revealed in the U.S. Air Force's own investigation, female cadets at the Air Force Academy had been subjected to physical and sexual harassment by fellow male cadets. Female cadets who reported these instances to their superior officers were often met with retaliation or indifference. A code of silence developed at two levels. First, the officers enacted a code of silence by not taking the female cadets' accusations seriously and not moving their complaints along the chain of command. Second, a code of silence developed among the cadets because of another value at the Academy—the belief that it was dishonorable to inform on another cadet who was a classmate.

While these six elements are common to many organizations, they do not create a complete list of situations in which personal, professional, and organizational ethics are violated. The two studies described below provide additional examples of the way in which ethical or unethical behavior is facilitated by the cultural values of organizations.

Seeger and Ulmer's (2003) analysis of the demise of Enron illustrate the ways in which a breach of professional and organizational ethics can negatively influence organizational culture. Leaders' choices and behaviors are visible to other organizational members, and as a result, are often seen as the moral barometers of an organization. Despite adopting a set of core values of respect, integrity, communication, and excellence—known through Enron as RICE—the values were neither modeled by leaders nor integrated into daily operations. Although promoted to external constituents, it was clear to employees that a different set of values governed internal activities as the company sought aggressive growth and exploitation of new opportunities. The espoused values of Enron's leaders—Kenneth Lay and Jeffery Skilling—were not the enacted values. Central to Enron's downfall was the fact that the culture did not practice the value of open communication—a mechanism for staying informed about and asking questions about organizational operations.

On a more personal level, some employees may create facades of conformity (Hewlin, 2003), or a false representation to appear as if they embrace organizational values. Why would employees do this? The primary reason is thought to be employees' need to maximize outcomes from organizational reward systems, particularly when performance evaluations are subjective. A façade hides individual values as employees manage emotional displays, carefully construct their interaction with others, and monitor their behavior and gestures to signal acceptance of organizational values and ethics. The potential for this type of conflict between personal and organizational values underscores the multidimensionality and complexity that must be acknowledged in any study of organizational culture. Simply because an employee is observed conforming or interacting in such a way as to support organizational values does not mean that the employee personally embraces those values. Organizational members are especially prone to developing facades of conformity when their organizations undergo significant change. An employee who initially perceived a person-organization fit may develop a façade to avoid repercussions at the unit and organizational level.

CURBING UNETHICAL TENDENCIES IN ORGANIZATIONAL CULTURE

How can leaders overcome the potential for unethical practices in their cultures? Deetz, Tracy, and Simpson (2000) offer four guidelines. First, the culture should allow for employee voice. Formal feedback mechanisms should be part of an organization's communication structure, and informal feedback mechanisms should be encouraged as well. Most important, any time leaders are considering changing some aspect of the culture, employees should be given opportunities to reflect and report on the ways in which those changes will influence their jobs and their roles in the organization. Leaders should not presume that a change perceived favorably by one level or function of the organization would be positively received by everyone. Second, organizational leaders should facilitate ongoing conversations with employees at all levels about organizational issues. The more open and upward the communication system, the more likely employees will feel secure in entering into a dialogue about what is happening and why. With this type of openness, leaders are more likely to discover how cultural elements are harming or discriminating against groups of workers. Third, organizational leaders should encourage deliberation—at all levels and in all groups of the organization. Consensus about organizational issues (including cultural elements) achieved through deliberation will result in greater employee commitment because they contributed to the process. Fourth, organizational leaders should consider a situational system of ethics rather than a law-based or universal system. While clearly more complicated to embrace and communicate, situationally based ethics may be more realistic for contemporary organizations that must be flexible to conduct business in a changing environment. Universal ethical systems are easier to communicate, but can create situations in which extreme, and potentially unethical, behavior can be easily rationalized.

In summary, organizational culture can both facilitate and undermine ethical decision making and other ethical behaviors. Most organizations use some type of structural elements—procedures, rules, monitoring practices, job design—to minimize opportunities for organizational members to behave unethically. However, each of these formal structural elements is limited in their scope or implementation making it possible for unethical behavior to emerge. An organizational culture that promotes assumptions and values that support ethical choices can fill in these gaps and deficiencies creating interdependence between formal and informal, structural and cultural elements (James, 2000).

Given the role of ethical issues in organizational life, Deetz (1985) and others have advocated that ethical issues and values should be a central component of organizational culture. Taking such a position does not demand that organizational leaders impose a set of ethical values on all organizational members. Obtaining a widely shared set of ethical values can also be achieved when broad ethical guidelines are promoted by leaders and subgroup members are given the responsibility and resources to develop and manage the ways in which the ethical guidelines best serve their work activities (Sinclair, 1993).

CAN ORGANIZATIONAL CULTURE BE MANAGED?

In summary to this section, then, answering the question, "Can organizational culture be managed?" is a reasonable way to conclude. Despite what organizational managers, executives, and leaders want to hear, the answer to the question is a resounding *maybe*. For many advocates, "organizational culture change promises to improve the performance of organizations through transforming values and thereby maximizing human asset utilization" (Ogbonna & Wilkinson, 2003, p. 1175). Organizational culture change can also be viewed "as a superior, cheaper form of control than bureaucratic control" (p. 1175).

Managers, executives, and leaders often want to create sharedness and unity within their organizations because doing so makes their organizations more manageable (Alvesson, 2002). But a unitary culture is unlikely to happen for six reasons (Morgan, 1997; Ogbonna & Wilkinson, 2003; Parker, 2000). First, given the variety of individual and societal views about the necessity of work, trying to prescribe meaning is doomed to failure. Meanings cannot be fixed even with the use of training, slogans, and fancy campaigns. Second, cultural change often requires that organizational members assume new work or organizational identities that are different from their current roles. Reconciling those differences is an individual process, not an organizational one. Third, to create a culture implies that this is a management prerogative. Given this exploration of organizational culture and recognition of the role of communication in creating and maintaining culture, it should be clear that all organizational members participate in setting these meanings. Moreover, when managers attempt to prescribe culture they are likely to bias the culture toward the organization's or their own interests while denying the interests of other groups. Total consensus is hard to achieve when someone's interests are not being considered. Fourth, organizations and their resulting cultures are processes, not things. Solidifying culture as an objective dismisses the organization's and organizational members' histories, as well as the many forms of turbulence with which organizations must contend in the external environment. Fifth, organizational culture is an evolved form of social practice; it is self-organizing and always evolving. Even when managers believe they do control their organization's culture, their control is not complete. Sixth, because organizational culture is not a discrete set of elements, it cannot be objectively created. Managers cannot create *the* interpretation of a ritual or control the acceptance of a norm.

Still, organizational leaders have a disproportionate influence on the organization and its culture (Parker, 2000). Studies of organization intervention practices show that the overwhelming majority of organizations engage in some type of planned cultural change and that managers have some degree of sophistication in developing ideas about cultural change, as well as implementing these change programs (Ogbonna & Harris, 2002a). However, managers who indicate that they desire cultural change may, in fact, be promoting structural change disguised as cultural change, and doing so in an attempt to minimize negative reactions. As Ogbonna and Wilkinson (2003) found, structural changes may lead to behavioral changes, but not necessarily create employee buy-in to the underlying assumptions and values guiding the change. Organizational culture and organizational structures are intertwined, but not wholly reciprocal.

From a managerial view, all organizational activity is strategic (Schoenberger, 1997). Thus, gaining commitment to a shared set of values is attractive to leaders, and leaders can succeed in these attempts if all organizational members are invited and encouraged to participate cooperatively in the organizing of the organization and its culture. While such outcomes cannot be predicted, our societal views of manager-employee relationships and the economic need to work are strong influences on the coordination of work activities.

Perhaps then it would be more fruitful to shift the responsibility for the management of an organization's culture from the role of CEO or president to that of a department or unit manager. Managers, at these more micro or local levels, can influence the people with whom they regularly interact. They are not highly visible to the public, do not control considerable resources, and generally do not rely on formal communication channels. Lacking these, however, local managers should have a better understanding of the working conditions of their subordinates, as they are involved with them in problem solving and managing departmental activities. Managers at this level are more intimately aware of employees—their performances, desires, and needs. More important, local managers should have a better understanding of what motivates their subordinates and how they react to changes in organizational activities. Managing culture at this level is likely to be more effective, as work departments or units are more likely to hold more shared assumptions and values than can be held by employees across the organization.

Managing organizational culture from the top level requires messages that can speak to a larger number of different groups. To do so, such messages would be broad and general increasing the certainty that they become translated differently with different groups of employees. Managing culture is not simply a stimuli-response activity (i.e., organizational executives unveiling radical change and employees throughout the organization accepting it) or the sole responsibility of top management (Alvesson, 2002). These notions coupled with the view that despite what the popular press proclaims, organizational change is more subtle than monumental (Alvesson, 2002), suggests that top-level managers are rarely fully in control of organizational change. It is true that organizational history has documented instances in which radical organizational culture change has taken place. More commonly, however, changes in organizational culture are more micro than macro, local than organizational, and minor than major. Most important, employees at all levels are part of the change process.

Regardless of where cultural change efforts are initiated or what the cultural change entails, cultural change is typically more difficult than easy to achieve. Barker, Melville, and Pacanowsky (1993), for example, detail the difficulties encountered at a telecommunication manufacturing company as its culture was altered by a shift to self-managed teams from a more traditional bureaucratic structure. Their case analysis suggests two recommendations for managers—at any level—considering cultural changes. First, cultural change is more likely to succeed when it is tied directly to some consequential change in business practices. Tying changes in assumptions and values to specifics of the day-to-day work routine relates the more abstract cultural change to a direct work experience. In this way, then, the cultural change is more meaningful. Second, managers need to acknowledge that cultural change must also occur at the interpersonal level, and that this type of change is difficult. That is, basic communication patterns among coworkers and between supervisors and subordinates are likely to be different when new values and assumptions are promoted. Managers expecting changes in routine day-to-day behaviors are likely to encounter some forms of employee resistance or defensiveness as they attempt new ways of doing things.

Moreover, any number of unintended consequences can result from a cultural intervention (Harris & Ogbonna, 2002). Two are described here as examples. First, when managers begin a cultural change program, they often start with a short-term program realizing later that change requires longer term efforts. In many cases, management ritualizes that approach by creating annual programs that create a hotbed of activity for a short period only to recede and lay dormant until the next yearly surge of activity. Thus, an unintended consequence is that cultural change initiatives become integrated with annual evaluations or yearly budget cycles, and, as a result, lose their effectiveness at initiating deep-level cultural change. Another unintended consequence occurs when managers plan cultural interventions without sufficient awareness of the diversity of cultural elements and the existence of multiple subcultures in the organization. When this occurs, interventions will lack relevance for many organizational members.

Another problem in changing culture is that employees hold at least two different sets of values. Adults, based upon their education and life experiences, have a set of personal values that guide their choices. These may be aligned or not with organizational values. The selection and retention process can create an initial alignment between the two sets of values. But, cultural change may introduce a shift of values that diminishes this alignment. The greater the discrepancy between personal values and new organizational values, the more difficulty individuals will have in accepting cultural change. In these cases, managers will need to rely upon their communication skills to clarify and describe the new values (Brightman & Sayeed, 1990), explain their benefits, and encourage workers to adopt them.

Finally, in the view of organizational culture presented earlier in this book, culture is created, maintained, and changed via communication—and all organizational members create the communication system in the workplace. As Sackmann (1990) argues, "each organizational member is a carrier and potential creator, developer, and change agent of culture" (p. 129). From this perspective, it is difficult to advocate for a direct link between management actions and cultural change. Systems of organizational communication are not top-down; they are also bottom-up, horizontal, and from the outside-in. Thus, organizational members participate in a system of messages and sensemaking that is open to influences other than managerial ones. In a longitudinal study of two food retailers, Ogbonna and Harris (2002b) found that employee reaction to and acceptance of management change interventions depended on a variety of factors. Internal to the organization were the differences between espoused and enacted behaviors, the type of coercive or exploitive tactics and training programs used in the cultural change process, employees' experiences with earlier cultural change initiatives, and the skill with which immediate supervisors managed the change. Organizational members also differed in their reactions based on their positions in the organizational hierarchy, their job function, gender, and the expectation that they held for being employed long term with the organization. Thus, cultural change initiatives are influenced by factors aside from managers' communication.

It should be apparent that cultural change is best viewed as a process. Two principles must be balanced in guiding an organization through a cultural change (Claver, Gasco, Llopis, & Gonzalez, 2001). One, the speed of change must be slow enough to overcome opposition or resistance. Moving slowly through the change process gives organizational members multiple opportunities to understand the changes and become involved in the process. Two, the speed of change must be fast enough that the change process has momentum and does not create gaps or holes leaving organizational members unsure of how to achieve their daily task activities.

Thus, we return to the question—Can organizational culture be managed?—and our answer—maybe. Managers are only part of an organization's communication system. The view of culture presented here is that culture is:

- dynamic,
- influenced by elements in the organization's external environment,
- developed through interactions of all organizational members,
- based on both direct and indirect influences,
- comprised of multiple cultural elements, and
- simultaneously shared and contested.

All of these elements create a system of influences that are not necessarily linked in direct causal patterns (Sackmann, 1990).

In this view of culture, managers cannot control it and can only potentially manage it. However, managers and other organizational leaders can be aware of their organization's cultures and make conscious attempts to influence what cultural elements are interpreted and how they are interpreted. Rather than looking for the *right* or *best* culture, managers should engage in scanning processes to reveal the meanings and interpretations that exist. The lenses described in Section 3 would be useful in those examinations. Managers can also use the lenses in Section 3 as frames to enhance the likelihood that certain ways of thinking, feeling, and behaving develop. By communicating what is important and why, managers can influence their organization's culture.

SUMMARY

It is likely that in your working experiences you will be charged with the responsibility, or you will need to take the initiative, for developing the culture for your organization or work unit. Taking a pragmatic approach to organizational culture can help you identify the ways in which you can influence your organization's culture. A great number of factors will affect how you can influence cultural formation and change. Just as managers are interested in creating a culture that promotes their views of organizational effectiveness, they are also interested in maintaining such a culture when it is established. Strategies are described for developing cultures and maintaining cultures. Cultural change in organizations is a fundamental aspect of organizing. There are three types of intentional culture change processes—evolution, revolutionary, and everyday reframing—that can be complementary. Several strategies are described for managing intentional cultural change processes.

A vision creates a realistic long-term path for the organization and can influence an organization's culture. Founders create a vision of the organization—a statement that describes the value of what is to be achieved, and that is turned into the organization's mission—where specifically the organization wants to go. Typically, these are accompanied by a strategic plan that details in the short-term how the organization will achieve its mission. The role of an organizational vision, mission statement, and strategic plan are central to how an organization operates. Organizations regularly revisit these cultural manifestations to fine-tune their organizational activities to their current organizational environment.

Socializing or assimilating new employees is the process by which new employees are integrated into the organization's culture. When employees are acculturated, they are likely to be more satisfied with the jobs, less likely to leave the organization, and have higher identification with the organization. Socialization, or orientation, processes cannot be completed on the first day, as new employees continue to learn about the organization, their job, and their work unit throughout their first year of employment.

Many believe that the primary job of organizational leaders is to create and manage culture. But leading an organization through the lens of organizational culture is a reframing of leadership itself, as leaders ask "What impact am I having on the social construction of reality in my organization?" and "What can I do to have a different and more positive impact?" Under a cultural lens, leadership is more organic, emergent, and reflective—it is a complex social process, not a mechanistic portrayal of leaders acting and subordinates responding. Leaders can attempt to invoke or influence cultural changes by interacting with employees, embracing new values and assumptions, listening to employee comments about the new values and assumptions, and listening and watching for their resistance to cultural change.

Organizational culture can both facilitate and undermine ethical decision making and other ethical behaviors. In the best of situations, our ethics are socially responsible, similar to, and supported by the values of our organizations. In other cases, personal and professional ethics can conflict with organizational values. Cultural elements can contribute to unethical behavior, but there are strategies for inhibiting unethical practices in organizations and creating an organizational culture that promotes positive values.

The ultimate question is: Can organizational culture be managed? Despite what organizational managers, executives, and leaders want to hear, the answer to the question is a resounding *maybe*. Managers, executives, and leaders often want to create a consensual organizational culture because doing so makes their organizations more manageable. But a unitary culture is unlikely to develop. In the view of organizational culture presented in this book, culture is created, maintained, and changed via communication—and all organizational members create the communication system in the workplace. Still, organizational leaders have a disproportionate influence on the organization and its culture. Managers and leaders can (a) be aware of their organization's cultures, (b) make conscious attempts to influence what cultural elements are interpreted and how they are interpreted, and (c) promote framing conditions to enhance the likelihood that certain ways of thinking, feeling, and behaving develop. By communicating what is important, managers can influence their organization's culture.

The Culture Toolkit: Methods for Exploring Organizational Culture

Why do people do what they do where they do it? That is the central question of any cultural investigation. Identifying, describing, and analyzing an organization's culture may be the objective of a scholarly study. Alternately, having the tools to examine the culture of your employing organization can help you reflect on that organization, and help you build interpretations that allow you to understand the complexity of the organization as an organizing process. Or an organization might ask some of its members or outside consultants to conduct a proprietary study. For a personal, or insider's, investigation, the questions might be: "What is my organization's culture?" "What is my role in the culture change process?" or "Are the espoused values the enacted values of my organization?" For a proprietary, or outsider's investigation, the questions might be: "How does this organization's culture facilitate or inhibit decision making?" or "In what ways does this organization's culture encourage employees to work toward organizational goals?"

A good cultural analysis integrates both insider and outsider perspectives. To get the best sense of an organization's culture, it is crucial to gain insider knowledge. However, an outsider's questions or point of view may reveal something that an insider takes for granted, as it can be difficult for insiders to uncover their own assumptions. Whatever the objective of your investigation, a culture analysis must go beyond the surface level or what is obvious to create an accurate and realistic portrayal of an organization's culture. The objective of a cultural analysis is to discover how communication is used in the organization. Fundamental questions that are a beginning point for any cultural analysis include: To whom is interaction directed? What is being communicated? How is that message or interaction being acted upon and interpreted? Do organizational members have similar or differing interpretations of the same interaction event?

There are two metaphors useful when conducting organizational cultural studies. The first is to think of an organization's culture as a jigsaw puzzle, with the pieces fitting together one by one until an interpretable picture is revealed. However, there are two important differences between a jigsaw puzzle and organizational culture. Typically, when completing a puzzle you know what the puzzle is supposed to look like. You have the completed picture on the puzzle box. Thus, your goal in putting the puzzle together is to figure out how to place the interlocking pieces in their appropriate places to reveal a very specific image. However, because organizational culture operates below the surface and is comprised of artifacts, values, and assumptions that people seldom talk about directly, there is no way to know before hand what you are trying to piece together. Moreover, the picture you are trying to piece together is likely to change as you work; and the pieces that comprise it may fluctuate or become blurred. In many ways, trying to identify an organization's culture is like putting together a puzzle without knowing what the picture is and without having all of the puzzle pieces—all while you expect the picture you are pursuing to change!

Another useful metaphor is to think of an organization's culture as a landscape that changes with the seasons. Not only is there seasonal change, change also occurs throughout the day. This sounds somewhat predictable. But when you figure in the environmental or climatic variables, such as rain, snow, sleet, wind, and temperature changes, it becomes considerably more complex. Although there are some general patterns to be expected (e.g., spring follows winter, it is generally rainier in the spring), the day-to-day variance can be considerable. While there are more enduring elements to an organization's culture, there are also anomalies that cannot be predicted; and cultural change may not be uniform throughout an organization.

Thus, studying organizational culture requires a delicate balance between viewing a culture as frozen at a point in time so it can be explored, and viewing a culture's dynamics and agreeing that no meaning can be fixed (Alvesson, 2002). Obviously, data collected at any one point can only represent that point in time. The organizational culture that is revealed through communication practices is in the present—any interpretation of past or future events is not the same as if you studied the organization's communication 6 months ago or 6 months in the future. The ideal would be to explore the organizing and dynamic elements of an organization's culture as it emerges from an organization's communication system. Eisenberg, Murphy, and Andrews' (1998) investigation of the cultural practices that resulted in the selection of a new provost was conducted over many months. More typically, studies of organizational culture are conducted over a much shorter timeframe.

When embarking upon an analysis of organizational culture, remembering the assumptions below can help you avoid being too dogmatic about viewing the culture as *this is the way it is*. Refusing to see emerging and shifting patterns will threaten the validity of your findings. Investigations and interpretations of organizational culture must allow for change, as cultural phenomena (Alvesson, 2002):

1. are related to history and tradition,

2. have depth, and can be difficult to grasp and account for,

3. require interpretation,

4. are collective and shared by members of groups,

5. are primarily ideational in character—meaning that they have to do with meanings, understandings, beliefs, knowledge, and other intangibles, and

6. are holistic, intersubjective and emotional—rather than being strictly rational and analytical.

STEPS IN CONDUCTING A CULTURAL ANALYSIS

Selecting an Organization

If it is not possible to conduct a study where you work, ideally you can select an organization you have interest in and one that complements your availability for observation. Your family, friends, and your school's alumni are good sources for helping you make connections. Ask your instructor for additional suggestions. When one of these resources helps you identify an organization, ask if you can use their name as a reference; also ask for a specific person to contact in the organization. In approaching an organization, visiting in person will likely make a better impression because you are asking the organization to allow an outsider in. Building a relationship with a gatekeeper is key to entering an organization.

What can you offer back to the organization that gives you entry? Although you may have a specific goal for the cultural analysis (i.e., you've been given an assignment by your instructor), you could offer to conduct additional data collection and analyses to satisfy a need of the organization. Most organizations, especially nonprofit organizations and government agencies, have cultural issues that need to be explored, yet lack resources to conduct such an investigation. Of course, the analyses you compile in a report can be attractive to an organization, as an outsider's view will almost certainly differ from an insider or managerial view.

If you are conducting a study of organizational culture for an academic project, be sure to check with the human subjects committee or institutional review board at your college or university. Before you can conduct such a project, it is likely that you will need to develop a research proposal (including how you will address participant confidentiality and anonymity), and obtain their approval. Informed consent procedures will likely be required. Your instructor can advise you about the procedures at your college or university. If you are conducting a study for your organization, be sure to clear your activities with your supervisor and, potentially, the human resources or personnel department. If your organization agrees to sponsor your investigation, organizational members who participate should be informed about the nature or purpose of the study. Your colleagues should also be able to decide if they want their identity revealed in the report. Whether for school or work, it is ethical for you to inform those you interview or observe who will receive a report of your findings from the cultural analysis.

Once you decide on an organization, you will have to determine if your study will include the entire organization or just one or several units of an organization. The amount of time you have in addition to the size of the organization will help you determine this. Observing and collecting cultural data takes time—often longer than initially anticipated. Generally, an in-depth view of a smaller unit of an organization is preferable to a broad but surface view of the entire organization.

Addressing Bias

Whether your cultural analysis takes an insider or outsider perspective, it is easy to succumb to potential errors or bias. Here are some of the more common mistakes, and helpful hints to prevent bias in data collection and analysis. First, be cautious about representing the culture of an organizational unit as the culture of the organization. It is possible that a division, department, or unit culture is an accurate representation of the entire organization if a consensus culture exists. However, if you have not collected data from other areas of the organization, you should note that and not overgeneralize from your findings.

Your entry into an organization is either guided by a gatekeeper, the person who agreed for you to do the study, or by virtue of your role in the organization. The data you collect will likely reveal these biases. If you are restricted in who you can talk with or who you can observe, try to obtain other perspectives on the organization's culture through publicly available sources. It is also important to remember that your observations reflect only the current conditions. Conducting interviews and analyzing documents can help you understand the history of the organization and the way in which its culture has developed. Remember that all methods of collecting data are partial or incomplete.

If you are conducting your analysis where you are employed, keep these potential problems in mind. It is difficult to be objective if you are involved with the organization; your experiences at work will influence both data collection and data analysis. There is also a possible limitation to your access, as sensitive information that management believes is inappropriate to otherwise share with you could be unintentionally revealed or discussed.

There are also issues to address if you are conducting your analysis at an organization in which you are not employed. Despite working elsewhere, it can still be difficult to be objective due to the tendency to view this organization through *your* organizational experiences. As an outsider you may also have limited access to sensitive information. Because you do not have a personal relationship with someone at the organization, organizational members may not trust you enough to reveal that their assumptions and values differ from those of management.

As an insider or outsider, there will be problems to be solved in collecting data, and biases to be addressed in analyzing data. The benefits from either the insider or outsider role will be balanced by challenges that also come with that role.

Preparing for and Collecting Data

The process of a cultural analysis begins long before you enter an organization. Much like a potential employee researches an organization before going for an interview, as a cultural researcher you should also enter an organization with some basic information.

Many organizations have websites and promotional materials that can provide a history of the organization, or a description of the products the company produces or the services it provides. At a minimum, you should know the location, size, purpose, product or service, business environmental conditions, and history of the organization. After collecting and reviewing this information, it can be helpful to list any tentative conclusions you have about the organization. Also if you are familiar with the organization's industry, or some of the employees, it can be helpful to write down everything you believe you know, and any assumptions you have, before observing and collecting data. This brings your assumptions to the surface allowing you to confirm or challenge your terministic screen, or perspective, as you collect data.

Once in the organization, try to view the organization, its members, and their interaction through naïve eyes. Try not to impose mental models on the process. The point of collecting data is to make sense of it from the perspectives of organizational members. It is not sufficient to just report what you see or hear, or to be satisfied with your initial interpretations. To better understand the organization's culture, you must collect enough detail so that patterns can start to emerge—sense is made out of the details.

A good way to acclimate yourself to the organization is to take a few minutes to describe, or even draw, the physical environment where you are observing or interviewing. How an organization is designed physically can influence organizational members' interactions and how the culture is developed. Record any interesting features of the space or layout; be sure to describe how the members interact within it.

Entering an organization and taking employees' time away from their work activities should not be treated lightly. Regardless of level or status, individuals are taking time to meet with you; being late will reduce the amount of time and data you can obtain.

Finally, try to get a representative sample of members. If possible, include organizational members at all levels in many job functions. However, when you speak with many organizational members do not introduce information from one interview into other interviews. Doing so could produce unintended consequences for those in the organization.

Interviews are a good way to gather information to both identify cultural elements and to assist in developing explanations of those elements. Open-ended questions are general and nondirective and accomplish two objectives: (a) they allow the interviewee to tell you what he or she believes is salient; and (b) they minimize the bias that can occur when you suggest or imply that a particular answer is preferred. Overall, open-ended questions give organizational members the freedom to express themselves. Thus, they are better for initiating dialogue and obtaining full descriptions from the participant's point of view.

In pursing a research project, especially one that involves individuals and their means of financial support, there are a few principles that should guide your activities and interactions with them. First, work to build trusting relationships. Your project will benefit from participants' truth and candor. Second, give people the opportunity to talk with you at a location that provides them privacy, if they desire it. Some individuals may be willing to talk about their perceptions of their organization's culture *if* they are confident that no one will overhear what they say. Third, report what people tell you in their words, not yours. It is easy, and tempting, when taking notes to generalize what was said to a common or shorter phrase. Doing so, however, moves the data from first to second hand; the former is more persuasive in substantiating your analyses.

Periodically throughout the data collection process, it is a good idea to create summaries of what you heard or observed. Try to write descriptions rather than explanations. For example, the descriptive notes that follow were taken at a leadership training session.

Description: At the training session, participants are randomly grouped at four tables. Groups are instructed to draw their vision of the ideal organization. In a loud voice, the trainer says "no words; everybody draws." The trainer hands large sheets of poster paper to each group; colored markers are already on the tables. Immediately after this instruction one person at Table A asks, "Who can draw at this table?" Each of the groups starts immediately on the task. Two groups are sitting around their tables. When someone starts to draw, some members are unable to see the drawing in its upright perspective. At the other two tables, members have stood up and are gathered at one side of the table so everyone has the same perspective on what is being drawn. As the groups work—they are given 15 minutes to complete this assignment—a second trainer walks around and says out loud to no one in particular "this is a very good class—particularly good, active, and enthusiastic." The first trainer is still standing at the front of the room. As the groups that are standing work it is difficult to hear their conversations as they huddle over their drawings. The sitting-down-groups are having some conversation; the members on the wrong side of the drawing participate less than others. Members in the standing-up groups laugh frequently and loudly.

These descriptive notes become articulated as an explanation by reflecting on the following questions after leaving the training session.

Questions: How are the two trainers working together? Are they working together? Why does the trainer want the groups to draw their visions rather than verbalize their vision? What kind of vision did she want the groups to develop? Did she mean that group members shouldn't talk about the vision as they create it? What is the purpose of the exercise?

After considering potential answers to these questions, the analysis is written in the form of a memo to capture the observer's interpretation of the activities and interaction at the training session.

Analysis: The two trainers appear to be comfortable working together, as if they've done this same exercise many times. Their instructions to the groups seemed cryptic, as if there was an ulterior motive (something that they were intentionally not telling the participants about the activity). Although the groups seem to know what to do (draw their vision), there's very little conversation about what the vision is that they're drawing. There are two different working patterns. The standing-up groups appear more cohesive as more members are contributing to the drawing by pointing out where new elements should go, handing markers to the person who is drawing, or giving verbal encouragement to the "artist." Still, the person who can draw or who controls the markers seems to also be in charge of creating the vision. At about 10 minutes into the task, the sitting-down groups haven't completed as much as the standing-up groups probably because the one person has had to create and draw the vision by him or herself with little or no input from the other group members.

Writing the description first helps you avoid making assumptions or generalizations too quickly. Asking yourself questions about the description helps you amplify both the description and explanation of what is occurring. Throughout the data collection and analysis process, view all analyses as temporary.

CULTURAL TOOLS

This section describes seven techniques, or tools, and identifies several quantitative surveys for exploring organizational culture. They can be used separately or in combination. Using several methods to produce different types of data is preferred. This creates the opportunity to view cultural elements from many views, as what we find is influenced by how we look, and our interpretations are influenced by what we find. Just as Section 4 encouraged managers to not look for the right or best culture, a cultural analysis should not look for *the* interpretation, as a single truth does not exist (Richardson, 2000).

Because of the complexity of organizational culture, it is best for a team to conduct the data collection. A team also excels at analyzing the data because team members can check and challenge one another's interpretations. To capture the most complete picture of an organization's culture, design your study to allow for data collection from organizational members at all levels and across functions and locations. Be sure to collect data at different times on different days, and, perhaps, at different work shifts. Taking these steps will enhance the quality of your research, your findings, and conclusions.

Organizational Culture Pyramid

The pyramid is a typology of cultural elements typically found in organizational cultures (e.g., pay, benefits, channel use, customer satisfaction). The four types of elements are central to the communicating and organizing processes that emerge in the artifacts, values, and assumptions of organizational culture. Using the layered pyramid model of organizational culture, the effect of one set of organizational elements on elements at other levels will become clearer. The pyramid contains four levels beginning with the most basic elements of an organization leading to the summit of the pyramid, the satisfaction elements. Each level will vary from organization to organization; and the importance of factors will differ as well. However, the basic structure of cultural elements should exist in any organization.

Basic Elements. The basic elements of an organization include those aspects of an organization that are tangible and similar for many employees. These elements are most frequently artifacts, including the organization's mission statement, and the organization's hierarchy or organizational chart. Basic elements also include essential details about the specific job—for example, job duties, work schedules, and the locations of the bathroom and break room. Policies about compensation, benefits, and parking are also basic elements. Most basic elements are generated by downward communication and are expected to be stable across individuals in the same role or function. Basic elements can be identified when you ask these four questions: What is the function of this job? What are the job responsibilities? How does this job fit into the organization? What rewards do people receive for doing the job?

Many organizations provide orientation for new employees that address these basic issues. Oftentimes, orientation includes a tour of the organization's property so employees can associate the hierarchical and functional structure with the physical structure. Gaining access to orientation materials or taking an organizational tour are good methods for understanding what basic elements are addressed and how.

Questions to use in analysis of basic elements include: How is organizational culture influenced by the presence of basic elements? How is information about the basic elements communicated? Is that communication adequate? Do organizational members view the formal structure (or any other basic element) of the organization similarly? Differently? Do employees know the organization's mission?

Process Elements. The process elements of an organization's culture focus on the transmission of messages and information in the organization. Mediums such as voicemail, email, bulletin boards, newsletters, memos, and meetings are included in the process elements level. Communication at this level of the cultural pyramid should help employees develop a clear understanding of their role and function in the organization, how their position or job is relative to other jobs within the unit and the organization, and how their position or job is aligned with the organization's objectives. In examining the influence of communication channels and messages on an organization's culture, be sure to assess the way in which individuals in a variety of roles and at a variety of levels use communication channels. Process elements can be identified when you ask these questions: To whom do employees communicate? How? About what? Are there rules for how employees communicate in this organization?

Because the process elements focus on upward, downward, and horizontal interaction, as well as formal and informal exchanges, questions that can be used to analyze process elements include: Who controls which messages and which channels? Are any organizational members restricted in their channel use and in the initiation of messages? Are there formal policies or informal rules for using channels? Are different channels used to communicate with coworkers, subordinates, or superiors?

Subjective Elements. This level includes issues such as trust, identification, cohesion, perceived quality of message, and personal value to the organization. These elements are based on both the task and relational networks individuals use and create in the organization. For example, one employee indicated, "I want to know who I can trust and who I can't. Other employees helped me figure this out." Subjective elements can be identified when you ask these four questions: How would you describe your relationships with your coworkers? Superiors? Subordinates? If you had difficulty completing a work assignment, who would you talk to? How do teams or groups work in this organization? What do you admire about this organization?

Questions that guide an analysis of subjective elements include: How do formal or task networks differ from informal or social networks? At what point did you feel that your supervisor trusted you with your job activities? How does the work unit manage conflict among its members? If a coworker takes a lengthy leave of absence, how does the rest of the work group cover that person's work? In what way does your supervisor contribute to the work completed by your unit?

Satisfaction Elements. Satisfaction elements have two primary components both of which are outcomes of work activities: job satisfaction and customer satisfaction. Here the focus is on internal and external communication, and their integration. Satisfaction elements can be identified with questions like these: What is the relationship between your interaction with customers or clients and your interaction with your coworkers (or supervisor)? What criteria do you use to assess your personal success on this job? What do you consider a reward for a job well done? What about this organization or this job encourages you? Frustrates you? How do you describe this organization to your friends and family? If you could change any one thing about your work or your work environment, what would that be?

Questions to guide an analysis of this level include: Is there alignment between employees' espoused and enacted values? Between their reports of management's espoused and enacted values? How do employees support or resist management criteria of organizational success? How is employee satisfaction related to organizational effectiveness? In what ways do employees identify with the organization, its espoused values, and the product or service it offers?

Once information about the four levels is collected, a deeper analysis can be developed from considering how the levels are related to one another. One way to conduct this analysis is to consider the layers as a support system to one another. From an employee's point of view, are basic and process elements essential to having their subjective and satisfaction elements met? Or, can subjective and satisfaction elements be met with deficiencies at the basic and process levels? Do elements at one level provide a sufficiently strong basis of support to the levels above it? Another way to use the pyramid is to trace the consequences or outcomes of one factor to the next level. For example, what communication channel and strategies (process level) were used to orient employees to their jobs and the organization (basic elements)? Or, in what ways has employees' use of communication technology (process elements) contributed to the creation of informal employee groups (subjective elements)? Are cohesive work units (subjective elements) evaluated as more productive units (satisfaction elements)?

Tell Me a Story

A simple way to initiate a cultural investigation is to ask organizational members to tell you their stories. Nearly everyone can tell a story about his or her work life—positive, negative, humorous, ironic. These stories reveal organizational members' social, emotional, economic, and historical interpretations of the culture. Simply asking "What story best describes your work environment?" or "What story do you tell most about where you work?" is an excellent tool for encouraging organizational members to talk about their experiences. Although not a typical question and answer form, soliciting and listening to stories is a type of information-gathering activity. Initiating the conversation with an open-ended question will elicit information that can be explored with other questions drawn from what the person is sharing. You can extend the conversation by asking additional open-ended questions. In asking questions try to use the same words, phrases, labels as presented in the story. If an organizational member uses the label *manager* you could confuse the storyteller by asking questions about the *supervisor.* If you were able to prepare for the interview by learning the name, title, and duties of the organizational member you are interviewing, you can ask questions to further your understanding of the person's role and the type of work they do in the organization.

Alternately, stories can be heard anywhere organizational members meet and talk about work, such as work breaks, lunch, and social activities after work. Organizational stories can also be collected from promotional or employee recruitment videos, public relations and marketing materials, from the text of speeches given by organizational leaders, and internal communication media like company newsletters or magazines.

Obtaining organizational stories allows you to use the narrative lens described in Section 3. To use this lens, you will need a set of questions to help you analyze the stories you collect. For example:

1. What is the preface to the story?
   a. Is there something that the storyteller wants you to understand before telling the story? Is some background information needed?

2. How is the story recounted?
   a. Beginning to end?
   b. Starts with the conclusion and traces back to the beginning?

3. What are the details of the story?
   a. Setting? Specific or general?
   b. Who are the people in the story? Are they named specifically or generally? What are their organizational roles?

4. What is the action of the story?
   a. What predicament or problem does the story address?

5. Whose voice is being heard?
   a. The storyteller's? Someone else's?
   b. Are there phrases or other terminology that are repeatedly presented?

6. What indication is there that the story is complete?
   a. Was there an outcome or point to the story?
   b. Was a moral of the story established?

7. Overall
   a. What was the intention of the storyteller in telling the story?
   b. If others were present, how did they respond to the story being told?
   c. How does this story fit in with others?
   d. How does this story fit in with other information you have collected about the culture?

How Do You Do That?

A particularly good method for uncovering values and assumptions held by organizational members is to focus on employees' routine tasks. By focusing on questions that answer "How do you do that?," the interviewer can uncover what the practice is and why it is performed in that manner. This tool can be used as an interview-only strategy. However, having the opportunity to observe employees perform the targeted task will help you develop more salient questions and look for contradictions in how work is performed and how work is explained.

For example, one of the most common tasks for a receptionist is, obviously, answering the phone. Helena has been the receptionist at the cooperative grocery store for about 5 years. In addition to answering the phone, she also sorts and delivers mail to the respective departments, gathers information and types up reports for each department, and assists in other special projects as assigned by the store's general manager. Because the store is a co-op comprised of member-customers, they call routinely to find out what the lunch specials are, what the deli has for take-home meals, and to get advice on nutritional supplements. If you were to interview Helena after observing her for a while, the interview schedule might look something like this:

1. How would describe the phone calls you receive from members? What is most routine? Unusual?

2. How do phone calls from members fit with your other organizational tasks? What takes priority? Why?

3. If you were instructing a new employee in answering the phone, how would you describe the task? What would you tell him or her is most important in answering the phone? Why is that important? Who believes it is important?

4. How would you describe the written and unwritten rules for answering the phone? What roles do the rules serve? Who are the rules important to? Who makes decisions about the rules?

5. If you could change anything about how phone calls are handled, what would that be?

6. What is the biggest mistake anyone has ever made in answering the phone?

Through these open-ended questions you should be able to develop a full description of how phone calls are handled, as well as a full explanation for why phone calls are handled the way they are. This type of interview should help in identifying organizational norms for this task, linking descriptions and explanations of the task to espoused values of the organization, and uncovering organizational assumptions.

Cultural Clue List

Cultural clues—that is, cultural forms and practices—can be found everywhere in an organization. You will be alerted to clues in their forms as artifacts. (See the list in Table 5.1.) Focusing on one clue helps initially direct your attention and investigation, and will often reveal fragments of other clues. By identifying and analyzing a set of clues, you can construct an understanding of salient communication practices that divulge information about the organization's culture. With this foundation it is easier to identify organizational values and assumptions. You can collect information about cultural clues through observations, conversations, or a combination of the two.

If you want to understand the organization's cultural practices of specific elements, you can generate questions about one or more clues to use in an interview or focus group. Or, use a less structured format such as an informal talk with an employee in the break room. All types and lengths of interviews and conversations can produce useful

Table 5.1   Cultural Clue List

Analogies	Myths/legends
Annual reports	Newsletters
Brochures	Organizational stories
Coffee machine or soda	Performance appraisals
machine/water fountain	Play
Compensation and pay	Policies/procedures
Computer or technology applications	Power
Decision making style	Rewards
Diversity	Rituals
Employee communication channels	Routine organizational situations
up/down	Break/lunch activities
Employee involvement/participation	Christmas Party
Employee selection	Company Picnic
Employee socialization/orientation:	First day at work
Evaluation process	Organizational change
Founding history/founder	Stressful work day
Grapevine/informal communication	Stories
channels	Storytelling process
Groups/teams	Underlying values of
Heroes/enemies	an organization
Humor/jokes	Use of meetings
Informal employees groups	Vocabulary
Baseball team	Voices
Bowling league	Blue collar/hourly
Informal rules governing day-to-day	Employee
behavior	Ethnicity/race
Language use/jargon	Female
Leadership style/philosophy	Male
Memos	Management
Metaphors	Professional/occupational
Mission statement/company philosophy	White collar/salary

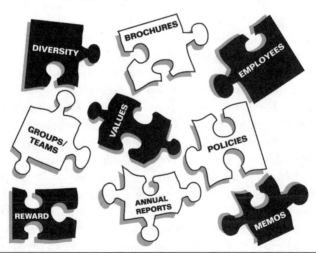

information. As you take notes (mentally or in writing), capture what is said, but also how it is said, and the location and environment of the interview or conversation. These pieces of information can shed light on your data and help you integrate information about one clue into a more in-depth analysis.

If you are observing, it may be more productive to let the first salient thing you observe direct your attention, until another clue becomes salient. This is an easier way of becoming familiar with an organization's culture than setting out to deliberately discover a particular artifact or identify the values that guide organizational members' interactions.

Prepare for the interview or conversation by developing a few open-ended questions that will help you explore the clues in which you are interested. Begin with broad questions and then move into more specific ones. However, do not be afraid to deviate from your plan of questioning if information about another salient or interesting clue is revealed. As you ask questions, provide a balance to give individuals the opportunity to talk about both positive and negative aspects of the cultural clue. While frustrations that organizational members experience can tell you a great deal about the culture of the organization, analyzing these relative to the positive aspects will create a richer analysis.

Archival Analysis

A great deal of data can be collected about an organization's culture through publicly available sources. Organizations often produce considerable artifacts that are easily secured. For example, most organizations have a Web presence and publish annual reports. Documents like these that are strategically designed and placed can reveal what an organization believes about its culture or what it wants its external stakeholders to believe about its culture. Many organizations, even nonprofits, produce advertising or marketing documents, as well as other promotional materials. These strategic communication forms contribute to understanding how the organization presents its culture to external audiences. Internal documents, especially those written by management, can also be strategic. Documents like formal reports, job descriptions, training manuals, newsletters, magazines, and policy and procedure handbooks can reveal what an organization believes about its culture, and what it wants its culture to be. On the other hand, other internal documents are more spontaneous than strategic. Memos and draft reports, logs of email or phone conversations, and notes written on whiteboards are likely to reveal a less edited view of the organization's culture—a view more reflective of what the organizational culture is really like.

Both descriptive and analytical articles about organizations are also available through the business and general news press (e.g., *BusinessWeek*, *The Wall Street Journal*, *The Chicago Tribune*). The most complete archival analysis, of course, would include documents from both organizational and external sources.

When data collection is complete, you could conduct a content or thematic analysis (see Keyton, 2001, for steps in conducting a content analysis). Some analyses of these data include:

1. Comparison of written documentation by job function or job level.

2. Level of commanding or directive language in the written documents.

3. Distinction between insider and outsider views of the organization.

4. Whose voice is represented? Whose voice is not represented?

5. The different or similar ways in which subcultures reference a prominent organizational artifact.

If you also have the opportunity to observe or interview organizational members, you should also consider the way in which:

1. Assumptions and values are espoused in written reports and how assumptions and values are enacted.

2. How cultural elements (especially artifacts) that receive frequent attention in written documents are treated in the work environment.

3. Cultural elements that are observed as meaningful in day-to-day organizational activity are presented (or ignored) in the written documents.

Mission Statement Analysis

Nearly every organization has a mission statement, a positioning statement, or statement of values—a written statement to capture the organization's purpose and business philosophy. Often a mission statement declares how the organization intends to interact with its customers and other stakeholders. Because a mission statement describes what an organization does, who it serves, and what makes it unique, it often represents management's view of the organization's culture.

Each of the statements below was taken from the organization's Web site. Mission statements can also be found in an organization's annual reports and other printed material, such as promotional materials and employee handbooks. Some organizations feature their mission statements prominently in their offices where employees and visitors can see it.

The Chicago Bulls organization is a sports entertainment company dedicated to winning NBA Championships, growing new basketball fans, and providing superior entertainment, value and service.

We aim to achieve our mission by working hard to emphasize the following core values:

- Mutual respect for each other, and a commitment to excellence, innovation, integrity and quality in everything we do.
- By providing our guests with superior entertainment *value* in a clean, secure, and comfortable environment—win or lose—regardless of their interest level in basketball.
- By helping our sponsors build their brands and grow their business.
- By treating our respective constituencies with respect, appreciation, and as we ourselves would want to be treated and serviced. In other words, by putting our fans and sponsors first every single day—and meaning it.
- By making our community a better place to live through our support of worthy social causes.
- By involving our guests in the game as active participants— not merely spectators.
- By knowing who and where our fans are, and reaching out to them.
- By working hard to make NBA basketball the most popular sport in our community and by selling and humanizing our players to everyone we meet.
- By being proactive and accountable in carrying out our mission.

The Chicago Bulls organization! Many people working together in a fiscally responsible way to grow our customer base and to win more World Championships.

Many people. One attitude. To dazzle our fans and sponsors.

FedEx Corporation will produce superior financial returns for its shareowners by providing high value-added logistics, transportation and related information services through focused operating companies. Customer service requirements will be met in the highest quality manner appropriate to each market segment served. FedEx Corporation will strive to develop mutually rewarding relationships with its employees, partners and suppliers. Safety will be the first consideration in all operations. Corporate activities will be conducted to the highest ethical and professional standards.

An organization's mission statement typically presents the big picture about the organization and is often geared more toward external audiences than employees. Even when it does specifically address employee and other internal issues, there is no guarantee that the mission statement reflects the organization's current practices. Mission statements are often based on ideals or values that organizations are striving to achieve. Thus, mission statements are an excellent place to begin if you want to identify the core values of the organization. After securing the mission statement, interviews and observations will help you answer the following questions:

1. Who wrote the mission statement? When?

2. Where is the mission statement printed, displayed, or promoted?

3. Does the mission statement accurately reflect what the organization does, who it serves, and what makes it unique?

4. What types of interactions or symbolic performances support the stated mission? What examples challenge or dispute the stated mission?

5. How does the mission statement influence or guide employees' actions with colleagues, supervisors, subordinates, and external stakeholders? In making decisions, providing leadership, or resolving conflicts?

6. In what ways are the values and ideals of the mission statement taught to new employees? Reinforced with existing employees?

7. Do organizational members at different levels or location, or in different roles interpret the mission statement differently?

8. Is there a managerial bias to the mission statement? How does an employee perspective differ from a management perspective?

What's the Real Culture?

It takes at least three steps to identify and verify an organization's culture. The first step is to identify what is included and excluded. One way to do this is to ask organizational members who is included in their organizational culture, as well as who influences their organization's culture. Your list might include:

- Employees
- Clients
- Customers
- Vendors
- Service providers
- Industry partners
- Industry critics
- Government agencies
- Media
- General public
- Shareholders
- Employees' families

This is an important step in identifying culture because of the centrality of communication to organizational culture. Thus, who is communicating, and from what roles and perspectives those messages are sent and interpreted will influence what is perceived as the culture. Making the distinction between who is included and who influences the culture might reveal boundary spanners who play a significant role in culture development, but are not formally members of the organization.

Asking organizational members across functions and levels to do this identification task will allow you to consider how the view of the organization's culture may differ based on organizational role. A deeper analysis can be obtained by collecting similar data from members of external constituencies. Doing so could reveal consensual or conflicting insider-outsider views of the organization. For example, it is not uncommon for contract workers (e.g., computer technicians) from one organization to complete their work activities onsite in another organization. How do these employees view the organization's culture? Can they potentially influence it?

All boundaries are socially constructed; thus, the boundaries of an organization's culture are likely to be blurry, to fluctuate, and to be permeable. This analysis can also address the ways in which onsite employees differ in their views of the organization's culture from employees who work in the field. Does cultural identification coincide with being physically present? What level of being communicatively connected creates a strong enough boundary to be considered a part of the culture?

After identifying who influences the culture, the second step is to determine if there is a difference between the espoused and enacted culture as perceived by those organizational members and external constituents. Any of the earlier described cultural tools can provide a method for obtaining this information.

Collecting information for steps one and two should lead you to the third step: Are there subcultures, and if so, what are they? How are they distinguished from one another? How are communication practices different or similar in these different groups? It is often easier to find evidence of shared assumptions and values because they will dominate the organizational environment and the interactions of its members. Identifying subcultures from a differentiation perspective can appear to be easily accomplished. But do not accept too readily the notion that subcultures only exist on predictable distinctions, such as managers vs. employees, professional vs. clerical workers, accountants vs. engineers. Recall that subcultures can be created along any dimension, and those dimensions may not be easily accessible to someone who does not have an insider's view of the organization.

With subcultures identified, now it is time to look at your information for evidence that ambiguity exists. Recall that from the fragmentation perspective, neither clear consistency nor clear inconsistency exists. For this part of your cultural analysis, it is a good time to review all of your notes again—especially notes that you earlier thought were irrelevant. Some information will not click into an interpretable pattern or paradox until we have had considerable time to reflect on the data collected as a whole. From this perspective, look for evidence that organizational members are part of shifting coalitions, continually forming and reforming based on shared identities, issues, and circumstances. Also look for tensions that appear to be irreconcilable. Sometimes organizational members will point to these as frustrations, ironies, contradictions, or unsolvable riddles.

Asking and answering, "What's the real culture?" will take time—both to collect enough data and to make credible interpretations. If it is possible, ask organizational members to read through or look over your interpretations. Getting their confirmation or rejection of your analyses is a crucial step in finding a plausible explanation of the organization's culture.

Quantitative Studies of Organizational Culture

There is considerable debate over whether organizational culture is best studied qualitatively or quantitatively. Often this debate is split along discipline lines with communication scholars advocating qualitative methods and management scholars advocating quantitative methods. That debate is ongoing and that split is not pure. Although more communication than management scholars conduct qualitative studies, both methodologies have been used in both disciplines.

However, given the multilevel and complex phenomenon that can be construed by subcultures in different ways, quantitative measures of organizational culture are limited to predetermined dimensions. As a result, findings from quantitative measures of organizational culture are more in line with the perspective that culture is something that an organization has rather than viewing culture as what an organization is. That said, surveys can be useful and efficient in tapping into an organization's culture, especially those aspects that are at the more superficial level such as norms and practices (Ashkanasy, Broadfoot, & Falkus, 2000).

There are two types of quantitative organizational culture surveys: those that classify organizations into a particular type of culture, and those that provide a profile of an organization's culture by describing a culture by its position on a number of dimensions. An in-depth analysis and comparison of quantitative measures are beyond the scope of this chapter. Other scholars have written extensively about one particular measure or have provided descriptive and evaluative comparisons among many. For example, Ashkanasy, Broadfoot, and Falkus (2000) compare 18 quantitative organizational culture surveys; Scott, Mannion, Davies, and Marshall (2003) evaluate 13 instruments for use in health care settings; and Rousseau (1990) reviews four organizational culture surveys commonly used by management scholars. More specifically, the Organizational Culture Inventory (OCI) is described in detail by Cooke and Szumal (2000). The quantitative survey used in the intercultural studies of organizational culture conducted by the Institute for Research on Intercultural Cooperation (IRIC) is described in detail by Hofstede (2001).

Most directly related to communication, the Organizational Culture Survey (OCS; Glaser, Zamanou, & Hacker, 1987; available in Rubin, Palmgreen, & Sypher, 1994) captures employees' perceptions of six dimensions believed to be prevalent in organizations' cultures: teamwork, morale, information flow, involvement, supervision, and meetings. A recent examination of the OCS (Schrodt, 2002) confirmed these dimensions and found that, in one sales organization, organizational morale was a significant predictor of organizational identification.

If you choose a survey instrument, review the items to make sure they are in vernacular consistent with the practices of the organization you are studying. Some minor changes may be needed. For example, if employees are called associates, that change should be made. Making more dramatic changes to a survey instrument can weaken its validity and reliability.

Selecting Data Collection Tools

The tool or tools you select to conduct an investigation of an organization's culture will depend partly on the questions you want to answer, what elements of culture you want to examine, the time that can be dedicated to the project, the availability of public information about the organization, your access to the organization and its members, and the number of people available to work on the investigation. Table 5.2 provides an overview of each tool, its strengths and weakness, and recommendations for using the tools.

In planning your investigation, remember that a more complete picture of an organization's culture will result when you can enter the organization and talk to or observe organizational members across all levels and functions. Moreover, multiple interviewers or observers will provide both a broader and deeper view of the culture. Thus, collecting data using different tools is recommended.

PUTTING IT ALL TOGETHER

After data collection is complete, there is still significant work to be done in analyzing the data to craft an interpretation of the organization's

Table 5.2   Cultural Tool Comparison

Cultural Tool	This tool is good for identifying:	Advantages	Disadvantages	Best use of this tool:
Organizational Culture Pyramid	Artifacts, values, and assumptions	Identifies relationships among different cultural elements	Requires observation	Provides naïve outsider a framework for making sense of organization's culture
Tell Me A Story	Values and assumptions	Organizational members find it easy to tell stories	Requires skilled interpretation as information is not first hand; point of story may not be obvious	To explore espoused vs. enacted values; understand culture from multiple views; investigate assumptions
How Do You Do That?	Values and assumptions	Easy to use with reluctant participants; they can talk about their work as they do it; good for exploring cognitive tasks	Requires considerable interview and observation time; open ended inquiry may lead investigation elsewhere	Helps investigator learn organization nuances
Cultural Clue List	Artifacts	Broad range of clues helps new investigators get started quickly	Easy to get lost in the detail and not connect to values and assumptions	Provides naïve outsider a framework for entering the organization's culture
Archival Analysis	Formal organizational artifacts; management's espoused values	Can track development of organization's culture	Will not reveal employee or other views of culture	As a framework before entering organization for other data collection

(Continued)

Table 5.2 (Continued)

Cultural Tool	This tool is good for identifying:	Advantages	Disadvantages	Best use of this tool:
Mission Statement Analysis	Management's espoused values	Can be done as outsider without entering organization; once inside, used as basis for identifying validity of espoused values	Not all aspects of organizational culture are directly tied to mission statement	As a framework before entering organization for other data collection; once inside, as a way to identify subcultures
What's the Real Culture?	Artifacts, values, and assumptions	Best for revealing most complete picture of culture	Time consuming; requires several observers	Extended studies; analysis of subcultures
Quantitative Measures	Surface manifestations of values; normative practices	Provides easily comparable data	Cannot reveal cultural nuances; can only identify subcultures by participants' report of demographic categories	Efficient data collection in large organizations; useful to determine where to focus qualitative efforts

culture. The most basic method is to identify themes that are revealed in the data. Are the themes similar or different? On what dimensions do the similarities and differences lie? It is easiest to work visually by listing out the themes on index cards and arranging them in a variety of ways until a pattern that makes sense is revealed. This pattern acknowledges your view of the organization. Now, consider if the pattern of themes or content of themes would change if different viewpoints were used. For example, separately consider the perspective of management, first line supervisors, and temporary workers. Or, consider the typology from the perspective of men versus women, employees who work with external stakeholders versus employees whose work is internally structured. Treat each pattern as viable, but tentative. Allow yourself to revisit these interpretations to make adjustments.

The next step is to consider how the patterns are tied together: Do they appear to be in some hierarchical ordering? Do the patterns conflict in any way? Typically, this is the most interesting aspect of the analysis. Returning to the puzzle metaphor, consider each theme a piece of the jigsaw puzzle. Now, what larger or macro themes are created when the pieces are considered in pairs, or in groupings of three or four? If the initial themes are connected, what holds them together? What distinguishes them from other themes?

Finally, is an overall picture of the culture beginning to emerge? Or do many macro themes emerge? If the data fit together, or are synchronous, it may be that the culture has a high degree of consensus or is integrated. If synchrony is low, then the culture may be divided and best characterized as differentiated or fragmented. One way to make the distinction between a differentiated and fragmented perspective is to analyze the gaps that exist. If the same gap exists for all employees, then the culture is more likely differentiated. If different gaps exist across employees, then the culture is more likely to be fragmented.

As a check on your analysis consider how your analysis would differ if you focused on the espoused culture. Compare that pattern to the pattern that emerges from the enacted culture. In analyzing the data do not try to force information to fit your preliminary analysis. If some data do not fit, set it aside momentarily. You cannot ignore information that does not fit, but you should not force a fit either. In the final analysis, your goal should be to account for all the information. If that is not possible, an alternative is to describe what cannot be integrated into the analysis and explain the multiple interpretations that were attempted. Reference sources for research design and data analysis are listed in the Appendix.

Writing Culture

The format of your final report will depend on the nature of your investigation, and your impetus for conducting it. Regardless, you will likely write a more detailed (and interesting) report if you first review examples of how other investigators present their findings. Your instructor can point to studies included in the references that have a style suitable for your project.

Culture is in the details, and it can be difficult to capture an interaction scene and environment, and realistically portray the organizational members and their communication for readers who have not shared in this experience. As you develop your analyses, be certain to include enough details to help your reader *be there*. For example, consider these questions as you write.

1. Have you situated the report in a specific organization? Industry? Location?

2. How can you describe the communication environment? What did it look like, feel like, sound like, smell like? What physical or other structural elements created this interaction space? Who was present?

3. Have you described the necessary details about the organizational members relative to your purpose or question? What do readers need to know about the organizational members you report on to view your findings as credible?

4. In describing interaction, have you described the accompanying nonverbal cues to help the reader interpret organizational members' verbal statements?

5. Do you have word-for-word quotes from organizational members that you have permission to use to substantiate your analysis?

Ideally, your description of the organizational scene should revolve around the communication of organizational members. Tying your analyses directly to excerpts of conversation or interviews, detailed descriptions of what you observed, or examples of organizational text will help readers *see* the organization, its members, and their communication practices that resulted in the artifacts, values, and assumptions of its culture.

SUMMARY

Why do people do what they do where they do it? That is the central question of any cultural investigation. Identifying, describing, and analyzing an organization's culture may be the objective of a scholarly study or a cultural analysis where you work or for another organization. Questions that might guide a personal exploration include: What is my organization's culture? What is my role in the culture creation process? Questions that might guide a proprietary exploration include: How does this organization's culture facilitate or inhibit decision making? In what ways does this organization's culture encourage employees to work toward organizational goals? In what ways does this organizational culture promote managerial values over values of other organizational member groups? The objective of a cultural analysis is to discover how communication is used in the organization. To whom is interaction directed? What is being communicated? How is that message or interaction being acted upon and interpreted? Do organizational members have similar or differing interpretations of the same interaction event? Both personal and proprietary studies of organizational culture should integrate data from both insider and outsider perspectives in answering these questions.

Advice for selecting an organization to study and for preparing and then collecting organizational culture data is provided. Seven qualitative data collecting tools are described. These tools can be used to identify cultural artifacts, values, and assumptions, and to provide a framework for their analysis. While each can be used singly, a more holistic view of an organization's culture can be achieved when multiple methodologies are used. Information about where to obtain surveys for collecting organizational culture data is also provided. After data collection is complete, there is still significant work to be done in analyzing the data to craft an interpretation of the organization's culture. Looking for themes and patterns across the data will reveal if, and how, the organizational culture is structured into subcultures. A cultural analysis is complete with the writing of your report.

Appendix

PART I: ORGANIZATIONAL CULTURE CASE STUDIES

Cases for Analysis

Article-length cases

Haasen, A., & Shea, G. F. (2003). *New corporate cultures that motivate.* Westport, CT: Praeger.

Keyton, J., & Shockley-Zalabak, P. (Eds.). (2004). *Case studies for organizational communication: Understanding communication processes.* Los Angeles: Roxbury.

May, S. K. (2003). Challenging change. *Management Communication Quarterly, 16,* 419–433.

Miller, V. D., & Medved, C. E. (2000). Managing after the merger: The challenges of employee feedback and performance appraisals. *Management Communication Quarterly, 13,* 659–667.

Peterson, G. L. (Ed.). (2000). *Communicating in organizations: A casebook* (2nd ed.). Boston: Allyn and Bacon.

Sypher, B. D. (Ed.). (1997). *Case studies in organizational communication 2: Perspectives on contemporary work life.* New York: Guilford.

Teboul, J. C. B. (2002). The language dilemma. *Management Communication Quarterly, 15,* 603–608.

Book-length cases

Bingham, C., & Gansler, L. L. (2002). *Class action: The story of Lois Jenson and the landmark case that changed sexual harassment law.* New York: Doubleday.

Browning, L. D., & Shetler, J. C. (2000). *Sematech: Saving the U.S. semiconductor industry.* College Station: Texas A&M University Press.

Bryce, R. (2002). *Pipe dreams: Greed, ego, and the death of Enron.* New York: PublicAffairs.

Conley, F. K. (1998). *Walking out on the boys.* New York: Ferrar, Straus and Giroux.

Ehrenreich, B. (2002). *Nickel and dimed: On (not) getting by in America.* New York: Metropolitan.

Freiberg, K., & Freiberg, J. (1996). *Nuts! Southwest Airlines' crazy receipt for business and personal success.* Austin, TX: Bard.

Kunda, G. (1992). *Engineering culture: Control and commitment in a high-tech corporation.* Philadelphia: Temple University Press.

PART II: RESOURCES FOR
RESEARCH DESIGN AND DATA ANALYSIS

Bartunek, J. M., & Louis, M. R. (1996). *Insider/outsider team research.* Thousand Oaks, CA: Sage.

Denzin, N. K., & Lincoln, Y. S. (2000). *Handbook of qualitative research* (2nd ed.). Thousand Oaks, CA: Sage.

Keyton, J. (2001). *Communication research: Asking questions, finding answers.* New York: McGraw-Hill.

Kvale, S. (1996). *InterViews: An introduction to qualitative research interviewing.* Thousand Oaks, CA: Sage.

Lindlof, T. R., & Taylor, B. C. (2002). *Qualitative communication research methods* (2nd ed.). Thousand Oaks, CA: Sage.

References

Alder, G. S. (2001). Employee reactions to electronic performance monitoring: A consequence of organizational culture. *Journal of High Technology Management Research, 12,* 323-342.

Allaire, Y., & Firsirotu, M. E. (1984). Theories of organizational culture. *Organization Studies, 5,* 193-226.

Alvesson, M. (2002). *Understanding organizational culture.* Thousand Oaks, CA: Sage.

Alvesson, M., & Berg, P. O. (1991). *Corporate culture and organizational symbolism: An overview.* New York: de Gruyter.

American Management Association. (2000). *Workplace testing and monitoring.* New York: Author.

Ames, G. M., Grube, J. W., & Moore, R. S. (2000). Social control and workplace drinking norms: A comparison of two organizational cultures. *Journal of Studies on Alcohol, 61,* 203-219.

Ashcraft, K. L., & Allen, B. J. (2003). The radical foundation of organizational communication. *Communication Theory, 13,* 5-38.

Ashcraft, K. L., & Pacanowsky, M. E. (1996). "A woman's worst enemy": Reflections on a narrative of organizational life and female identity. *Journal of Applied Communication Research, 24,* 217-239.

Ashforth, B. E., & Humphrey, R. H. (1995). Emotion in the workplace: A reappraisal. *Human Relations, 48,* 97-125.

Ashkanasy, N. M., Broadfoot, L. E., & Falkus, S. (2000). Part Two: Measurement and outcomes of organizational culture and climate. In N. M. Ashkanasy, C. P. M. Wilderom, & M. F. Peterson (Eds.), *Handbook of organizational culture & climate* (pp. 131-145). Thousand Oaks, CA: Sage.

Bantz, C. R. (1983). Naturalistic research traditions. In L. L. Putnam & M. E. Pacanowsky (Eds.), *Communication and organizations: An interpretive approach* (pp. 55-71). Newbury Park, CA: Sage.

Bantz, C. R. (1993). *Understanding organizations: Interpreting organizational communication cultures.* Columbia: University of South Carolina Press.

Barge, J. K., & Little, M. (2002). Dialogical wisdom, communicative practice, and organizational life. *Communication Theory, 12,* 375-397.

Barker, J. R., & Cheney, G. (1994). The concept and the practices of discipline in contemporary organizational life. *Communication Monographs, 61,* 19-43.

Barker, J. R., Melville, C. W., & Pacanowsky, M. E. (1993). Self-directed teams at Xel: Changes in communication practices during a program of cultural transformation. *Journal of Applied Communication Research, 21*, 297-312.

Bartunek, J. M. (1988). The dynamics of personal and organizational reframing. In R. E. Quinn & K. S. Cameron (Eds.), *Paradox and transformation: Toward a theory of change in organization and management* (pp. 137-162). Cambridge, MA: Balliner.

Bate, P., Khan, R., & Pye, A. (2000). Towards a culturally sensitive approach to organization structuring: Where organization design meets organization development. *Organization Science, 11*, 197-211.

Becker, H. S., & Geer, B. (1960). Latent culture: A note on the theory of latent social roles. *Administrative Science Quarterly, 5*, 304-313.

Bennis, W. (1969). *Organizational development: Its nature, origins, and prospects.* Reading, MA: Addison-Wesley.

Bettenhausen, K., & Murnigham, J. K. (1985). The emergence of norms in competitive decision-making groups. *Administrative Science Quarterly, 30*, 350-372.

Bingham, C., & Gansler, L. L. (2002). *Class action: The story of Lois Jenson and the landmark case that changed sexual harassment law.* New York: Doubleday.

Bloor, G., & Dawson, P. (1994). Understanding professional culture in organizational context. *Organization Studies, 15*, 275-295.

Boden, D. (1994). *The business of talk: Organizations in action.* Cambridge, England: Polity Press.

Boje, D. (1991). The storytelling organization: A study of storytelling performance in an office supply firm. *Administrative Science Quarterly, 36*, 106-126.

Boje, D. M. (1995). Stories of the storytelling organization: A postmodern analysis of Disney as "Tamara-land." *Academy of Management Journal, 38*, 997-1025.

Bormann, E. G. (1983). Symbolic convergence: Organizational communication and culture. In L. L. Putnam & M. Pacanowsky (Eds.), *Communication and organizations: An interpretive approach.* (pp. 99-122). Beverly Hills, CA: Sage.

Brightman, H. J., & Sayeed, L. (1990). The pervasiveness of senior management's view of the cultural gaps within a division. *Group & Organization Studies, 15*, 266-278.

Brown, M. H. (1990). Defining stories in organizations: Characteristics and functions. In J. A. Anderson (Ed.), *Communication yearbook 13* (pp. 162-190). Thousand Oaks, CA: Sage.

Bruner, J. (1991). The narrative construction of reality. *Critical Inquiry,* (Autumn), 1-21.

Bryman, A. (1996). Leadership in organizations. In S. R. Clegg, C. Hardy, & W. R. Nord (Eds.), *Handbook of organization studies* (pp. 276-292). Thousand Oaks, CA: Sage.

Byrnes, N. (2004, January 19). What's beyond for Bed Bath & Beyond? *BusinessWeek, 46*, 50.

Cable, D. M., Aiman-Smith, L., Mulvey, P. W., & Edwards, J. R. (2000). The sources and accuracy of job applicants' beliefs about organizational culture. *Academy of Management Journal, 43,* 1076-1085.

Callahan, J. L. (2002). Masking the need for cultural change: The effects of emotion structuration. *Organization Studies, 23,* 281-297.

Carbaugh, D. (1988a). Comments on "culture" in communication inquiry. *Communication Reports, 1,* 38-41.

Carbaugh, D. (1988b). Cultural terms and tensions in the speech at a television station. *Western Journal of Speech Communication, 52,* 216-237.

Chatman, J. A. (1991). Matching people and organizations: Selection and socialization in public accounting firms. *Administrative Science Quarterly, 36,* 459-484.

Chatman, J. A., & Jehn, K. A. (1994). Assessing the relationship between industry characteristics and organizational culture: How different can you be? *Academy of Management Journal, 37,* 522-553.

Child, J. (1981). Culture, contingency and capitalism in the cross-national study of organizations. In B. Shaw & L. Cummings (Eds.), *Research in organizational behavior* (Vol. 3, pp. 303-356). Greenwich, CT: JAI.

Claver, E., Gasco, J. L., Llopis, J., & Gonzalez, R. (2001). The strategic process of a cultural change to implement total quality management: A case study. *Total Quality Management, 12,* 469-482.

Cohen, A. (1974). *Two-dimensional man: An essay in the anthropology of power and symbolism in complex society.* London: Routledge & Kegan Paul.

Conley, F. K. (1998). *Walking out on the boys.* New York: Farrar, Straus and Giroux.

Cooke, R. A., & Szumal, J. L. (2000). Using the Organizational Culture Inventory to understand the operating cultures of organizations. In N. M. Ashkanasy, C. P. M. Wilderom, & M. F. Peterson (Eds.), *Handbook of organizational culture & climate* (pp. 147-162). Thousand Oaks, CA: Sage.

Coopman, S. J. & Meidlinger, K. B. (2000). Power, hierarchy, and change: The stories of a Catholic parish staff. *Management Communication Quarterly, 13,* 567-625.

Cooren, F., & Taylor, J. R. (1997). Organization as an effect of mediation: Redefining the link between organization and communication. *Communication Theory, 6,* 219-259

Corsini, V., & Fogliasso, C. (1997). A descriptive study of the use of the black communication style by African Americans within an organization. *Journal of Technical Writing and Communication, 27,* 33-47.

Cox, T. (1993). *Cultural diversity in organizations: Theory, research, and practice.* San Francisco: Berrett-Koehler.

Czarniawska-Joerges, B. (1992). *Exploring complex organizations. A cultural perspective.* Newbury Park, CA: Sage.

Deal, T. E., & Kennedy, A. A. (1982). *Corporate cultures: The rites and rituals of corporate life.* Reading, MA: Addison-Wesley.

Deetz, S. A. (1985). Ethical considerations in cultural research in organizations. In P. J. Frost, L. F. Moore, M. R. Louis, C. C. Lundberg, & J. Martin (Eds.), *Organizational culture* (pp. 253-270). Beverly Hills, CA: Sage.

Deetz, S. A. (1988). Cultural studies: Studying meaning and action in organizations. In J. A. Anderson (Ed.), *Communication yearbook 11* (pp. 335-345). Newbury Park, CA: Sage.

Deetz, S. (1992). *Democracy in an age of corporate colonization: Developments in communication and the politics of everyday life.* Albany: State University of New York Press.

Deetz, S. A., & Kersten, A. (1983). Critical models of interpretive research. In L. L. Putnam & M. E. Pacanowsky (Eds.), *Communication and organizations: An interpretive approach* (pp. 147-171). Newbury Park, CA: Sage.

Deetz, S. A., Tracy, S. J., & Simpson, J. L. (2000). *Leading organizations through transition: Communication and cultural change.* Thousand Oaks, CA: Sage.

Denison, D. R. (1990). *Corporate culture and organizational effectiveness.* New York: John Wiley.

Denison, D. R. (1996). What is the difference between organizational culture and organizational climate? A native's point of view on a decade of paradigm wars. *Academy of Management Review, 21*, 619-654.

Dickson, M. W., Aditya, R. N., & Chhokar, J. S. (2000). Definition and interpretation in cross-cultural organizational culture research. In N. M. Ashkanasy, C. P. M. Wilderom, & M. F. Peterson (Eds.), *Handbook of organizational culture & climate* (pp. 447-464). Thousand Oaks, CA: Sage.

Dickson, M. W., Smith, D. B., Grojean, M. W., & Ehrhart, M. (2001). An organizational climate regarding ethics: The outcome of leader value and the practices that reflect them. *The Leadership Quarterly, 12*, 197-217.

Dougherty, D. S. (2001). Sexual harassment as [dys]functional process: A feminist standpoint analysis. *Journal of Applied Communication Research, 29*, 372-402.

Douglas, P. C., Davidson, R. A., & Schwartz, B. N. (2001). The effect of organizational culture and ethical orientation on accountants' ethical judgments. *Journal of Business Ethics, 34*, 101-121.

Eisenberg, E. M. (1984). Ambiguity as strategy in organizational communication. *Communication Monographs, 51*, 227-242.

Eisenberg, E. M., Murphy, A., & Andrews, L. (1998). Openness and decision making in the search for a university provost. *Communication Monographs, 65*, 1-23.

Eisenberg, E. M., & Riley, P. (2001). Organizational culture. In F. M. Jablin & L. L. Putnam (Eds.), *The new handbook of organizational communication: Advances in theory, research, and methods* (pp. 291-322). Thousand Oaks, CA: Sage.

Feldman, D. C. (1984). The development and enforcement of group norms. *Academy of Management Review, 9*, 47-53.

Ferris, G. R., Hochwarter, W. A., Buckley, M. R., Harrell-Cook, G., & Frink, D. D. (1999). Human resources management: Some new directions. *Journal of Management, 25,* 385-415.

Fitzgibbon, J. E., & Seeger, M. W. (2002). Audience and metaphors of globalization in the DaimlerChrysler AG merger. *Communication Studies, 53,* 40-55.

Gagliardi, P. (1986). The creation and change of organizational cultures: A conceptual framework. *Organization Studies, 7*(2), 114-134.

Gibbs, J. P. (1965). Norms: The problem of definition and classification. *American Journal of Sociology, 70,* 586-594.

Gibson, M. K., & Papa, M. J. (2000). The mud, the blood, and the beer guys: Organizational osmosis in blue-collar work groups. *Journal of Applied Communication Research, 28,* 68-88.

Gilsdorf, J. W. (1998). Organizational rules on communicating: How employees are—and are not—learning the ropes. *Journal of Business Communication, 35,* 173-201.

Glaser, S. R., Zamanou, S., & Hacker, K. (1987). Measuring and interpreting organizational culture. *Management Communication Quarterly, 1,* 173-198.

Glisson, C., & James, L. R. (2002). The cross-level effects of culture and climate in human service teams. *Journal of Organizational Behavior, 23,* 767-794.

Goodall, H. L., Jr. (1990). A theatre of motives and the "meaningful orders of persons and things." In J. A. Anderson (Ed.), *Communication yearbook 13* (pp. 69-94). Thousand Oaks, CA: Sage.

Goodman, E. A., Zammuto, R. F., & Gifford, B. D. (2001). The competing values framework: Understanding the impact of organizational culture on the quality of work life. *Organization Development Journal, 19*(3), 58-68.

Harper, G. R., & Utley, D. R. (2001). Organizational culture and successful information technology implementation. *Engineering Management Journal, 13*(2), 11-15.

Harris, L. C., & Ogbonna, E. (2002). The unintended consequences of culture interventions: A study of unexpected outcomes. *British Journal of Management, 13,* 31-49.

Harter, L. M. (2004). Masculinity(s), the agrarian frontier myth, and cooperative ways of organizing: Contradictions and tensions in the experience and enactment of democracy. *Journal of Applied Communication Research, 32,* 89-118.

Hatch, M. J. (2000). The cultural dynamics of organizing and change. In N. M. Ashkanasy, C. P. M. Wilderom, & M. F. Peterson (Eds.), *Handbook of organizational culture & climate* (pp. 245-260). Thousand Oaks, CA: Sage.

Helms, M. M., & Stern, R. (2001). Exploring the factors that influence employees' perceptions of their organisation's culture. *Journal of Management in Medicine, 15,* 415-429.

Hewlin, P. F. (2003). And the award for the best actor goes to . . . : Facades of conformity in organizational settings. *Academy of Management Review, 28,* 633-642.

Hochschild, A. R. (1997). *The time bind: When work becomes home and home becomes work.* New York: Metropolitan.

Hofstede, G. (1981). Cultures and organizations. *International Studies of Management and Organization, 10*(4), 15-41.

Hofstede, G. (2001). *Culture's consequences: Comparing values, behaviors, institutions, and organizations across nations* (2nd ed.). Beverly Hills, CA: Sage.

Huang, J. C., Newell, S., Galliers, R. D., & Pan, S. (2003). Dangerous liaisons? Component-based development and organizational subcultures. *IEEE Transactions on Engineering Management, 50,* 89-99.

Hylmö, A., & Buzzanell, P. M. (2002). Telecommuting as viewed through cultural lenses: An empirical investigation of the discourse of utopia, identity, and mystery. *Communication Monographs, 69,* 329-356.

Ibarra, H., & Andrews, S. B. (1993). Power, social influence, and sense making: Effects of network centrality and proximity on employee perceptions. *Administrative Science Quarterly, 38,* 277-303.

Isaac, R. G., & Pitt, D. C. (2001). Organizational culture: It's alive! It's alive! But there's no fixed address! In R. T. Golembiewski (Ed.), *Handbook of organizational behavior* (2nd ed., pp. 113-144). New York: Marcel Dekker.

Jablin, F. M. (2001). Organizational entry, assimilation, and exit. In F. M. Jablin & L. L. Putnam (Eds.), *The new handbook of organizational communication* (pp. 732-818). Thousand Oaks, CA: Sage.

Jacques, E. (1951). *The changing culture of a factory: A study of authority and participation in an industrial setting.* London: Tavistock.

James, H. S., Jr. (2000). Reinforcing ethical decision making through organizational structure. *Journal of Business Ethics, 28,* 43-58.

Jameson, D. A. (2001). Narrative discourse and management action. *Journal of Business Communication, 38,* 476-511.

Janis, I. L. (1982). *Groupthink: Psychological studies of policy decisions and fiascoes* (2nd ed.). Boston: Houghton Mifflin.

Jones, O. (2000). Scientific management, culture and control: A first-hand account of Taylorism in practice. *Human Relations, 53,* 631-653.

Katz, J. P., Swanson, D. L., & Nelson, L. K. (2001). Culture-based expectations of corporate citizenship: A prepositional framework and comparison of four cultures. *International Journal of Organizational Analysis, 9,* 149-171.

Kaufman, B. (2003). Stories that sell, stories that tell: Effective storytelling can strengthen an organization's bond with all of its stakeholders. *Journal of Business Strategy, 24*(2), 11-15.

Keyton, J. (1994). Designing a look at women. *The Mid-Atlantic Almanack, 3,* 126-141.

Keyton, J. (2001). *Communication research: Asking questions, finding answers.* New York: McGraw-Hill.

Keyton, J., Ferguson, P., & Rhodes, S. C. (2001). Cultural indicators of sexual harassment. *Southern Communication Journal, 67,* 33-50.

Kirby, E. L., & Krone, K. J. (2002). "The policy exists but you can't really use it": Communication and the structuration of work-family policies. *Journal of Applied Communication Research, 30,* 50-77.

Kouzes, J. M., & Posner, B. Z. (1987). *The leadership challenge: How to get extraordinary things done in organizations.* San Francisco: Jossey-Bass.

Kroeber, A. L., & Kluckhohn, C. (1952). *Culture: A critical review of concepts.* Cambridge, MA: Harvard University Press.

Kuhn, T., & Ashcraft, K. K. (2003). Corporate scandal and the theory of the firm: Formulating the contributions of organizational communication studies. *Management Communication Quarterly, 17,* 20-57.

Kuhn, T., & Corman, S. R. (2003). The emergence of homogeneity and heterogeneity in knowledge structures during a planned organizational change. *Communication Monographs, 70,* 198-229.

Kuhn, T., & Nelson, N. (2002). Reengineering identity: A case study of multiplicity and duality in organizational identification. *Management Communication Quarterly, 16,* 5-38.

Kunda, G. (1992). *Engineering culture: Control and commitment in a high-tech corporation.* Philadelphia: Temple University Press.

Larson, G. S., & Pepper, G. L. (2003). Strategies for managing multiple organizational identifications: A case of competing identities. *Management Communication Quarterly, 16,* 528-557.

Levey, J., & Levey, M. (2000a, Jan/Feb). Executive summary: Corporate culture and organizational health: A critical analysis of the reasons why investing in people is a wise business investment. Retrieved December 21, 2003 from http:// www.wisdomatwork.com/BUSINESS/ center/report.html

Levey, J., & Levey, M. (2000b, Jan/Feb). Reflections for leaders: Corporate culture, organizational health, and human potential. Retrieved December 21, 2003, from http://www.wisdomatwork.com/BUSINESS/center/EAPA.html

Lewin, K. (1951). *Field theory in social science.* New York: Harper & Row.

Lindsley, S. L. (1999). A layered model of problematic intercultural communication in U.S.-owned maquilaodras in Mexico. *Communication Monographs, 66,* 145-167.

Lutgen-Sandvik, P. (2003). The communicative cycle of employee emotional abuse: Generation and regeneration of workplace mistreatment. *Management Communication Quarterly, 16,* 471-501.

Martin, J. (2002). *Organizational culture: Mapping the terrain.* Thousand Oaks, CA: Sage.

Martin, J., & Frost, P. (1996). The organizational culture war games: A struggle for intellectual dominance. In S. R. Clegg, C. Hardy, & W. R. Nord (Eds.), *Handbook of organization studies* (pp. 598-621). Thousand Oaks, CA: Sage.

Mathys, N. J. (2002). A conversation with C. Richard Panico: Leading an ethically-based organization. *Journal of Leadership and Organization Studies, 9*(2), 89-101.

McKenna, T. (2003, June). Culture as a competitive weapon. *National Petroleum News, 96*(6), p. 13.

McMurray, A. J. (2003). The relationship between organizational climate and organizational culture. *Journal of American Academy of Business, 3,* 1-8.

McNeal, G. J. (2000). Organizational culture and African American nurse faculty productivity: A comparative study. *Journal of Cultural Diversity, 7,* 114-127.

McPhee, R. D., & Zaug, P. (2001). Organizational theory, organizational communication, organizational knowledge, and problematic integration. *Journal of Communication, 51,* 574-591.

Meares, M. M., Oetzel, J. G., Torres, A., Derkacs, D., & Ginossar, T. (2004). Employee mistreatment and muted voices in the culturally diverse workplace. *Journal of Applied Communication Research, 32,* 4-27.

Meyer, J. C. (1995). Tell me a story: Eliciting organizational values from narratives. *Communication Quarterly, 43,* 210-224.

Michela, J. L. & Burke, W. W. (2000). Organizational culture and climate in transformations for quality and innovation. In N. M. Ashkanasy, C. P. M. Wilderom, & M. F. Peterson (Eds.), *Handbook of organizational culture & climate* (pp. 225-244). Thousand Oaks, CA: Sage.

Miller, K. (2002). The experience of emotion in the workplace: Professing the midst of tragedy. *Management Communication Quarterly, 15,* 571-600.

Mills, T. L., Boylstein, C. A., & Lorean, S. (2001). "Doing" organizational culture in the Saturn Corporation. *Organization Studies, 22,* 117-143.

Mitchell, M. A., & Yates, D. (2002). How to use your organizational culture as competitive tool. *Nonprofit World, 20*(2), 33-34.

Mohan, M. L. (1993). *Organizational communication and cultural vision: Approaches for analysis.* Albany: State University of New York Press.

Morgan, G. (1997). *Images of organization.* Thousand Oaks, CA: Sage.

Mumby, D. K. (1988). *Communication and power in organizations: Discourse, ideology and domination.* Norwood, NJ: Ablex.

Murphy, A. G. (1998). Hidden transcripts of flight attendant resistance. *Management Communication Quarterly, 11,* 499-535.

Murphy, A. G. (2001). The flight attendant dilemma: An analysis of communication and sensemaking during in-flight emergencies. *Journal of Applied Communication Research, 29,* 30-53.

Myers, K. K., & Oetzel, J. G. (2003). Exploring the dimensions of organizational assimilation: Creating and validating a measure. *Communication Quarterly, 51,* 438-457.

Nelson, R. E., & Gopalan, S. (2003). Do organizational cultures replicate national cultures? Isomorphism, rejection and reciprocal opposition in the corporate values of three countries. *Organization Studies, 24,* 1115-1151.

Ogbonna, E., & Harris, L. C. (2002a). Managing organizational culture: Insights from the hospitality industry. *Human Resource Management Journal, 12,* 33-53.

Ogbonna, E., & Harris, L. C. (2002b). Organizational culture: A ten-year, two-phase study of change in the UK food retailing sector. *Journal of Management Studies, 39,* 673-706.

Ogbonna, E., & Wilkinson, B. (2003). The false promise of organizational culture change: A case study of middle managers in grocery retailing. *Journal of Management Studies, 40,* 1151-1178.

Ogbor, J. O. (2000). Organizational leadership and authority relations across cultures: Beyond divergence and convergence. *International Journal of Commerce and Management, 10,* 48-73.

O'Reilly, C. A., III, Chatman, J., & Caldwell, D. F. (1991). People and organizational culture: A profile comparison approach to assessing person-organization fit. *Academy of Management Journal, 34,* 487-516.

Pacanowsky, M. E., & O'Donnell-Trujillo, N. (1982). Communication and organizational cultures. *Western Journal of Speech Communication, 46,* 115-130.

Pacanowsky, M. E., & O'Donnell-Trujillo, N. (1983). Organizational communication as cultural performance. *Communication Monographs, 50,* 126-147.

Parker, M. (2000). *Organizational culture and identity: Unity and division at work.* Thousand Oaks, CA: Sage.

Penman, R. (2000). *Reconstructing communicating: Looking to a future.* Mahwah, NJ: Lawrence Erlbaum.

Peters, T. J., & Waterman, R. J. (1982). *In search of excellence.* New York: Harper & Row.

Pothukuchi, V., Damanpour, F., Choi, J., Chen, C. C., & Park, S. H. (2002). National and organizational culture differences and international joint venture performance. *Journal of International Business Studies, 33,* 243-265.

Putnam, L. L. (1983). The interpretive perspective: An alternative to functionalism. In L. L. Putnam & M. E. Pacanowsky (Eds.), *Communication and organizations: An interpretive approach* (pp. 31-54). Newbury Park, CA: Sage.

Putnam, L. L., & Fairhurst, G. T. (2001). Discourse analysis in organizations. In F. M. Jablin & L. L. Putnam (Eds.), *The new handbook of organizational communication: Advances in theory, research, and methods* (pp. 78-160). Thousand Oaks, CA: Sage.

Quinn, M. Q. (1988). The vision shines through. *Journal of Extension.* Available online: http://www.joe.org/joe/1988summer/fut1.html

Rafaeli, A., & Worline, M. (2000). Symbols in organizational culture. In N. M. Ashkanasy, C. P. M. Wilderom, & M. F. Peterson (Eds.), *Handbook of organizational culture & climate* (pp. 71-84). Thousand Oaks, CA: Sage.

Ragins, B. R. (1995). Diversity, power, and mentorship in organizations: A cultural, structural, and behavioral perspective. In M. M. Chemers, S. Oskamp, & M. A. Costanzo (Eds.), *Diversity in organizations: New perspectives for a changing workplace* (pp. 91-132). Thousand Oaks, CA: Sage.

Richardson, L. (2000). Writing: A method of inquiry. In N. K. Denzin & Y. S. Lincoln (Eds.), *Handbook of qualitative research* (2nd ed., pp. 923-948). Thousand Oaks, CA: Sage.

Rigby, D. (2003). *Management tools 2003.* Retrieved January 18, 2004 from http://www.bain.com/management_tools/strategy_brief.pdf

Rosenfeld, L. B., Richman, J. M., & May, S. K. (2004). Information adequacy, job satisfaction and organizational culture in a dispersed-network organization. *Journal of Applied Communication Research, 32,* 28-54.

Rousseau, D. M. (1990). Assessing organizational culture: The case for multiple methods. In B. Schneider (Ed.), *Organizational climate and culture* (pp. 153-192). San Francisco: Jossey-Bass.

Rubin, R. B., Palmgreen, P., & Sypher, H. E. (Eds.). (1994). *Communication research measures: A sourcebook.* New York: Guilford.

Sackmann, S. A. (1990). Managing organizational culture: Dreams and possibilities. In J. A. Anderson (Ed.), *Communication Yearbook 13* (pp. 114-148). Thousand Oaks, CA: Sage.

Sackmann, S. A. (1991). *Cultural knowledge in organizations: Exploring the collective mind.* Newbury Park, CA: Sage.

Sackmann, S. A. (1997). Introduction. In S. A. Sackmann (Ed.), *Cultural complexity in organizations: Inherent contrasts and contradictions* (pp. 1-48). Thousand Oaks: Sage.

Sass, J. S. (2000). Characterizing organizational spirituality: An organizational communication culture approach. *Communication Studies, 51,* 195-217.

Scheibel, D. (1994). Graffiti and "film school" culture: Displaying alienation. *Communication Monographs, 61,* 1-18.

Schein, E. H. (1983). The role of the founder in creating organizational culture. *Organizational Dynamics, 13-28.*

Schein, E. H. (1992). *Organizational culture and leadership* (2nd ed.). San Francisco: Jossey-Bass.

Schein, E. H. (1996). Culture: The missing concept in organization studies. *Administrative Science Quarterly, 41,* 229-240.

Schein, E. H. (1999). *The corporate culture survival guide: Sense and nonsense about cultural change.* San Francisco: Jossey-Bass.

Schein, E. H. (2000). Sense and nonsense about culture and climate. In N. M. Ashkanasy, C. P. M. Wilderom, & M. F. Peterson (Eds.), *Handbook of organizational culture & climate* (pp. xiii-xxx). Thousand Oaks, CA: Sage.

Schoenberger, E. (1997). *The cultural crisis of the firm.* Cambridge, MA: Blackwell.

Schrodt, P. (2002). The relationship between organizational identification and organizational culture: Employee perceptions of culture and identification in a retail sales organization. *Communication Studies, 53,* 189-202.

Scott, T., Mannion, R., Davies, H., & Marshall, M. (2003). The quantitative measurement of organizational culture in health care: A review of the available instruments. *HSR: Health Services Research, 38,* 923-955.

Seeger, M. W., & Ulmer, R. R. (2003). Explaining Enron: Communication and responsible leadership. *Management Communication Quarterly, 17,* 58-84.

Semler, S. W. (1997). Systematic agreement: A theory of organizational alignment. *Human Resource Development Quarterly, 8*(1), 23-40.

Shockley-Zalabak, P. (2002). *Fundamentals of organizational communication: Knowledge, sensitivity, skills, values.* Boston: Allyn and Bacon.

Shockley-Zalabak, P., & Morley, D. D. (1994). Creating a culture: A longitudinal examination of the influence of management and employee values on communication rule stability and emergence. *Human Communication Research, 20,* 334-355.

Siehl, C., & Martin, J. (1990). Organizational culture: A key to financial performance? In B. Schneier (Ed.), *Organizational climate and culture* (pp. 241-281). San Francisco: Jossey-Bass.

Sinclair, A. (1993). Approaches to organizational culture and ethics. *Journal of Business Ethics, 12,* 63-73.

Smircich, L. (1983). Concepts of culture and organizational analysis. *Administrative Science Quarterly, 28,* 339-358.

Smith, F. L., & Keyton, J. (2001). Organizational storytelling: Metaphors for relational power and identity struggles. *Management Communication Quarterly, 15,* 149-182.

Sobo, E. J., & Sadler, B. L. (2002). Improving organizational communication and cohesion in a health care setting through employee-leadership exchange. *Human Organization, 61,* 277-287.

Sorensen, J. B. (2002). The strength of corporate culture and the reliability of firm performance. *Administrative Science Quarterly, 47,* 70-91.

Soupata, L. (2001). Managing culture for competitive advantage at United Parcel Service. *Journal of Organizational Excellence, 20*(3), 19-26.

Stackman, R. W., Pinder, C. C., & Connor, P. E. (2000). Values lost: Redirecting research on values in the workplace. In N. M. Ashkanasy, C. P. M. Wilderom, & M. F. Peterson (Eds.), *Handbook of organizational culture & climate* (pp. 37-54). Thousand Oaks, CA: Sage.

Stephens, J., & Behr, P. (2002, January 27). Enron's culture fed its demise: Groupthink promoted foolhardy risks. *The Washington Post,* p. A01.

Stevens, S. (1983). 10 incentive mistakes to avoid at all costs. *Sales & Marketing Management, 130*(5), 78-86.

Stohl, C. (1995). *Organizational communication: Connectedness in action.* Thousand Oaks, CA: Sage.

Stohl, C. (2001). Globalizing organizational communication. In F. M. Jablin & L. L. Putnam (Eds.), *The new handbook of organizational communication: Advances in theory, research, and methods* (pp. 323-375). Thousand Oaks, CA: Sage.

Stohl, C., & Cheney, G. (2001). Participatory processes/paradoxical practices. *Management Communication Quarterly, 14,* 349-407.

Sutton, R. I. (1991). Maintaining norms about expressed emotions: The case of bill collectors. *Administrative Science Quarterly, 36,* 245-268.

Suzuki, S. (1997). Cultural transmission in international organizations: Impact of interpersonal communication patterns in intergroup contexts. *Human Communication Research, 24,* 147-180.

Taylor, J. R., & Van Every, E. J. (2000). *The emergent organization: Communication as its site and surface.* Mahwah, NJ: Lawrence Erlbaum.

Testa, M. R., Mueller, S. L., & Thomas, A. S. (2003). Cultural fit and job satisfaction in a global service environment. *Management International Review, 43,* 129-148.

Tompkins, P., & Cheney, G. (1985). Communication and unobtrusive control. In P. Tompkins & R. McPhee (Eds.), *Organizational communication: Traditional perspectives and new directions* (pp. 179-210). Beverly Hills, CA: Sage.

Triandis, H. (1983). Dimensions of cultural variation as parameters of organizational theories. *International Studies of Management and Organization, 12,* 139-169.

Trice, H. M., & Beyer, J. M. (1993). *The cultures of work organizations.* Englewood Cliffs, NJ: Prentice Hall.

Trujillo, N. (1992). Interpreting (the work and the talk of) baseball: Perspectives on ballpark culture. *Western Journal of Communication, 56,* 350-371.

Ulijn, J., O'Hair, D., Weggeman, M., Ledlow, G., & Hall, H. T. (2000). Innovation, corporate strategy, and cultural context: What is the mission for international business communication? *Journal of Business Communication, 37,* 293-317.

United Way of America. (2004). *United Way community impact agenda.* Retrieved January 30, 2004, from http://national.unitedway.org/aboutuw/ciagenda.cfm

Vandenberghe, C. (1999). Organizational culture, person-culture fit, and turnover: A replication in the health care industry. *Journal of Organizational Behavior, 20,* 175-184.

Waldron, V. R. (2000). Relational experience and emotion at work. In S. Fineman (Ed.), *Emotion in organizations* (2nd ed., pp. 64-82). Thousand Oaks, CA: Sage.

Weick, K. E. (1979). *The social psychology of organizing* (2nd ed.). Reading, MA: Addison-Wesley.

Weick, K. E. (1985). Sources of order in underorganized systems: Themes in recent organizational theory. In Y. S. Lincoln (Ed.), *Organizational theory and inquiry* (pp. 106-136). Beverly Hills: Sage.

Weick, K. E. (1995). *Sensemaking in organizations.* Thousand Oaks, CA: Sage.

Weick, K. E. (2001). *Making sense of the organization.* Malden, MA: Blackwell.

Wilderom, C. P. M., Glunk, U., & Maslowski, R. (2000). The high performance organizational climate: How workers describe top performing units. In N. M. Ashkanasy, C. P. M. Wilderom, & M. F. Peterson (Eds.), *Handbook of organizational culture & climate* (pp. 193-209). Thousand Oaks, CA: Sage.

Witmer, D. F. (1997). Communication and recovery: Structuration as an ontological approach to organizational culture. *Communication Monographs, 64,* 324-349.

Zammuto, R. F., Gifford, B., & Goodman, E. A. (2000). The cultural dynamics of organizing and change. In N. M. Ashkanasy, C. P. M. Wilderom, & M. F. Peterson (Eds.), *Handbook of organizational culture & climate* (pp. 261-278). Thousand Oaks, CA: Sage.

Zoller, H. M. (2003). Health on the line: Identity and disciplinary control in employee occupational health and safety discourse. *Journal of Applied Communication Research, 31,* 118-139.

Zorn, T. E., Page, D. J., & Cheney, G. (2000). Nuts about change: Multiple perspectives on change-oriented communication in a public sector organization. *Management Communicating Quarterly, 13,* 515-566.

Index

About the Author

Joann Keyton (Ph.D., The Ohio State University, 1987) is Professor of Communication at The University of Kansas. Specializing in group and organizational communication, her current research interests are relationship issues and collaboration in organizational teams, models of community leadership, organizational culture, and organizational responses to sexual harassment. Her research has been published in *Journal of Applied Communication Research, Management Communication Quarterly, Communication Studies, Small Group Research, Southern Journal of Communication, Communication Yearbook,* and numerous edited collections. She has published texts on group communication (Oxford) and research methods (McGraw-Hill), as well as an organizational communication case book (with Pam Shockley-Zalabak; Roxbury). Professor Keyton has served on the editorial boards of *Communication Monographs, Communication Studies, Journal of Applied Communication Research, Small Group Research,* and *Southern Communication Journal;* she is the editor of the *Journal of Applied Communication Research,* volumes 31–33.